Spinner V

Cataloging–in–Publication Data

McCabe, Marsha
Spinner: People and Culture in Southeastern Massachusetts, Volume V
192 pp., illus., 22cm
1. History – Massachusetts – Pictorial Works
2. Photography – Southeastern Massachusetts – History
3. Oral History – Massachusetts – Regional Works
I. Thomas, Joseph D.   II. Title
Library of Congress Catalogue Number: 96-92236

ISBN: 0932027 - 318 cloth
ISBN: 0932027 - 30x paper

@ 1996 by Spinner Publications, Inc. All rights reserved.
First Printing, published 1996.
Printed in the United States of America
Spinner Publications, Inc., New Bedford, MA

Book Design, Electronic Typesetting, Image Editing and Scanning
Joseph D. Thomas & John K. Robson

Cover Design: Colleen Berry, John K. Robson, Joseph D. Thomas

Spinner Volume V

People and Culture in Southeastern Massachusetts

Edited by

Marsha McCabe & Joseph D. Thomas

with

John K. Robson & Ruth J. Caswell

Spinner Publications, Inc.

New Bedford, Massachusetts

Foreword

Welcome to the world of Spinner, our fifth in the *Spinner* volume series, featuring the history and culture of the cities and towns of southeastern Massachusetts.

It's been almost 17 years since our first book, *Spinner I,* rolled off the press. Still, our purpose hasn't changed. Our aim is to tell the story of our region through the voices of those who have lived here, especially those whose stories are not often told in history books.

We hope to fill in the gaps left by historians who have penciled history as a succession of great wars, great men, political acts, social upheavals, discoveries, inventions and so forth. Spinner hopes to supplement that history with stories that include the subtle inflections of everyday life. Through oral history, we meet and celebrate people in different ethnic groups; we uncover the history of buildings, neighborhoods and farms; we look at photographic collections and diaries of historic value.

These sources give us insight into families and neighborhoods, industry and the workplace; they reveal the workings of our public institutions; our relationship to land and sea; the growth of urbanization and the role of politics. In particular, they give us insight into the souls of the people who settled in this corner of Massachusetts. In *Spinner V,* through the photography of Milton Silvia, we see news events, politicians, and rock festivals. But we also see a lonely elderly man staring out his rooming house window, a child loving an animal, workers showing pride in their work, a city teeming with life.

Spinner promotes the arts of the region and collaboration among artists. We welcome the voices of new writers and the vision of new photographers and graphic artists.

In keeping with this mission, in the pages of *Spinner V,* community historian, Ken Champlin, adds a poignant chapter to our ongoing history of neighborhoods. In "Between Heaven and Hell," Ken revisits the devastating fire in Fall River when Notre Dame church, a cherished landmark on the Fall River skyline, burned to the ground in 1982, taking a good part of "the Flint" neighborhood with it.

Interviews with neighborhood people reveal what the church meant to the French-Canadians who originally settled here. Built by ordinary mill workers, the church, with its magnificent paintings and stunning architecture, was their "temple to God." Over the years, the church tells the story of a changing neighborhood. Ken searches out the people in the old Flint neighborhood who lost their homes and asks: How have they rebuilt their lives? Is there still life in the Flint?

Drawing on oral history, old newspapers and family scrapbooks, "Judgment Day," brings back New Bedford's colorful Mayor Edward Peirce. It sheds light on a chapter of New Bedford history that has always seemed murky and unfinished. Did a former mayor of New Bedford really run for office from jail? The answer is yes. Ned Peirce's daughter, Nancy, tells his tragic story and defends his honor.

Mayor Peirce's story is the larger story of America, a man who reached the pinnacle of success, only to be brought down by the opposing forces of his time. Taking time out from umpiring a prison softball game in 1955, the incarcerated mayor reflected: "The drive and ambition of one with a goal can be treacherous and can catch up with him. What time do you have to think clearly on the outside, to really meditate? You think you're pretty smart. I did. But you're really thinking in one track and see only what's in front of you.

"Yes, my plans for the future are not concerned with how am I going to make a dollar, but with how, with what outlook, will I live. Look at me. I don't know what it was, luck, brilliance, the help of the Good Lord. But I had $1 million before I was 30. Yet, a few years later, in 1936, I was working on the WPA. And within eight years of that, I was in the Massachusetts Senate."

Spinner has uncovered two extraordinary journals of local and international interest. Natalie Kaplan's story was filed in a box in the UMass Dartmouth Jewish archives, silent and waiting for discovery. "Unforgettable Days" is Natalie's account of her girlhood in Russia and her conscription into the Red Army as a nurse, before emigrating to New Bedford with her husband, Dr. Boris Kaplan. When Boris died young and unexpectedly, Natalie struggles as a single parent to raise two daughters.

"The Fall River Nanny," came to us by way of Florence Brigham, that city's beloved librarian and historian. When Mrs. Brigham submitted the diary to us, she said: "This is the Fall River *I* remember. There aren't many of us who remember it that way."

When a young Englishwoman, Annie Ward, came to America from England in 1914 and worked as a nanny for a mill owner, she left behind a journal that recalls Fall River at a quieter time in its history. Her journal is an account of domestic life in an affluent household, of the gaiety of night life in Fall River, in particular, the old Academy Building as a cultural center. In contrast to her life in Fall River, Annie's letters from home are more bleak as England is being drawn into World War I.

Sometimes, people's life stories may seem mundane. But to Spinner, the simple tales of immigration, making a life and working hard is the essence of our books. We ask our citizens to look back and share their stories. Two such accounts give us a glimpse of life at two area institutions, St. Mary's Home for Children in New Bedford and Sol-e-Mar Children's Hospital in South Dartmouth. Though closed for many years, these places continue to hold an almost mythical place in the local mind. They remind us of the strength and character many residents developed as a result of their childhood struggle. We revisit these old institutions through words and photographs.

In "At St. Mary's Doorstep," Raymond Rivard tells about his teenage years as a resident there. Unlike many others who recall the rigidity and harsh discipline at the Children's Home, Raymond remembers St. Mary's as a place that gave him sustenance and saved his life.

"Children of Sol-e-Mar" is a fond recollection of life at the Sol-e-Mar Hospital for crippled children. Three young girls who lived there and formed a lifelong friendship tell their story to freelance writer Christine Woodhouse. Through photographs and oral history, we learn of the days before penicillin, when children were struck down by polio and insidious bone and joint diseases. Sol-e-Mar was a gift from Amelia Jones to the stricken children of Greater New Bedford.

The history of our local farms tells the story of people's relationship with the land, with neighbors and nature, with crops and animals, and with methods of buying, selling and bartering. In "Heritage Harvest," Kerry Downey Romaniello shows how the culinary worlds of the Indians and settlers mixed and mingled, bringing us the jonnycake, the clambake and more. Three area farms that have survived are spotlighted: Gray's Grist Mill, the Smith Long-Acre Farm (now the Westport River Vineyard and Winery) and Ashley's Peaches in Acushnet.

Photographs are the heart and soul of Spinner. In these pages, we display a rich assortment of more than 350 photographs obtained from area archives and personal collections. A special feature, "Milton Silvia: As I Saw It," showcases a treasury of photographs taken during Milt's long career with *The Standard-Times.* They document a half century of life in southeastern Massachusetts. In "Trolley Days," by John Ackerman, pictures and personal accounts bring back the days of the city streetcars.

Old newspapers? Other people's trash and recyclables are Spinner's treasures. Newspapers are living history. In "The Progress of Bloomerism," author Paul Cyr tracks the coming of the new fashion through New Bedford's newspapers and discovers the Whaling City is more tolerant than most. Also, the rise and fall of bloomers said less about fashion than about women's position in society.

What to do with a valedictory address delivered at Russells Mills High School in Dartmouth in 1894? This one is not a throwaway. Teenager, Carrie Sherman, delivers a moving address in "The Old Order Changeth." The document seems to presage her death a short time later.

Finally, Spinner relies on oral history to create a portrait of "Rum Running in Westport." Though rumrunning was a principal occupation of many in that town, it is still a well-kept secret. What was life like in Westport during Prohibition? What does local lore have to say? Plenty—but no names, please.

This is the world of Spinner: words and photographs, oral histories and journals, books and newspapers, memoirs and memorabilia. It is a world we all have in common as human beings.

Acknowledgments

The Editors and Staff of Spinner Publications wish to express their gratitude to the organizations and individuals whose generous support made *Spinner V* possible. We would especially like to thank the publisher, editors, correspondents and staff at *The Standard-Times*. The newspaper continues to generously support our research efforts. We are also grateful to the Massachusetts Cultural Council, and the State Senators and Representatives who have supported the Council's funding efforts. Without the grant support provided by the Council (since 1983), Spinner Publications would not exist.

Grant Sources
- Massachusetts Cultural Council
- New Bedford Arts Council
- Dartmouth Arts Council
- Westport Arts Council
- Crapo Foundation

Spinner V Staff
- Joseph D. Thomas
- Marsha McCabe
- John Robson
- Darlene Pavao
- Melissa MacLeod
- Ruth Caswell
- Susan Grace
- Claire Nemes
- Jay Avila

Major Contributors
- Milton P. George
- Daniel Georgianna
- Donna Huse
- Milton Silvia
- Jane Thomas
- Karen Whoriskey

Authors & Artists
- John Ackerman
- Kenneth Champlin
- Paul A. Cyr
- Jennifer Dulude
- Ruth Edwards
- Robert A. Henry
- Nina Downey Levesque
- Davison Paull
- Kerry Downey Romaniello
- Christine Woodhouse

Organizations/Businesses
- The Standard-Times
- New Bedford Free Public Library
- Notre Dame de Lourdes Church
- St. Luke's Hospital Medical Library
- University of Massachusetts Dartmouth
- Center for Jewish Studies at UMass Dartmouth Library
- Fall River Herald News
- Fall River Historical Society
- Providence Journal-Bulletin
- Brown University
- Oberon Company
- Southeastern Regional Transit Authority (SRTA)

Other Contributors
- Joan Barney
- Nicholas Beraudo
- Colleen Berry
- Mark Berube
- Florence Brigham
- Robert V. Boutin
- Tony Braz, Jr.
- Lee Butterworth
- Everett Caswell
- Robert Cosgrove
- Rachel M. Deschene-Costa
- Gail Couture
- Lucille Gomes Crispim
- Donald Edwards
- Russell Forand
- Tina Furtado
- Mary Giles
- Janet Grindley
- Ralph Guild
- Susan Hill
- Jack Hirschmann
- Bonnie Hsu
- James H. Jenkins
- Barbara Kaplan
- William Kells
- Eleanor Smith King
- Albert Lees, Sr.
- Paul Levasseur
- Barbara J. Little
- Carlton Manchester, Sr.
- Roland Masse
- Timothy McTague
- Caroline Medeiros
- Mary Soares Mello
- Walter Mitchell
- Claudette Moorhouse
- Reverend Frank Morse
- Ab Palmer
- Richard Paull
- Brenda Pinkney
- Elsie Lareau Ponte
- Albert Proulx, Jr.
- Joseph G. Reedy
- Raymond & Lorraine Rivard
- Esther Roderick
- Robert & Carol Russell
- Mary Sadlier
- Dennis & Louise Sentner
- Katherine Simon
- Barbara Sylvia
- Paul Thibault
- Joseph E. Toole
- Archer Tripp
- Diane & Ernie Ventura
- Grayton Waite
- Robert Waxler

Contents

4. Foreword

6. Acknowledgments

8. Between Heaven and Hell .... Ken Champlin
Fall River residents reflect on the catastrophic fire that took historic Notre Dame de Lourdes church and 30 buildings, leaving hundreds homeless.

40. Children of Sol-e-Mar .... Christine Woodhouse
Three young girls meet and form a lifelong friendship at this convalescent hospital for crippled children in the days of polio and other illnesses.

54. Judgment Day .... Marsha McCabe
The daughter of New Bedford mayor Edward C. Peirce recalls her dad, who was sent to jail on charges of protecting gamblers, and defends his honor.

72. Westport Rum Runners .... Davison Paull
Rum running was the principal occupation of a good many Westporters who are still careful about what they reveal. Fear of the mob remains in these parts.

84. The Old Order Changeth .... Carrie Sherman
Dartmouth's Carrie Sherman gives a moving valedictory speech to the graduates of Russells Mills High School in 1894.

88. Milton Silvia: As I Saw It .... Marsha McCabe
Photographic essay representing the 50-year career of photojournalist Milton Silvia, former *Standard-Times* staff photographer.

108. At St. Mary's Doorstep .... Raymond Rivard
"If you don't behave, we'll send you to St. Mary's!" Raymond Rivard remembers St. Mary's Home as a place that gave him sustenance and saved his life.

118. Unforgettable Days .... Jennifer Dulude
Natalie Kaplan's story begins in Russia as a conscripted nurse in the Red Army. Her story continues in New Bedford where she struggles to earn a living.

134. The Progress of Bloomerism .... Paul Cyr
A merry romp through New Bedford's old newspapers in search of "the bloomer girl." The city is surprisingly tolerant in regard to the new fashion.

142. Trolley Days .... John Ackerman
Remember trolleys? The beloved streetcar returns in words and pictures—trips to beaches and Lincoln Park, childhood pranks and fond memories.

156. Heritage Harvest .... Kerry Downey Romaniello
The mixed culinary worlds of the Indians and settlers bring us the jonny cake, the clam bake and more; and a visit to historic local mills and farms.

170. The Fall River Nanny .... Annie Ward
Annie Ward, a young Englishwoman, works as a nanny for a mill executive. She leaves a journal full of romance, turmoil and old Fall River days.

186. Bibliography

187. Index

Robert Cosgrove's award-winning photograph freezes the fall of Notre Dame de Lourdes' steeple, Fall River, Massachusetts, May 11, 1982.

Between Heaven and Hell

Kenneth Champlin

The fire that destroyed Fall River's beautiful Notre Dame de Lourdes Church and much of the neighborhood in the Flint section, on May 11, 1982, did not destroy the spirit of the people residing there. In this first person account, Ken Champlin, Fall River native, talks about the hellish day of the fire and its aftermath. Has the Flint survived? How have these people rebuilt their lives?

Notre Dame Church, along with a good section of the Flint, burned down today. I was in the public library doing research on the Flint when I heard the news. I hurried over to Government Center to watch the view eastward from the Office of Historic Preservation. The church was engulfed in flames and the south tower had already fallen. By the time I walked/ran to the Flint, just the shell remained of Notre Dame with fire fanning out from the church, towards the west and south.

— Journal entry, Ken Champlin, May 11, 1982

The parish of Notre Dame de Lourdes in Fall River figured in our family conversation from my earliest days of childhood. The memories of my mother, aunt and grandmother were woven around a collection of family photographs, a fragile cloth of family, work, parish and neighborhood recollections.

Pictures of barber uncles cutting hair, children in tenement yards, textile workers with shuttles, "Tin Lizzies," weddings, graduations and other events were accompanied by the stories of the French-Canadians, of the follies and achievements of brothers and sisters, aunts and uncles, of the virtue and pettiness of nuns and priests. Recounted, in essence, were the lives of the saints and sinners of Flint Village.

I last visited the church in 1979 in the company of Fall River poet and writer, Stephen Ronan. Stephen, carrying his camera, wanted to check out the world-famous paintings on the ceilings by Italian

Flint inferno. *This view, looking east, shows most of the Flint Village in Fall River's East End. The church stood on a small hill and seemed to rise above the neighborhoods. A landmark feature that could be identified from miles away, Notre Dame helped define the character of the parish city.*

Hank Seaman, The Standard-Times

master artist Ludovic Cremonini. I noticed the exterior of the church was badly in need of restoration. While tugging at the locked door, I wondered if the interior had fared as badly. Above me rose a wall of granite ashlar, badly buckled.

Three years later, the decision to restore the church brought joy to parishioners and city preservationists. The announcement was made on February 11, 1982, the feast day of Our Lady of Lourdes. To reach the $1 million goal over a four-year period, the parish sought a pledge of $1,000 from 500 individuals and families (or $5 per week) which would bring in a half million dollars. Blue and white bumper stickers heralding the campaign appeared on cars everywhere in the city.

The campaign was a rousing success and the workmen were ready to go. There was much to be done. The massive gutters, granite masonry, stained glass windows and two 235 feet high wooden steeples, covered by copper sheeting, were badly in need of repair and restoration. The installation of a comprehensive fire detection system was also under consideration.

Work began in late March. Dramatic scaffolding crisscrossed the structure. Steel vines of staging climbed 100 feet between the steeples on Notre Dame Street and a network of pipe rose up the north wall of St. Joseph Street.

On May 11, one of the workers atop a pipe staging was using a blowtorch to heat soldering irons in a compact portable oven. The oven had been placed in the massive gutter, where it was thought to be safe because it was surrounded by metal.

"We really don't know just how the fire started," said supervising contractor Bernard Gendreau.

"We do know that pine boards of varying lengths and sizes were used behind the metal gutters in a fashion common in the roofing of nineteenth century buildings," said reporter Aime Lachance. The boards may have been ignited by a spark from the blowtorch.

The employee using the blowtorch worked for Universal Roofing Co. of New Bedford. The company went out of business when it burned to the ground shortly after the Notre Dame fire.

Notre Dame de Lourdes Parish

Edmour Poirier

Notre Dame de Lourdes Church, circa 1980. *The Bedard Street neighborhood is visible at far right foreground.*

Restoration in progress (left), **Gendreau Construction Company, March 1982.**

John Sheckler, The Standard-Times

Clock tower and steeples ablaze.

Doomed dome (below left). Dome of the church where Sister Carole Ann saw flames chasing Cremonini's angels and saints.

Rapid fire (below right). View on Notre Dame Street shows the fire spreading to houses along Bedard Street (left). The church was consumed in 90 minutes.

First steeple tumbles (opposite page, left). Firemen look on with awe and with the realization that the church is lost. View looks east down Bedard Street from Notre Dame Street.

Backyard oven (opposite page right). In the backyards on Bedard Street, firemen scramble in vain to save houses.

The residents of Bedard Street woke to a cool gloomy dawn, the gray sky clearing by noon. A crisp wind from the north stirred the new foliage of trees on the grounds of Notre Dame. The most popular view of the old church was the angle of its north wall and the front, with the brown shingles and white trim of the street's triple-deckers to the right.

That afternoon, Notre Dame School principal, Sister Helene Dussault, and Sister Carole Ann were conducting a First Communion class in the rear sanctuary of the upper church. Just before 2:20, Claire Pelletier, busy in the parish rectory, noted smoke rising from the northeast corner of the church roof. She informed the assistant pastor, Rev. Normand Grenier, who met up with the sexton, Roland Masse, and both men ran the few yards from the rectory to the church.

Mr. Masse and the workmen bolted past the Communion class to grab fire extinguishers positioned throughout the church. At first startled, then alarmed, the Sisters gathered the children together.

Sister Carole Ann glanced up at the dome one last time to behold Cremonini's angels and saints peering down, their figures seeming to flee from an orange glow emanating above the circular stained-glass window. The two Sisters led their class from the sanctuary, crossing through the sacristy. From there, they descended a staircase to the lower church and exited through an exterior stairwell near the rectory.

Paul Turcotte, 7, saw flames coming through the sacristy ceiling. While hurrying down the stairs, he thought he heard a muffled explosion from within the church.

Because of heavy smoke, Mr. Masse and the workmen could not gain access to the loft via the steeple. The crackling sound first heard by Conrad Gendreau, of wood burning unseen beneath the slate roof, soon became the rooftop flames seen by the school children. It was 2:30 PM when Mr. Masse reentered the church to remove the Blessed Sacrament from the sacristy tabernacle, and he too saw flames coming from the ceiling.

Notre Dame de Lourdes Parish

David Souza, The Standard-Times

The residents of Bedard Street saw the sky darken for the second time that day. A dreamlike rain of burning embers wafted from those storm clouds, landing in tenement yard lilac bushes as the first fire trucks responded to the alarm called in by workers.

The wail of fire trucks was heard throughout the city, the first alarm at 2:25 PM, another at 2:27, and a third at 2:29. Finally, the general alarm came at 2:48 PM.

When the firefighters arrived, three were ordered up to the roof of the church to investigate. Lt. Robert Viveiros and Pvts. Dean Kimball and Thomas J. Moore followed one of the workmen up. Mr. Kimball

David Souza, The Standard-Times

Ron Rolo, The Standard-Times

13

David Souza, The Standard-Times

Bedard Street goes up in flames. *An estimated 70 families and 300 people were left homeless. At right, a tangle of hoses and exhausted firefighters are no match for the raging fire.*

removed a skylight, but they were ordered down when the heat and smoke became too much.

According to *The Standard-Times* newspaper: "As they scrambled down a ladder, air somehow began streaming into the church, which up to then had been a smoldering oven. In a matter of seconds the old wood inside the church exploded into flames…The fire just picked up and blew all the windows out. Once the air got in, it went up like a match."

At that moment the wind picked up again from the north. The smoke turned to a cottony orange and the firefighters were forced to retreat from Bedard Street. Fire engines exited so quickly that hoses were snapped off at the hydrants.

Detective Sgt. Robert Peladeau and three other detectives knew they had only a few minutes to get the residents out of the triple deckers. "There were so many heroes out there," said Sgt. Peladeau.

David Souza, The Standard-Times

Everyone seemed to have a camera that day, including Bob Cosgrove, the mail room clerk and custodian at the Fall River *Herald News* who had dreams of being a professional photographer.

He was riding shotgun in a companion's car, headed towards the flaming church. Positioning himself as close to the church as possible, he captured the plunge of the church's twin steeples in a series of photos which ended with the shattering of the north spire upon the church porch. First published in the Fall River *Herald News*, the star photo was eventually picked up by the Associated Press and received national and international exposure.

The three-hour inferno provided photographers ample opportunity to shoot. Firefighters, held at bay by the firestorm on Bedard Street, dropped back to Notre Dame Street. The church

The Standard-Times

Fire and water. *On Bedard Street, firefighters hose down rooftops (top) and battle a hurricane of fire (left).*

Ron Rolo, The Standard-Times

Mike Valeri, The Standard-Times

War zone. *Firefighters came from throughout the region to do battle. At right, men from East Taunton and Taunton fire companies survey ruins of Bedard Street.*

From the air *(opposite). The rear of the church is a smoldering ruin, looking west from Eastern Avenue.*

and the vest-pocket neighborhood to the south were lost. Fire Chief Louis Shea and his crew met the wall of flames with a wall of water at Pleasant Street. At least 26 fire departments from cities and towns in Massachusetts and Rhode Island responded. Warren, Rhode Island's new ladder truck was baptized in the "water curtain" thrown over the flames. One and a half million gallons of water were pumped on the fire.

Daylight faded. The dying north wind seemed to calm the small scattered fires in the granite foundations, which appeared quarry-like under the alchemic humus of water and incinerated wood. Notre Dame de Lourdes, a structure that took 16 years to build, was gutted in less than a half hour. "The Last Judgement" and 18 other paintings perished in the fire. A carillon of 20 bells, weighing more than nine tons, fell with the steeple. Of the 13 stained glass windows, one survived.

Mike Valeri, The Standard-Times

Hank Seaman, The Standard-Times

Notre Dame de Lourdes Parish

The magnificent church had been built by working people, the French-Canadian parishioners in the Flint district of Fall River. It was their "temple to God." According to Roland J. Masse, who wrote a brief history in a cherished memorial booklet, Notre Dame's third pastor, Father Prevost, arrived in Flint Village in 1888 to find his parish in dilapidated condition. He set about building a suitable house of worship, a temple to God, and succeeded beyond his wildest dreams.

Mr. Louis Destremps, a parishioner and noted architect, began designing a church in which there would be no supporting pillars to obstruct views of the services. By using a system of trusses, beams, buttresses and metal rods with turnbuckles, Mr. Destremps was able to get by with one interior column. The ceiling of the nave was supported from the attic, and the transept represented a false dome when viewed from the inside. Destremps would later design at least two other Fall River churches using this same architectural style, St. Roch's and Blessed Sacrament.

The cornerstone was laid on May 30, 1891 and work continued for the next 16 years. Mr. M. J. Castagnoli, a master sculptor, was commissioned to produce the interior plaster work, the long-admired columns, cornices and bas-reliefs.

While Castagnoli was laboring on the walls, the master artist, Ludovic Cremonini, executed 18 paintings on canvas, using parishioners as models. All but one were done in the style of the Renaissance artist, Titian. The large arch over the sanctuary was based on the style of Raphael. His most famous painting was "The Last Judgement," produced on several canvases that were joined and mounted on the ceiling of the church nave (77 feet long and 55 feet wide). It portrayed Christ on the last day, rendering judgment on mankind.

The Brothers Casavant of St. Hyacinthe, PQ, Canada were commissioned to build and install a great organ. The high romance organ, put in place in 1906, had over 3,000 pipes and 70 voices. Some 1232 light bulbs were set in the ceiling.

On November 29, 1906, Bishop Harkins of Providence dedicated the new temple of God.

In 1924, a jubilee year, a carillon was installed in the south steeple. From the Harvard Foundry of Ville-Dieu, France, this nine-ton set of bells numbered 20. On the inside, the most striking improvement was the installation of stained glass windows. The Maumejean Brothers of Paris created 13 windows 7-feet wide by 27-feet high, depicting the life of Christ.

The only stained glass window that survived the fire was in Boston being repaired. It has found a home in the new church.

The Standard-Times

Notre Dame de Lourdes, 1918. *The tall spires were damaged by the 1938 hurricane. The original steeples were 310 feet high but were cut and repaired to a new height of 235 feet.*

Church interior *(opposite page). The classically designed interior was adorned with 1232 lights. The church was supported from its roof and the ceiling was fastened to it with the help of trusses. A system of steel rods and turnbuckles kept the walls in place. This allowed for only one interior column, so parishioners could view the church without obstruction.*

Cremonini's "The Last Judgement" *(left). One of Cremonini's most famous paintings, "The Last Judgement" took one year to paint and was made on 7 small canvases, assembled and fastened to the ceiling by hammer and tacks.*

"Flight Into Egypt." *Notre Dame's only surviving stained glass window was being repaired at the time of the fire. The church's windows were built in Europe by Maumejean Brothers in 1924.*

Milton Silvia, The Standard-Times

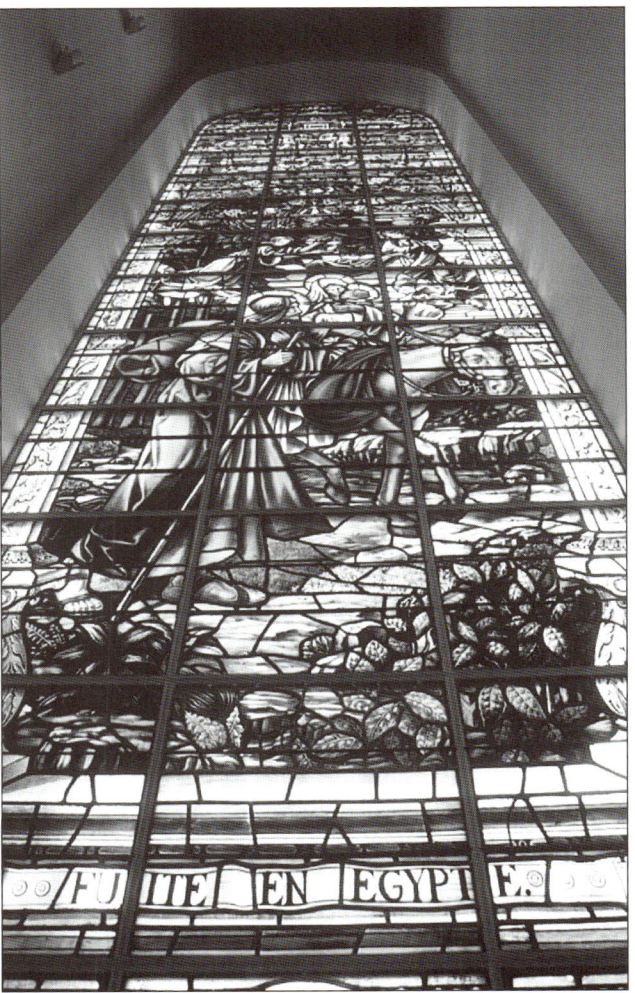

John K. Robson

Hank Seamen, The Standard-Times

Red Cross relief. At 10AM Wednesday morning, the American Red Cross and other agencies opened a disaster relief center in the old Espirito Santo Church on Alden Street, appealing to the public for funds, canned goods and clothing.

Christ the Redeemer. Standing before the ruins, the statue of Christ the Redeemer seems to beg us to understand the horror of what has taken place. The statue survived the devastation.

Shades of a wartime ruin (opposite page). This powerful photograph brings to mind the haunting images of the devastation in Europe during World War II. Ironically, National Guard Sergeant Henry Froment is standing in the same halls where he made his First Communion and Confirmation just a couple of decades earlier.

Returned to the Flint today to observe the destruction firsthand. The shell of the church was still smoldering and the scaffolding had melted under the heat of the flames, particularly on the front, where it lay crumpled down the front steps like the blackened skeleton of some prehistoric animal. The south wall of the church was perched eerily above the charred timbers of tenements and small shops along Pleasant Street—A tenement on Bedard had been wrought by the flames into a brittle iron-black bird cage…more like a sketch of a houses's outline in charcoal than real wood, stone and brick. We walked away from a group of men, one of whom shouted, "To hell with the church. Fall River's got plenty of churches. What about people like me who got burned out?"

— Journal entry, Ken Champlin, May 12, 1982

What about the people? Thirteen multi-family dwellings on Bedard Street were among over 30 buildings either destroyed or damaged. Some 109 families, a total of 300 people, were displaced. Property damage was estimated at $15 million.

Most of the victims moved in with relatives. Other families, stunned and bereft, filed slowly through the auditorium doors of Jesus Mary Academy on St. Joseph Street, seeking shelter for the night. One hundred and forty-six guardsmen of the 211th field artillery, ordered into the streets by Governor Edward J. King, took over the neighborhood. Fall River Police Chief Raymond Conroy placed 50 of his officers on duty.

Ron Rolo, The Standard-Times

The city began working overtime, gathering statistics to get disaster relief for the victims. Twenty businesses, most located on Pleasant Street's 1500 and 1600 blocks, were either ruined or damaged. Being designated a disaster area would allow people to apply for low interest, Small Business Administration loans. Specifically intended for the under-insured or uninsured, these federally funded loans carried interest rates of 8%-11% on loans up to $500,000 for a business and $55,000 for a homeowner. The chief executives of the major banks agreed to offer special short term loans as well.

The Fall River Community Development Agency and state representatives Robert Correia, Thomas Norton and Charles Sylvia drafted a fire aid bill, which provided low-income families with rental assistance. The bill also sought a $1 million reimbursement from the state to the city, to defray the costs of firefighting and overtime for the police and National Guard. In the Senate, Mary Fonseca introduced legislation that would allow the Fall River Tax Assessor's Office to grant abatements for those whose property was destroyed or damaged in the fire. The city council quickly approved the legislation in accordance with Massachusetts home rule provisions.

The city established two sites to process the paperwork for the various relief programs. Families and individual householders applying for SBA loans were directed to Park Superintendent Daniel Rapoza's office at the Red Cross center. Another office addressing the concerns of small business owners, operated by Robert Karam and the staff of Jobs for Fall River, met at the Flint branch of the Fall River Public Library.

Mike Valeri, The Standard-Times

Joseph D. Thomas

The day after. Four views of the remains of Notre Dame show the gnarled staging in front of the church entrance (above) and the rubbled foundations of the houses that once stood on Bedard Street (right).

In one of his articles for the Fall River *Herald News*, Aime Lachance observed, "From the lips of a youngster came the question to a parent, 'How could God let this happen?'"

Maybe one should consider what God didn't allow to happen. In the midst of such destruction, not one life was lost.

Still, one feels emptiness upon surveying the vacant parking lot where hilltop tenements once stood. Here one discerns a rent in the built fabric of the Flint. The weave only becomes whole again where the gentle, sloping bend of Choate Street triple-deckers comes into view. The obvious questions arise. Thirteen years after the fire, what became of the former residents of Bedard Street? Did the parishioners rebuild? Did the neighborhood survive? Did the city provide?

In the days following the fire, Father Blais said to his parishioners: "It was in the blood of our forefathers to build after they had lost a Notre Dame Church by fire in the early 1890s, and it is in our blood now." And so it was. The cornerstone of the new church is dated 1986.

How did the people fare? This is another story. To nineteenth century French-Canadians, "in the blood" meant survivance, survival of the French church and the French language. In the aftermath of the fire, survivance would assume its most literal and universal meaning—survival.

I believe now as I did 14 years ago that neighborhoods decline when their mythology is lost. The mythology of a neighborhood can be rebuilt by reconstructing its past. Life has continued in the Flint, and the fire has become part of the story.
— Journal entry, Ken Champlin, August 1995

Joseph D. Thomas

Joseph D. Thomas

Joseph D. Thomas

Robert V. Boutin

Robert Boutin and his wife Marilyn owned four houses and a garage on one large lot on Bedard Street. For nine years, they lived in one of the apartments at 21 Bedard. The fire drastically changed the lives of all twelve families in the tenement houses, including the Boutin's. All four houses were lost.

BACK IN 1973, I only paid $65,000 for the entire property, and the Lafayette Bank was the only bank even willing to talk to me.

I never had a problem renting. Ninety-nine percent of the time, we got very, very good people over there. One woman had lived there since 1912 or 1915. She moved to a nursing home shortly before the fire. Two sisters had been there since the 1930s.

I was at my wife's store and got to the fire just about the time the firemen did. I went up Bedard Street and the kids were coming out of school. The slate was popping off the roof and I told the kids to go through the Bedard Street yards, over the fence and out Pleasant Street, which was the safest way for them.

After that, I picked up all of my barrels because Tuesday was barrel day and I put them in the back where they belonged. The firemen were all over the place by that time. They had gone into my apartment houses and told people to shut their windows and leave. My carpenter had been out there fixing some porches and we started double checking to see if people were out. We broke down a few doors and he wasn't too happy with that. He figured he'd get in trouble.

At that point, it looked like everything was going. We found two elderly women who didn't want to leave. They were in a front apartment on the second floor, right on the street side of the six-family tenement. We took them down the stairs, but they were very concerned about making sure their door was locked. When we got to the landing for the first floor, we couldn't go down the 11 steps there.

A big piece of sheet metal, about twice the length of the hood of a car, had blown off the steeples. The copper sheeting was still smoldering. It was really eerie. So we took one of the ladies over the banister onto the bulkhead, and we had to be careful because there were some old ladders there.

The other lady panicked. Real nice lady but she panicked and she wouldn't go. I figured I wasn't going to leave until she was over. So I grabbed her in the touche and she went flying over. The carpenter had just returned from the back of the property and he caught her, which was great.

The carpenter and I stayed for a while and tried to hose the place down, but the hose got burnt. Shrapnel from the roof started cutting the hose. You could see the wall of flames coming up through the back yards. I went into the house to take a peek at it for the last time. We had just painted the front house and it looked nice. We had put central heating in, stuff like that, and we had just finished our own apartment that very day! I was hoping the houses in the back could be saved but I didn't realize the fire chief had already said there was a certain line they were going to stop at and my house was within the burn area.

So I went inside, took my TV set from the bedroom and put it in the basement along with some silverware my wife had, which she bought when we got engaged, and our marriage certificate and threw an old plastic cloth or something over them. Then I figured I was going to go out the front door. Believe it or not, the front door would not open, which was a good thing because there was stuff flying all over the

John K. Robson

Robert Boutin, 1995. *The former Bedard Street resident peruses Notre Dame history in his Pleasant Street office. "The church had a purpose in its day. It showed pride. The French-Canadians were really looked down on. This church was considered very special. It was not only religion. It had to do with themselves being important. Even communist Chinese television carried the fire. And they mentioned it, not because it was a church, but because it was something that the peasants, basically, put up, people who were considered very lowly. And it's true, that's what it was all about."*

place. I think my guardian angel was with me not to let the front door open.

I returned to the basement and found a crash helmet down there from when I was a kid and had a little mini-bike. I put that on. I found an old sweater that I put on, then I went out the alley and around to look at the south side of the house and looked down the driveway. I started to hear bells go off and they were falling from the steeple. I knew I had to get the heck out of there. You couldn't see anything through the smoke.

There was a flat building connected to Poirier's Bakery and I climbed onto that and over the bakery. I started a ruckus with the firemen when they were on the roof. They were not pouring any water on my house and I said to them, "Look, put some water there, will ya?" At least I figured I could save my house. The firemen said, "Oh, no, no. This is all we're doing." So we had a few choice words at that point and they called a policeman over. The policeman said, "I know how you feel, pal, but you've got to get off the roof."

I said, "You don't know how blankety-blank I feel. This is not your blankety-blank house. This is my house!" He said, "I don't care. You're getting arrested if you don't get off the roof."

After the fire we moved to the caretaker's building at Jesus Mary Academy and stayed for three months. I'm not sure it was a good idea because we could see the rubble every day. That was depressing.

When we went to the so-called refugee center at Espirito Santo Church, everyone from my property had long faces except me and Mr. Charette. My wife Marilyn said, "Gee, Mr. Charette's taking it very well." We had been concerned because he had a heart condition. It turned out his mother gave him a tenant's policy years ago and he just kept renewing it!

Our two-family house had a homeowner's policy that covered furniture and clothes. Our tenants, who all stayed with relatives, got $350 up front, which was something.

Just days after the fire, Marilyn and I went to Mass in the auditorium of Jesus Mary Academy. The curate, Father Grenier, was all upset. He's since left the priesthood, you know. And he says, "Gee, I'm sorry I burnt your house." I said, "No, it's all right, I've got insurance and I'm going to buy a house on Meridian Street." "What one?" he asked. "The first house I see on Meridian Street that I like," I said.

That day I went driving up Meridian Street, saw a house for sale and two weeks later, we came back and bought it! And now I wouldn't move out of

Fire sail. High winds quickly brought devastation. Robert Boutin's rental property on Bedard Street succumbs to the inferno.

Joseph E. Toole

Meridian Street for all the tea in China! It's wonderful. There are deer in the backyard, wildlife and everything.

We had no intention of rebuilding there after the fire. Other people wanted to and it was a catastrophe for them. There were no sewers on Bedard Street—it's all ledge, all granite and the politics of the day said, "No, you can't rebuild," not just because of the sewers but also because the frontage did not meet present zoning.

Eventually exceptions were made for private developers with political connections. Later they were made for everyone because the city wanted new construction. It was ridiculous.

The church finally bought all the Bedard Street house lots for $10,000 each, a total of $60,000, without the permission of the Bishop, but that's another story. If we sold our lots to the church, we were told the city would take them back. We figured it would be a long, cold day in hell before the city government in a Catholic city would be able to take away that land. We'd picket City Hall! Obviously they didn't make the move and the Diocese acted very quickly once they realized the city's interest. They weren't too happy at first that the pastor had signed the offer agreements, but later, they ran with it. We did get a fair price. We did better selling to the church.

I was baptized in Notre Dame church, then we moved to my mother's parish. I was 17 before I walked into the church again, and my 19-year old brother had never been inside at all! But my father told us all the stories. I said, "Dad, I don't understand all these stories," and he said he'd take us to midnight Mass, but it's in French. We didn't speak French, but we understood it, so we went. And my wife and I didn't go again until we moved to the parish when I was 26.

Before the church burned, Father Grenier came to the house for a pledge. I said, "Look, I'll pledge this amount of money. But if you tear the church down and build a small white church, I'll give you twice as much." He was mortified, "How can you do that? How can you even say that?" I said, "I wasn't raised in this parish. It's my father's parish and I know it's a beautiful church with beautiful artwork, but we cannot afford it anymore. How are you going to get the money from people who are living in tenements with space heaters to keep a monstrosity church like this?"

The church had a purpose in its day. It showed pride. The French-Canadians were really looked down on. This church was considered very special. It was not only religion. It had to do with themselves being important. Even communist Chinese television carried the fire. And they mentioned it, not because it was a church, but because it was something that the peasants, basically, put up, people who were considered very lowly. And it's true, that's what it was all about.

But today we don't need that. We could not have kept the school and the church open. The restoration drive would have succeeded in fixing the church and destroying the parish because you just could not keep it up. You would have had to put in all new boilers, eventually, too. Remember how large it was? How high? How beautiful? It was special, but it was a work of art. How many bingos can you do?

The problem was that the church had been shut to the public for years. They never promoted it. Parishioners had been telling friends about the artwork for years, but they never really opened the church up. One time I went to a meeting of the Historical Society and spoke to some elderly ladies who were not even Catholic. Their father had taken them to Notre Dame Church so they could lie on the pews and look at the paintings on the ceiling.

Robert Cosgrove

Bedard Street engulfed.

Mike Valeri, The Standard-Times

Anguish, shock and awe. *Mr. & Mrs. Paul Doiron watch their house burn. Mr. Doiron is Robert Boutin's uncle.*

Their father understood how beautiful it was. But that was rare. French-Canadians, some from the North and South Ends, had never been in the church. If they had succeeded in creating a following of people who were art enthusiasts, then it might have worked. Not just religion, but for the art.

We used to have students from New York City architectural and engineering schools come to Fall River to study the trestle work, the type of loft. There were no columns in that church. People in architecture knew that was a special place.

A friend of mine said one of the prophets on the wall was his grandfather or great-grandfather. And there's a priest being cast into hell who was also a real person. He was in charge of the artist, Cremonini, who was getting paid either by the hour, the week, or the month. The priest was told to hurry him up, which aggravated the artist. From what I understand, when Cremonini unveiled that picture, the priest noticed it was his face and tried to get it changed, but the pastor said, "You can't change a work of art."

The devil in "The Last Judgement" was modeled after a fish peddler from Pleasant Street. All the people in the paintings were parishioners. There used to be a Franco-American hall in one of the buildings on a side street off Pleasant and they say that's where most of the paintings were done. That's what my father told me and he heard it from my grandfather Boutin. My mother's older sister is a Lapre and she married a Destremps. His grandfather, Louis Destremps, was the architect of the church.

Notre Dame parish expanded when the other two French-Canadian parishes, St. Mathieu's and St. Roch's, closed down. All those people can join this parish now, and they are not going to walk to church like we did, because it's so far. They need a parking lot. It's like any business. If you don't have a parking lot and air conditioning, you're not going to make it.

When you go into the new church, on the left there's a plaque with part of the cornerstone of the old church. A little piece of the facade of the Notre Dame in Paris, which was being restored, was brought from France, together with a rock from Lourdes, from the stream, from St. Bernadette. All that together makes a connection. In the new church, too, on the Bedard Street side over the door, is a stained-glass window which depicts the very first church, the just-burned church and the new one.

The fire made me jump into real estate with both feet. On Bedard Street, we just had rentals. That's all I did. Seventeen apartments and four stores, counting our Pleasant Street property. We actually made our money on that. That's what Boutin Reality was.

After the fire we had our business in three different locations, all of them generally in downtown. I went down to the Chamber of Commerce and I talked to the men at SCORE. They were wonderful,

Milton Silvia, The Standard-

"The Last Judgement," detail. *A close-up of Cremonini's masterpiece shows Mary at Christ's side, interceding for souls in purgatory. The saved are on His right and the damned are on His left. Hell (not visible), at the base, is guarded over by Satan, and awaits the fallen angels. The painting was said to be the largest interpretation of "The Last Judgement" in the world* [The Standard-Times, 7/10/66].

like grandfathers. Mr. Felder and Mr. Davol, I think. They said go back to the Flint, get a storefront, get a sign out there. The same landlord I was renting from downtown had this storefront opening up, so we moved over here.

When we came here to the Flint, business just started shooting up for us. We do a lot of business selling houses to people from New Bedford who are used to the Flint and used to shop here. People know us in the Flint, that's a big plus. They come, their children look for homes. So we have a niche here. We would never leave the Flint.

Albert Proulx, Jr., 65 Bedard Street

I WAS AROUND 14 or 15 and the fire was an adventure to a kid, but not to an adult. I knew I'd better get out of there when the stained glass window facing our doorway blew out. I told my stepmom to get out of the house, and I wanted to move my Dad's car, 'cause he was at work. By the time I got the keys, the fire department had already draped their hoses over it and wouldn't let me take it.

The car was a fire barrier for them, something to hide behind as the flames came out of the house. My father had just rebuilt that car and it irritates me to this day. When we returned to the house, it had burnt to the ground. The bar of the weight set in my room looked like a pretzel. All the appliances were melted down to nothing.

We ended up living with my grandfather in Somerset for several months and I continued to go to school in Fall River. We got some help, a pair of pants this week, maybe a shirt next week. We got a new package of underwear. We took our vouchers and I went with my dad to get beds. I remember the guy telling my father they would only give beds to me and my brother Christopher. The adults ended up sleeping on the floor most of the time.

My parents were divorced long ago and I lived with my mother, mostly, in Newport. Around the time of the fire, I had come to live with my father. I hadn't seen my father from ages six to twelve, so we had a lot of time to make up. He had bought me a lot of new possessions. I lost these and all the trophies I had won in sports.

My father was devastated more than anybody. The day after the fire he sat and cried most of the day. He had worked hard most of his life, at Arkwright Finishing, and he was mostly out of debt when the fire hit. He had to start all over and go into debt again so we could get back some of the stuff we needed.

Things started getting better for him, then something happens, like Arkwright closing. Twenty-seven years and they tell you goodbye! And you've got nothing again.

Shortly after the fire, I ended up moving back to Newport to live with my mother. Today I work as a nurse at the Corrigan Mental Health Center. Every time I drive down Eastern Avenue, I have to look up Bedard Street, and I can still see the empty lot.

Katherine Simon

ALL THE PEOPLE who lived on Bedard Street had lived there for years, like I did. Their parents had lived there, and their children continued to live there so that everybody knew everybody. Now I'm the only one still there. I had no choice but to stay. There were no ifs, ands or buts. I lived there all my life. If the house could be fixed, and they said it could, then I'd stay. People said, "Go take your money and live in an apartment." But I couldn't see that. I just couldn't see myself living away from there.

John K. Robson

Albert Proulx, Jr. and son, 1995.

Katherine Simon, 1995.

John K. Robson

There's always a big wind on Bedard Street, and the wind carried the fire down the street, but it stopped at my house. On the top floor where I live, there was water damage. The firemen's hoses were still running through the house when I returned that evening. On the bottom floor, one side was completely destroyed and the other side suffered from smoke damage. But the house was saved. The three-tenement house next door, which I also owned, was completely destroyed.

The young man who lived downstairs with his wife and child moved to Oak Grove Avenue and has since passed away. He was not a well man. Two of my tenants, two ladies, went to live in Barresi heights, then found apartments in their new neighborhood. They almost had nervous breakdowns thinking about the fire. There was nothing left for people to come home to except a hole in the ground.

I got a second mortgage with the Community Development Agency to refurbish the house. The Red Cross, St. Vincent de Paul, Almac's, Edgar's Department Store, the Salvation Army—all gave us something. I kept saying I didn't want anything because I lived alone, I had enough furniture in the house and I figured there were poorer families, but they gave to everybody equally.

Here's a for instance: The package was a couch and a chair and a table. Two side tables and a coffee table. Television, toaster, mixing bowl, silverware, glassware, coffeemaker. If you needed clothing or bedding, it depended on how many were in the family. If there was a man in the family, he got clothes, underwear, outerwear, shoes.

I'm a Protestant Congregationalist and belong to the First Congregational Church, but I feel as if Notre Dame was my church too. I've been in and out of there with the kids I grew up with. In fact, I used to pray in French because I didn't think the Lord understood English since it was a French church! There will never be another church like it.

That summer of 1982, nothing bloomed in the yard because they were throwing everything out—wood and concrete and glass. But after the house was built and the yard was surfaced over, a year later, things that my father had planted—he died in 1949—all bloomed that second year. And still blooming. So what can you say? Life goes on. Nobody died. Everybody was given a start. People still had their jobs. God doesn't pick and choose. It's just what happened.

Rental property of Katherine Simon ignites. "What can I say? Life goes on. Everyone was given a start. People still had their jobs. God doesn't pick and choose. It's just what happened."

Joseph E. Toole

Dennis Sentner & Lucille Sentner (mother)

Dennis Sentner installs sprinkler systems. Lucille Sentner is retired. The Sentner's lost two houses on Bedard Street. The houses were insured, but not the contents. "We just never thought of getting insurance for personal property," said Lucille. After the fire, the Sentners stayed with a cousin in Westport for a month, then moved to County Street in Fall River, where they live today.

Dennis

THE DAY OF THE FIRE, May 11, was my birthday. My 25th birthday. Biggest candle I ever had. We lost everything. I had a four-wheel drive truck in the yard that burned, and we lost our rental income. The only thing I had left was on my back.

The Salvation Army and factories throughout the city donated clothing and shoes. People were decent. They were there when you needed them. We were fortunate enough to have a big family and other relatives that lived on the street.

We tried to reclaim some of the things we lost by digging in the foundation and found a few things like my brother's coin collection in a bottle. A friend, Pierre Castonquay, was helping us and one night he went home to take a shower, took off his shoe and found a little blessed Mary medallion that belonged to my mother, in his shoe! We also found a silver wedding anniversary plate and a Bible with the edges burnt.

Losing everything hurts. It hurts. You never forget something like that. But you've got to move ahead.

Lucille

THE HOUSES WE LOST were originally my grandmother's, then my uncle took the property, then my brother, then we took it. My grandmother had another house further down Bedard, where she lived. She had a lot of houses built—triple deckers. My uncle Ernest Gaudreau built them. The Gaudreaus, for the most part, built Bedard Street. It was basically the whole family, cousins and what not, on this street.

Steve Varnum, The Standard-Times

Recovered memories. *Denise Sentner Hartnett, Dennis's sister, holds a photograph from her school graduation.*

Joseph E. Toole

Hank Seaman, The Standard-Times

One of the Sentner houses gets hosed down *(far left). The Sentner's had a long tradition of living on Bedard Street. "It will always be home to me," said Lucille Sentner.*

Sifting through debris. *Mark Sentner was able to salvage some old coins and jewelry from the rubble of their home.*

Dave Souza, The Standard-Times

Joanne Estrella and Dennis Maloney. Bedard Street residents console each other.

The day after (right). While neighbors assess the damages and begin the cleanup, water still runs on the smoldering remains along Bedard and Notre Dame Streets.

One son lived on the second floor in our house and a married daughter on the third floor. I was born in the front house. When I got married, my husband was in the service and we would travel to a place maybe two years, then come back to Fall River. The minute the kids saw the church, it was, "Memere's church! Memere's church!" I was baptized in Notre Dame, had my First Communion there and was married there. Everything!

After the fire, they wanted us to go into the project. I came out of there because I didn't like it. I wasn't going back. After the fire, I wanted to rebuild on the same spot, but the city said we couldn't because of the zoning. My husband figured he was too old to borrow and he didn't want to rebuild. It was hard to leave. This place isn't home to me. Bedard Street will always be home.

Marc Berube, 43 Bedard Street

Marc Berube is now an architecture student at Trinity College, Hartford.

LOOKING BACK ON IT, the fire was actually a good event for me—It forced a change in my life. I had been with Aetna in Fall River for eight years as a computer supervisor. There wasn't much opportunity for advancement. The fire was a life changing event. You see, I was ingrained in the community. Then, all of a sudden, I wasn't. So it gave me a little bit of freedom. I thought, "Well, I really don't have anything at all." So at 27, I'm starting from scratch. What do I want to do with my life?"

In the aftermath of the fire, I was more open to possibilities. I applied for a job in Hartford and was able to get a management position, which never would have happened had I stayed in Fall River. In the year before I moved, I got an apartment in a wonderful neighborhood in the Highlands, in one of those old Victorian mansions with turrets and everything, a place I always wanted to live.

Surprisingly enough, in all the years I lived on Bedard Street across from Notre Dame Church, I had only been in there once, when a friend got married. I belonged to St. Jean's, where I attended parochial school, then Bishop Connolly High School. I used to speak French, but not anymore, though I still understand it.

Joseph D. Thomas

The windows in my living room looked out onto the towers and the stained-glass windows, which were beautiful when they were lit up for Masses. It was a very comforting feeling to live next to the church, although the church eventually set the neighborhood on fire.

I had renter's insurance and was paid $8,000, which I thought was more money than I could ever use. I found out it doesn't buy a whole lot. $8,000 went fast when I even had to buy dishes, socks and underwear as well as the big things. The only thing I owned were the clothes I had worn that day, and my car, which was worthless. I also lost two cats in the fire. There are, of course, personal things I miss like pictures, including baby pictures my mother had given me. Family wedding pictures. I bought a set of fire photos and they are with me in Hartford.

Robert Cosgrove

Bob Cosgrove took the sensational photos of the fall of Notre Dame's steeples. His photo series was eventually carried by the Associated Press and shown around the world. "The fire was basically the climax of my photographic career," he says. Bob works as a pressman at the Herald News *and lives on Chicago Street with his wife and child.*

I WAS IN THE RIGHT PLACE at the right time—and in the right car when I took those pictures. I had the day off and they were getting rid of some old desks in the *Herald* office. A friend had a utility trailer and we went to the office to get a desk. When I pulled out of the loading dock, I could see smoke coming from the other end of the city. At that time, I really didn't go anywhere without my camera.

We dropped the desk and trailer off at his uncle's house and headed up toward Pleasant Street in his grandfather's car. His grandfather was a retired fire chief and his car still had the "Portsmouth Fire Chief" plate on the front. When we got down to the corner of Pleasant Street and Eastern Avenue, where they were re-routing all the traffic, they flagged us right through and I was able to take those pictures!

John K. Robson

Robert Cosgrove

Robert Cosgrove and his award-winning photos. *Notre Dame's steeples fall like fiery comets as they hit the earth. "I was in the right place at the right time—and in the right car when I took those pictures."*

Robert Cosgrove

Robert Cosgrove

Robert Cosgrove

Bakery on fire (right). The fire skirted down Notre Dame Street to Pleasant Street where it touched Poirier's Bakery (at left) and other businesses.

Poirier's Bakery, 1995. Ray and Paul Thibault stand outside their bakery on Pleasant Street. "We had wedding cakes in the oven when the fire broke out," said Paul. The brick building survived the fire and pastry was given to harried firefighters and the Salvation Army. The bakery, originally owned by Emour Poirier, was established in 1916, and is perhaps the only French bakery left in Fall River.

Paul Thibault, owner of Poirier's Bakery.

THE DAY OF THE FIRE, I was 24. We were all working in my father's bakery down the street from the church. We had wedding cakes in the oven. We could see the fire, but we couldn't leave the bakery empty, so we kept running back and forth.

The firemen tried to stop the fire at the back of this building and had their hoses on the roof. Considering the amount of water they pumped, we didn't have much water damage, probably because the building is mostly made of brick. But you could smell smoke in the bakery for a long time afterwards.

All the pastry we had, we gave to the firemen and to the Salvation Army. It was all good—It didn't

Ron Rolo, The Standard-Times

smell or taste smoky. But the Board of Health said we couldn't sell it. We lost two wedding cakes when the gas and electricity went off. We also had to get rid of a lot of flour in open bags.

Our four-tenement house at 64 Notre Dame Street, owned by my father, burned right to the ground. I lived on the first floor, my sister and her husband and two kids lived on the second floor.

All our business tenants on Pleasant Street left. Gene Hubert's Aluminium Products moved out from next door (in this building), and Texeira's Barber Shop, which had burned out down the block, moved in. Terry's Beauty Shop and Lindsey's Antiques, and I think, maybe a curtain shop, George and Paula Sue—those were all in a building next door. We lost that property in the fire, three stores and an apartment upstairs. We put in a parking lot there. It was just too expensive to put up another building.

We had insurance on the buildings but not on our personal property. We got a lot of assistance from the Salvation Army but didn't need government loans because we didn't lose the business. We were all working in the bakery—me, my father and my two sisters.

John K. Robson

Joseph E. Toole

After the fire, I lived in Somerset for a while with my father, then six months later, I moved upstairs over the bakery, where we had two apartments made. I would have liked to move out to Assonet, someplace like that, but we already had a piece of land here so we built a house on our lot about three years ago.

The church didn't buy our lot because of the location. I had to find out about the zoning from the city because all the gas, water and sewer lines had been closed. I had new lines put in from Notre Dame Street and the house is back of the bakery so it's close to work.

Eventually my wife and I will move out to the country but we'd keep the bakery here because it's so well known. When I remarried, my wife already had two kids—a son who just left for boot camp this morning and a daughter who is now 12.

I bought the bakery from my father last January, a business he had bought from his boss, Emour Poirier, in 1966. When Mr. Poirier owned the bakery, people used to leave him their bean pots on Saturdays and pick up their baked beans on Sunday.

We're the only French bakery left in Fall River. It's all Portuguese around here now. We still make wedding cakes, birthday cakes, pastries. Our specialty is French-Canadian meat pies and chicken pies. We make chourico pies, just to keep up, which sell pretty good. We have our regulars coming in all the time. When we close for vacations, they come in and load their freezers up with meat pies. The bakery's keeping us alive.

Rachel M. Deschene-Costa, owner of Paradis Funeral Home on Pleasant Street.

I WAS WORKING the day of the fire at my father's funeral home. We lived upstairs and the funeral home was downstairs. There was a wake going on that day so we took the body out and took it somewhere until we knew things were right. The funeral was the next morning. Everybody met at the Catholic Memorial Home where the Mass was to take place originally.

We had a summer house in Westport and every year my father would do something to it because he wanted to live there when he retired. After the fire, he wanted to move to the Westport house.

On our Pleasant Street building, the roof was gone and the building was gutted to the outside walls, except for one room, the room we eventually added on to. We spent the first night with my sister who lived off County Street. The following morning we were considered missing because we never reported anywhere.

We didn't only lose a business, we lost a home. There's a lot of sentimental meaning to that. We took out an SBA loan because no matter how much insurance you have, it never covers what you lost, never. We've always had a good business here, and you don't move a business that's doing well. You can move one block and not do as well. That was an old

John K. Robson

Rachel Deschene-Costa, 1995. "We didn't only lose a business, we lost a home. There's a lot of sentimental meaning to that."

Fire on Notre Dame Street (top left). The home of Paul Thibeault at 64 Notre Dame Street incinerates.

wives' tale of dad's, and our families and the people we deal with are here. This is our home, no matter how you look at it.

They say that things are in God's hands. St. Joseph was in the window in the front room the whole time my father lived there. The chimney fell down across the room, but St. Joseph only had a broken toe!

I was in my late 20s at the time and a student. My father felt he had lost his whole life. He said to my mother that night, "I've lost everything.' She said, "No, we have each other and we'll go on from here."

From May to August, we lived in a one-bedroom apartment on Downing Street that belonged to my father's brother. We slept on mattresses and box springs and army cots. Every morning we got up, put the beds away and used the front living room for our funeral home office. We sold caskets, basically, out of a book or out of Pilgrim Casket on No. Main Street. People understood that we didn't have a choice.

We had construction going on in two places at once: on the house in Westport and the damaged building on Pleasant Street. At the time of the fire, my father was in the process of buying out Corriveau Funeral Home on County Street. So we relocated to County Street during the reconstruction, then Corriveau came with us to Pleasant Street. We moved to the Westport house in August and the business was back on Pleasant Street by October. The first funeral out of here was the original hair dresser that dad had hired.

My father bought the business about 40 years ago. The original Mr. Paradis passed away and his daughter or daughters were running it. I bought the business from him in 1987.

I'm married now with four children and I still miss living on Pleasant Street. I know what it's like to live and work in the same building. I'm the mother of the family so my life entails a lot more than a man's. If I still lived on Pleasant Street, I would be with my kids more often. It would be easier, but I'm surviving it.

A week or two after the fire, dad was having a medical problem and I made him promise that if he wasn't going to be all right, not to rebuild this building. I wasn't ready to go on in the business without him. It would have destroyed me. But if he could put the building back together, and he could enjoy it with me, then we could go on together. And he kept that promise. He hung on for a long time.

Dad grew up in the Flint, lived on Downing Street, was baptized, took Communion and Confirmation in Notre Dame. He was married here and buried in this church two weeks ago. We've always been members of the Notre Dame parish.

We survived it all. Actually, a dream of mine was always to make this building a little bit bigger. Tough way to have a dream, though.

Ron Rolo, The Standard-Times

Funeral pyre. Firefighters attack the Paradis Funeral Home on Pleasant Street. During the fire, the Deschenes had to hastily remove a body, preventing an inadvertent cremation from taking place.

Roland Masse, sexton of Notre Dame.

THE OLD CHURCH could seat 1,000 people comfortably, but we never had more than 400 in there at one time. I would stand in the sanctuary, giving out Communion at Mass, and look out on the congregation and say to myself, "My God, the church is empty."

The parish population was getting smaller all the time. We could have restored the outside, but the inside? The parish could not afford to do that. That's why we were reaching out to the community for aid. We had had problems with vandals setting fires and that's why the church was locked up, theoretically, after morning services. It was open on Sunday mornings, but again, that was the time of services. After the last Mass, you'd lock it up.

A visitor would have to stop in the rectory or catch me outside and ask to get into the church. Then you'd bring them in. We were in the process of forming touring groups and planning a small gift shop downstairs. The church was a work of art. We could show people the paintings on the ceilings, the stained glass windows, the walls.

The statuary was all plaster of Paris cast—nothing hollow. It came from the House of DePrato out of Chicago, purchased through St. Michael's Liturgical Arts in Dedham. Castagnoli did all the decorative plaster work—the plastered columns, the frieze all around the cornice work, the plaster work around the windows. I think he cast the angels that held up the large painting. Angel heads here and there. He had his molds and he brought them with him.

The loss of the church was priceless in the sense that you can't restore it. You can't make a Cremonini. There are four of his murals in the Public Library: "The Spirit of America," "The Spirit of Massachusetts," "The Spirit of Fall River," and "The Spirit of the United States." They're arch paintings. Also, he did a portrait of a Fall River woman from the Highlands which is hanging in one of the public reading rooms and there's a small landscape in an office or closet somewhere. Durfee High School also has a very large Cremonini, not by Ludovic, but by his son.

Cremonini's "Last Judgement" was totally different from Michaelangelo's, but may be inspired by it. The former is darker and tends to the blue, blue-gray. Cremonini's was more pink, reddish shades, rusts.

Cremonini used people he saw attending services as models, and he would walk up and down Pleasant Street. If he saw an interesting face, he'd ask that family to please come and model. Eventually, he had too many visitors in his studio in the sacristy, so he rented a store on Pleasant Street and painted there.

People used to come in and say, "I want to see Cremonini's 'Moses' because my grandfather is the guy that posed." So I'd tell them, "Hey, I think Cremonini did at least two 'Moses' in the church. What one is your grandfather? Is it this one or that one?" "Well, I don't know," they'd say. "But my grandfather said he posed for Moses." Cremonini also did work at Notre Dame University in Indiana.

The wreckers had trouble knocking the old church down. During the fire, the granite in the south wall kept shattering and shattering and shattering when the cold water hit the hot stone. The north wall looked fine but sooty. Still, they had trouble knocking that south wall down. They began using a ball to bash the walls down but the ball broke. They removed the ball and put an actual bucket on and began dismantling it stone by stone. The bucket would come down, grab a stone, lift it off, and continue. That's how they demolished the church—slowly.

Roland Masse, sexton. Serving Notre Dame Church since 1979, Roland Masse was baptized in the parish and knows its history probably better than anyone. Behind him is a wooden model of the church, on display in the Heritage Room.

John K. Robson

Notre Dame used to be referred to as "the cathedral." Well, we're not the cathedral anymore! Which I think upset downtown a bit.

The windows of the old church had been leaking and a company from Boston said, "Let us restore one window and we'll show you the quality of our work." They removed two windows, taking out the stained glass. They left one window in the church in its crate and took the other to Boston, "The Flight Into Egypt," restoring nine or 12 sections of it. They returned them and those nine sections burned in the fire; the other sections stayed in Boston.

We asked them to ship back those remaining sections and we found a color photograph of that window. When it was time to rebuild, we gave those sections to the Rohlf Studios of New York and told them, "Now reproduce the sections that are missing from this picture." So they restored it, had new frames made and installed it in the new church, but that was the only stained glass window that was saved. And it was not one of the prettiest, just the one in the worst condition.

The fire brought a lot of people back who wanted to see their roots. And it got a lot of people already here talking to each other more, probably because they had to go through the same hardships. For Masses, we were going to Bishop Connolly High School, to JMA across the street, then to Mount St. Joseph. Just the physical setup of these places brought people closer together.

Bishop Cronin made it clear: "That we're not in the business of building museums but of building churches. We're not going to rebuild Notre Dame. We'll simply raze it and build a new church that will suit the needs of the parish." And so we did.

The anticipation of building a new church got people focusing on a common idea. You know— What are we going to be doing? What are we going to be getting? And what is it going to be like? After we moved into the new building, the interest was in adding more things to the church. At first, we didn't have any stained glass in the new church. The statuary, the carvings, a lot of things hadn't arrived. So, each week people were saying, "What's new in church this week?" Or, "Here come two more windows!"

The new windows are based on those in Canterbury Cathedral in England. They were designed by an Englishman, Mr. Cole, who came from Canterbury to have a look at the building—his designs would be shipped here, then Rohlf Studios would make the

Site of new church, 1984. Soon after the fire, the granite shell of the church was leveled—as it was determined to be unsafe to rebuild—and construction was underway at the same site for the new church.

Notre Dame de Lourdes Parish

Notre Dame de Lourdes Parish

windows in New York. They put them in as they were made. Maybe six would be ready; then four weeks later, the truck would show up again so the spaces were being filled slowly, except for that rose.

For some reason, the architect rejected Mr. Cole's design for that rose window. So Rohlf Studios put two of their in-house artists on the project—two women. The theme was based on the Litany of the Blessed Virgin in which you have about 48 different titles attributed to Mary. There are 20 wedges in the window and each wedge is a different title of the Blessed Virgin. So that's what that window is about.

The old church was facing Notre Dame Street, the center of the city. In 1888, when they started the foundation work, Eastern Avenue was a dirt trail. I think it was called Eight Rod Way—only half the width it is now. There was no Eastern Avenue as such. And the pastor at the time decided he wanted his church facing a paved street so he faced it to the west.

Today, of course, everybody would drive by and say, "How come we're looking at the back of the church, when we're on the main drag?" So Father Blais said, "I'm sick and tired of looking at the rear end of my church all the time. I want to come out of the rectory and see the front of the church!" So now the new church faces the rising sun, it faces east.

The sanctuary lamp you see there, lit, near the tabernacle, has three angels hanging from the bottom of it. The angels are from the sanctuary lamp in the old church. We had them attached to the new lamp. On the altar itself are two candlesticks we found in the ashes of the fire. We sent them back to the original company and had them refurbished. So from the old church we have the old window, three angels, the two candlesticks and the ciborium we use at Mass.

The new church has practically no wood in it at all, only in the pews, the catwalk in the attic and the cabinets in the sacristy. That's it. Everything else is metal studs, cement block, sheet rock or plaster.

Many people who are not excited by the exterior of the church are surprised when they come inside to see the interior. Very spacious, comfortable. Not ornate like the old one was. It's a different style, very contemporary. The chapel on the side is intimate, basically done in blues so it's very soft in there, very calm.

Notre Dame de Lourdes Parish

Notre Dame de Lourdes Parish

John K. Robson

Roof construction and framework, 1985 (top), **and cornerstone.**

New dome (top left). Workers construct the roof of the new church, a modern design with a glass-paneled, domed roof.

Open house at the new Notre Dame de Lourdes, 1985 (left).

Christ the Redeemer, 1995. The only remaining structure belonging to the former national historic landmark church is the statue of Christ. Today, He ushers in the parish's second century with a new house to watch over. Though the statue hasn't moved, it is now located behind the church which fronts Eastern Avenue.

Notre Dame parish probably could have been merged into Immaculate Conception, but the problem was we had more people and there was a question of space. We have about 2,000 people and one-and-a-half priests. In the old days, we had 10,000 people and six priests. Also, people were bound to ask what happened to the insurance money from the old church. Why can't we rebuild our church if we have the money? And I think, really, the Diocese didn't want to face that kind of a headache.

We still say six French Masses a week, Monday through Saturday at 8:00AM. We no longer teach French in our grammar school. That's the shame. But the other grammar schools teach French, like St. Anne's and, I believe, St. Jean Baptiste. Yet we have Mass in French. You figure it.

There will be no more French in a few years. It's not so much when the older generation passes away, it's when you no longer have priests who can speak French. That's the problem. The Mass is being said in French by older priests. We have one who's 85, another 75, who both say Mass in French. So once the older priests are gone… Let's put it this way, everybody in this parish speaks English. There is no need to have a Mass in French and some people who attend that early Mass don't understand it

There are still a lot of French ethnic people in this neighborhood, but most don't consider themselves French. You consider yourself an American of Canadian ancestry, not French ancestry. So, it's really French-Canadian and you call yourself "Franco-American." It probably should be Canadio-American! Oh, yeah, there's still a lot of identity with the old culture, but that fades with time. How many more generations will it take? Maybe one more.

In ten years you will not see any more French Masses in Fall River. They'll be finished. So many people have moved to the suburbs, which is why our parish population is falling. They are moving to Westport, Somerset, Swansea. They want to get out of the inner city and into the country.

We have so many Cambodians in the area now, down here at the bottom of Mason Street and St. Joseph. And many are not Christian, they follow their own religion. Fall River never had many black people, but now we have quite a few and many of them are Baptist. They may live in the area but they're not our parishioners. So you're bringing in other ethnic flavors to the area.

No, I don't think the fire at Notre Dame caused the end of the French. The fire was just a part of it, an aid to the end—but not a major one.

Epilogue

"No man is an iland, intire of it selfe; every man is a peece of the Continent, a part of the maine; if a Clod bee washed away by the Sea, Europe is the lesse, as well as if a Promontorie were, as well as if a Mannor of thy friends or of thine owne were; any mans death diminishes me, because I am involved in Mankinde; And therefore never send to know for whom the bell tolls; It tolls for thee."

-John Donne

The Notre Dame fire was remarkable in that not one life was lost in the conflagration itself. But there is yet another part of the story. The fire took nearly three months to claim its only victim, Alphonse Picard. With his 1965 Chevrolet assuming the anima of a sole mute witness, the 57-year-old homeless man ended his life.

An article in the Fall River *Herald News* indicates that the man, once a machine operator at Dover Stamping, had been despondent in the months following the fire. Mr. Picard was laid to rest in the Notre Dame Cemetery, whose ground was truly consecrated by the flaming embers of the old neighborhood where he lived.

Perhaps this article will provide a measure of closure for these events. By placing them in the context of local history, we can give a last glance back in respect.

Ken Champlin grew up in Fall River and earned a B.A. from UMass Amherst. Trained as an historical researcher by the former Fall River Office of Historic Preservation, he made his first contribution to Spinner *in 1982. Over the years, he has produced an archive and a history for the Fall River YMCA, tours for Fall River Heritage State Park, the Fall River Office of Tourism and the Victorian Society of America. He also provided research for* Victorian Vistas: Fall River, 1886-1900. *He lives in the Globe section of Fall River.*

The new Notre Dame de Lourdes, shortly after completion, 1986.

Notre Dame de Lourdes Parish

Sol-e-Mar Children's Hospital, 1949.

Children of Sol-e-Mar

CHRISTINE WOODHOUSE

In many ways, Caroline Medeiros, Elsie Lareau and Lucille Gomes were like any other adolescent girls growing up in the 1930s. They went to school together, played jacks together and even got into mischief together. However, in a very important way, these girls were different from the other kids. They all had orthopedic conditions that demanded a kind of care they couldn't receive at home.

For this reason, the three girls came to live at the Sol-e-Mar Convalescent Hospital in Clark's Cove, South Dartmouth. Because they were around the same age and all arrived about the same time, they developed a close bond that still exists today.

Sol-e-Mar did more than just provide physical therapy and a homey atmosphere for crippled children like Caroline, Elsie and Lucille. The hospital was dedicated to treating the whole child—mentally, socially and spiritually. When it first opened in June, 1924, the hospital promised to make the children useful citizens. And by all accounts it did.

Annual Ball, 1930s.

Portable recreation *(opposite page, top and bottom). With emphasis on sunshine therapy, Sol-e-Mar's policy required outdoor recess and recreation for everyone, in summer or winter—including the bedridden. The kids looked out for one another. "They need no prompting to help each other dress, if help is needed. Some tads are so stiffly braced with steel and plaster of paris that they cannot bend over to tie shoes or fasten garters...Big girls tie hair ribbons for little girls."* [Morning Mercury 1/31/32]

Dartmouth Police Association Party, 1949. *Children gather with local police, parents and volunteers for fun and sunshine. On a regular basis, civic groups, community members and celebrities were invited to the hospital to become involved with the children. Parties and picnics were especially popular. These events were coordinated by the Sol-e-Mar Vounteers, a well-organized group of local people who devoted many hours to recreation with the boys and girls, planning special projects and fund-raising for equipment. At the time of this photograph, the Volunteers were led by Mrs. Gilbert F. Fernandes, president.*

Caroline, Elsie and Lucille are in their 70s today, but they still remember Sol-e-Mar in vivid detail. Though their sufferings as young children must have been immense, they show no signs of disability today. They attribute their present good health to the years of great care they received at Sol-e-Mar.

Lucille Gomes Crispim, a lively 11-year-old when she came to Sol-e-Mar in 1930, was admitted for scoliosis. Though she was also weak from malnutrition, her handicaps did not curb her appetite for trouble. She is remembered as a rascal and still loves to talk about the day she wandered off into a festive, foreign world not far from the hospital grounds

The children were not allowed beyond certain limits in the large yard. Lucille was playing outside with some friends when she heard friendly, laugh-

St. Luke's Hospital Medical Library

ing female voices off in the distance. Sol-e-Mar was fairly secluded so they generally didn't see anyone outside of the hospital staff. Lucille convinced some of the other children to go on an expedition to see just what was going on. So, off they limped, crutches and all.

What they discovered were folks at a Portuguese feast. Their eyes widened, amazed by the heapings of food they saw being carried out of the big, open house, and the good smells. They walked up eagerly, wanting to see what it was all about.

The women spotted the crippled children and burst into tears. Lucille and her friends were surprised and confused, but Elsie Lareau, who could speak Portuguese, came to the rescue. She quickly explained how they had wandered off from Sol-e-Mar. This calmed and reassured the women, and the children were able to walk back to the hospital without a big fuss.

Some time later, the children were playing outside when they heard the sound of music and singing. Soon, they saw the Portuguese women from the feast, carrying a large Portuguese sweet bread baked in the shape of a life-sized child. The women had been so impressed by the children, they decided to bring the bread and the celebration to them!

Sol-e-Mar had been blessed by this kind of community support since its beginnings. Over the years, groups like the Kiwanas Club and the New Bedford Firefighters Charities, Inc. supported the hospital with fundraisers. Sol-e-Mar Volunteers, a group dedicated solely to the well-being of the hospital, organized events like the immensely popular annual ball. Proceeds allowed the Volunteers to make large purchases like new beds or a whirlpool bath.

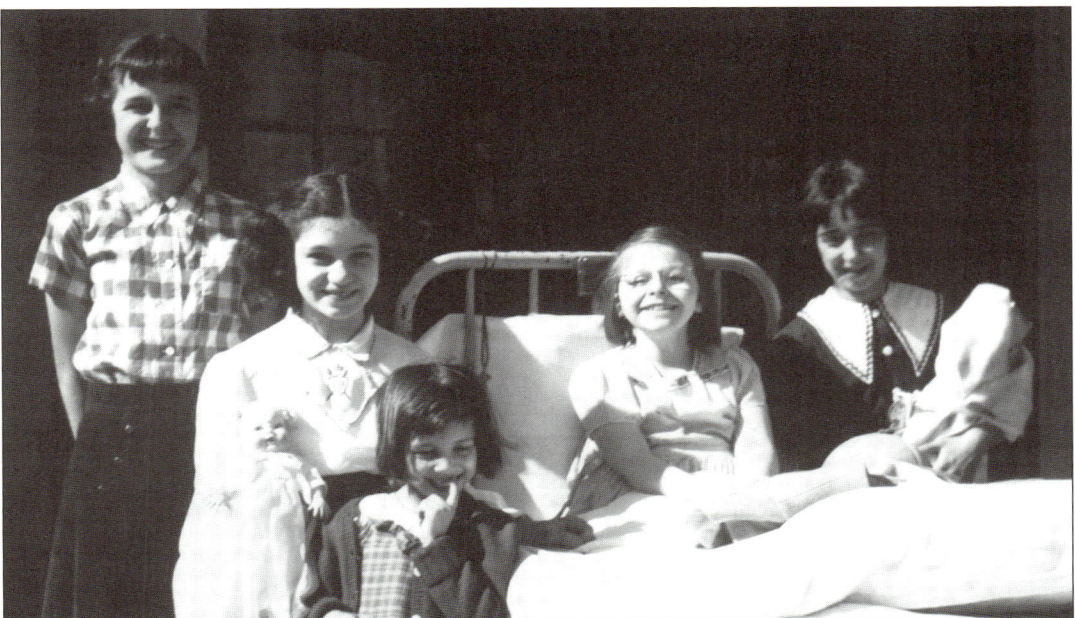
St. Luke's Hospital Medical Library

St. Luke's Hospital Medical Library

Sol-e-Mar's Beginnings

Sol-e-Mar Hospital became a reality, thanks to the generosity of one woman, Amelia H. Jones. Amelia Jones' family was already well known for its wealth and philanthropy when she donated the family's 166 acre farm in South Dartmouth to St. Luke's hospital in 1923.

As a young child, Amelia Jones traveled to Europe with her foreign-diplomat father. Their visit to a hospital in Portugal named Sol-e-Mar made a lasting impression on her. Amelia learned that the name Sol-e-Mar meant "sun and sea" in Portuguese and these natural elements were the hospital's primary therapies. She was struck by the simplicity of the care, of using sunlight and salt water to help heal children. Many years later, she would put this theory to use.

Before Sol-e-Mar was established, Miss Jones operated a summer camp on her farm in South Dartmouth. Its location on an inlet of Buzzard's Bay offered an abundance of sun and sea and was ideal for children recovering from surgery and in need of treatment. The farm also offered acres of beautiful meadows and woods for the children to play in.

As the number of children increased, Miss Jones was keenly aware that the families of these ailing

The Standard-Times   *The Standard-Times*

Amelia Jones, 1934 (left) and 1920 (right).

The idea to build a hospital came from Dr. William R. MacAusland, a surgeon who began orthopedic work at St. Luke's Hospital in 1910. "We used the cellar of St. Luke's and once a week, for many years, we gave orthopedic treatment to the poor people of New Bedford, the Cape and Islands." Soon it became apparent that more permanent facilities were needed. Besides special care, "persons with tubercular or infantile disease of the bone must have fresh air, sunlight, good food and kind words.

"So I went to Miss Jones and virtually wept on her shoulder. She wrote that she would give $25,000. But that wasn't enough to scratch a cow's back, so I waited. I put her name down in my appointment book to get a letter from me every six months. In response to these appeals, she raised her offer to $50,000, then to $100,000 and after seven years, we had a long talk. She said, 'I'll give you my farm and $1,000,000.' That was exactly what was needed. Miss Jones made her gift with the understanding that the hospital would be exclusively for crippled children."

Sol-e-Mar hospital. Built in 1924 on 166 sloping acres of woods and meadow, the children's hospital along Clark's Cove in South Dartmouth consisted of an administration building (center), flanked by a boy's pavilion (left) and girl's pavilion (right). At the far right is the infant's pavilion, which was added in 1931, and the isolation ward behind it.

Designed by architects Kendall and Taylor of Boston, Sol-e-Mar's original capacity was for 40 children, 20 in each ward. Two months after the arrival of the original seven patients, there were 31. Soon, the hospital filled to capacity and the infant's ward was built, increasing total capacity to 80.

children were not able to provide the kind of special care they needed. She felt the need of a larger, more specialized facility.

Amelia Jones organized Sol-e-Mar as a branch of St. Luke's Hospital and the new buildings sprouted up in woodsy Clark's Cove. Staffed with nurses, doctors, attendants and teachers, Sol-e-Mar opened its doors in 1924 to afflicted children in New Bedford and adjacent towns, ages two to 14. Many enjoyed free care, thanks to Ms. Jones' endowment. The new hospital offered treatment for infantile paralysis, rickets, scoliosis, osteomyelitis, malnutrition and other orthopedic conditions.

The Sol-e-Mar name, "sun and sea," remained the centerpiece of the children's treatment. Their physiotherapy was a robust combination of many things besides medicine: fresh air, healthy diet, rest, massage and exercise. In the summer months, the children enjoyed regulated sun exposure as well as exercises in the salt water. In the winter, they received Alpine lamp treatment as a substitute for the sun. The farm itself played a role in the children's treatment. Each child was required to drink one quart of milk a day and on Sundays they feasted on vanilla ice cream from the Gulf Hill Dairy farm.

St. Luke's Hospital Medical Library

Dairy farm, 1929. *In addition to drinking fresh milk from cows kept on the hospital farm, the children took part in tending the animals.*

State of the art design. *Sol-e-Mar was the latest in hospital designs with an abundance of windows, each ward opening on three sides with open solariums designed to let in the curative processes of the sun year-round.*

"A fairy road, red and gold oak leaves overhead, filtering autumn sunshine and blue glimpses of sea, winds from the Dartmouth highway to a group of many-windowed pavilions set like a group of fairy mushrooms in the woods at the edge of Clark's Cove." [Morning Mercury 10/26/24]

St. Luke's Hospital Medical Library

Choir, 1930s. *On Tuesday and Friday afternoons, school was followed by a singing hour under the instruction of Mrs. Laura Ware. On Wednesday afternoons the same hour was given to religious instruction.*

Recovery and Enrichment

Sol-e-Mar managed to provide a well-rounded education for its young patients at a time when many adults in the larger community went uneducated. Teachers were provided by the New Bedford School Department. The children performed in plays and concerts, worked on arts and crafts, enjoyed singing lessons twice a week and even created their own Sol-e-Mar rhythm band. All children who were able, including bed patients, received a classroom education as well as religious instruction.

St. Luke's Hospital Medical Library

Integrated class. *A typical Sol-e-Mar classroom had children of various disabilities learning together. The hospital's aim was to encourage children to manage their handicaps and be self-reliant. Even children bound fast to their beds were encouraged to keep up with the others, and it was considered a privilege to wheel a friend to and from the classroom.*

Seated in the foreground is Doris Oliver, who died while at Sol-e-Mar. Behind her to the right is Lucille Gomes Crispim, and to the left is Caroline Sylvia Medeiros.

"The regular course of study of the public schools is followed as far as conditions permit by Ms. Myra H. Clark. The children love just to look at her in her pretty dresses like the green swiss one with the green sweater she wore the other day. Those who went to public school before they came to the hospital tell her naively, 'I like your school, but I didn't like the other.' There, they were trying to keep up with well children." [Morning Mercury, 10/26/24]

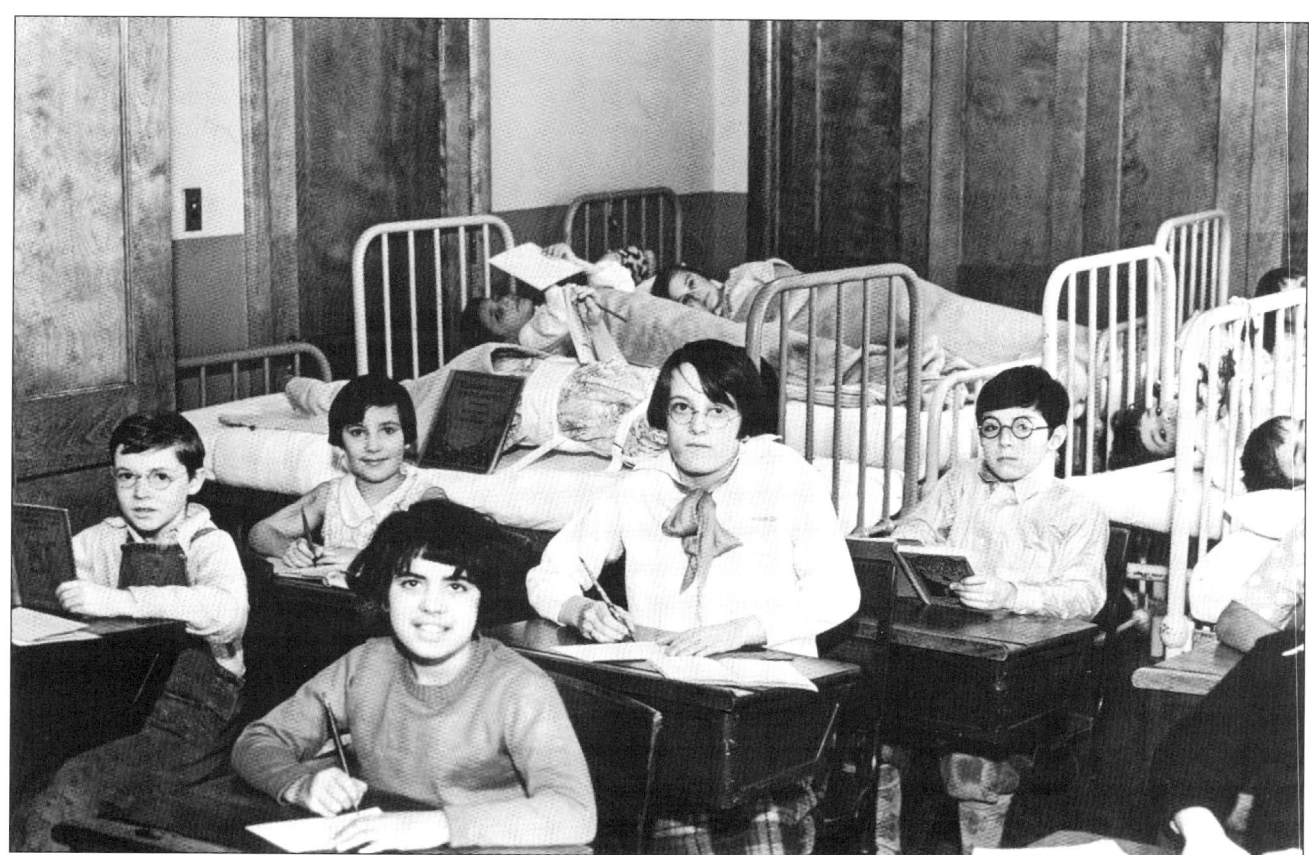

Margaret Francis Collection

Christine Woodhouse

Christine Woodhouse

Christine Woodhouse

Christine Woodhouse

Caroline Medeiros felt fortunate to be able to walk on her own and she helped to wheel the beds of others to the classroom. Her friend, Lucille, however, thought it a privilege to be wheeled to class. Lucille was envious of the children who attended class in bed so she decided to become one of them. One morning she refused to get out of bed, complaining of an ache in her side and she was quite happily wheeled to class.

Eleanor Smith King attended school while in bed every day and she does not recall it as fun. She came to Sol-e-Mar in 1932, when she was just five, and was put in a cast from the neck down because of a serious osteomyelitis infection. She remembers Sol-e-Mar less vividly than the other three women, probably because of her young age and severe condition. Eleanor shows no signs of disability today. At 68, she is healthy and leads an active life.

Extracurricular life at Sol-e-Mar was abundant and colorful. The children showed their talents at plays and concerts and were often entertained by others. They had famous visitors like the cowboy Tom Mix, Clarabell the clown from the Howdy Doody Show and Clarence C. Nash, the voice of Disney's Donald Duck. They enjoyed special privileges such as visits to Old Iron Sides (not open to the public at the time).

Elsie Lareau Pont played Maid Marion in Sol-e-Mar's production of Robin Hood and is still able to recite her lines. Elsie, at 11, suffered from multi-osteomyelitis. The memory of numerous painful treatments, including extensive surgery on her legs, arms and back is still with her. But this plucky little girl endured everything with a brave face and, in the end, says she enjoyed her childhood at Sol-e-Mar.

Girls of Sol-e-Mar. *Clockwise from left are Caroline Medeiros, Lucille Gomes Crispim, Elsie Lareau Pont and Eleanor Smith King.*

Sol-e-Mar children. *"Patients who first enter the hospital are isolated for three weeks to guard against children's diseases. After that they are anxious to play together. Friendships more often develop than animosities which are short-lived."* [Standard-Times]

Private Collection

Lucille as Robin Hood, 1931 (right). *Activities and personal hobbies were an important part of the therapy. In addition to producing their own plays, children made their own costumes, worked in clay, finger painting, weaving, plastic work, knitting, belting, woodworking and much more. Lavish displays of artwork adorned the inside, and individual gardens graced the outside. All reports on Sol-e-Mar indicate that life in a hospital could be fun.*

Caroline Medeiros, age 3.

Private Collection

Robin Hood was played by the effervescent Lucille Gomes. She was taught archery to enhance the play's authenticity and encourage her physically. With a smile, she recalls falling victim to stage fright on the big night and losing her voice. She opened her mouth and nothing came out.

Lucille notes today how much she learned about nature from living out in the beautiful seclusion of Sol-e-Mar. By spending so much time outside in the garden and woods, the children learned how to identify different flowers and plants. They also learned about the relationship between living things, the earth, the sea and the sun.

Working at Sol-e-Mar

Barbara Little of North Dartmouth worked as a nurse's aide at Sol-e-Mar in the summers of '48 and '49. Barbara was a student at Barrington College in Providence, RI (then known as the Providence Bible Institute), and was considering a future career in nursing. Her experience at Sol-e-Mar helped make her decision for her and had a profound effect on her life. She loved caring for the children so much, she went on to become an RN.

She learned the meaning of professionalism from two nurses in particular, Miss Coon and Miss Grace Lyman. Miss Coon was highly skilled in supervising the care of children in her ward. Her younger sister, Beverly (now Beverly Dickenson), also a nurse's aide, became a close friend of Barbara's. Their paths crossed again years later in the visiting nurses' field when they both became RNs.

Barbara remembers Miss Lyman for her kindness and compassion when handling the children at Sol-e-Mar and, in turn, the children were devoted to her. Lucille Gomes Crispim

Private Collection

Private Collection

Private Collection

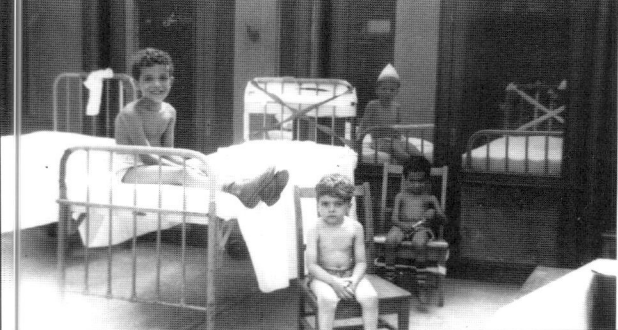
St. Luke's Hospital Medical Library

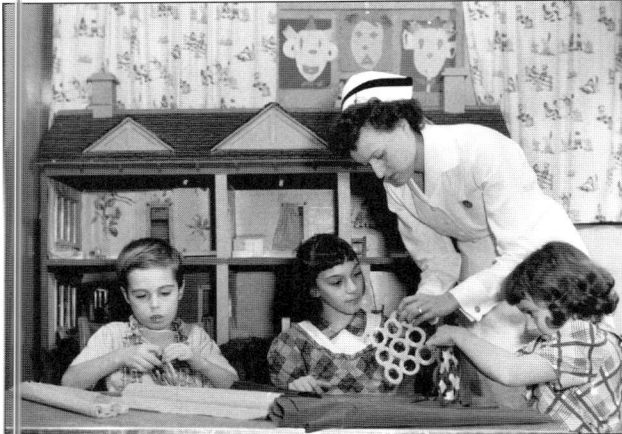
St. Luke's Hospital Medical Library

recalls making her a May basket which she and her friends hid in the woods until it was finished. Their surprise was spoiled by the ants that got into the chocolate before Miss Lyman.

Mary Soares Mello, an attendant at Sol-e-Mar from 1929 into the 30s, started working in the kitchen washing dishes and serving the nurses' tables. Miss Ross, a nurse, took a liking to Mary and was responsible for her promotion to the baby ward. Miss Ross was so impressed with Mary's work with afflicted infants that she wanted to help put her through nursing school. However, Mary didn't meet the secondary school education requirements and was unable to go on.

Her vivid memories of Sol-e-Mar never left her. Even after she married and had children, she talked constantly of her experience there. Because of what she saw there, she became a very protective mother and resisted buying her children bikes or roller skates because of the fear they would be hurt. Though she was often forced to give in when her husband bought them anyway, she stood her ground with ice skates.

A little girl Mary had cared for at Sol-e-Mar had fallen while ice skating and badly hurt her leg. Mary became close to the girl, enduring the pain with her when her leg failed to heal. The girl later died and proved to Mary that ice skating was not only dangerous, it could be fatal.

Memories of the children at Sol-e-Mar stay with Barbara Little too. She recalls a small girl named Carol, about four or five-years-old, recovering from polio. Carol's mother had died so her minister came to visit her quite frequently. Barbara's heart went out to the quiet, likable child. She played with her and read to her often, inspiring her bright young mind to prosper and grow.

Ms. Lyman, 1933 *(left). Sol-e-Mar nurses are remembered for their kindness and compassion in handling crippled children. Much skill was needed to handle polio patients and special classes were held for training nurses.*

Mary Soares Mello *(right). Ms. Mello began as an attendant washing dishes. She so impressed her supervisors, she was promoted to work with patients in the baby ward.*

Fourth of July Party Scene, 1948 *(middle). The children celebrate the holiday on the patio where they were often wheeled to enjoy the sunshine and fresh air.*

Occupational therapy, 1949 *(below). In addition to their regular courses of study, the children at Sol-e-Mar received occupational therapy. Miss Kathryn Gibbs would co-ordinate play with their classes and physical needs.*

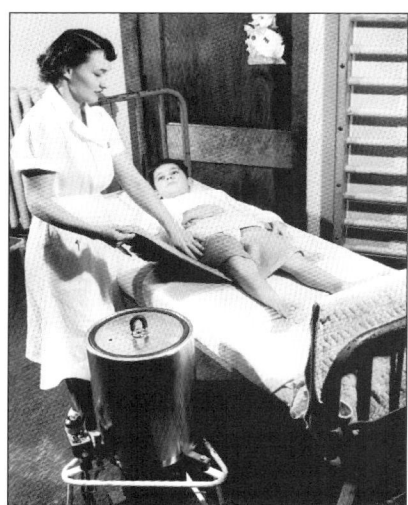

St. Luke's Hospital Medical Library

Advanced treatments. *One new treatment at the time was the Kenny Method, which called for hot cloths, steamed and dried in a special machine and placed on the patient. The chest, abdomen, limbs, arms and other parts of the body were wrapped, leaving only the joints free, so the stimulated blood would flow through the affected parts.*

"There is one large pool at the hospital made entirely of aluminum, with steps down one side and a long ramp on the opposite side. It is amazing what immersion does for paralyzed limbs, the nurse explained, for the patient can move around in the water and even walk up the steps out of the water. But this mobility is only temporary." [The Standard-Times, 1947]

Infants' pavilion, circa 1938. *Soon after it was built, Sol-e-Mar filled to capacity. A new infants' pavilion opened in 1931. However, the ward never held its capacity of 40 beds, and in 1938 the infants' pavilion was closed.*

The nurse's aides were responsible for bathing, dressing and feeding the children, difficult tasks because many children had fragile bones and had to be handled carefully. Supervising them on the playgrounds was another strenuous task because they wanted to run and jump and play just like anyone else their age. Fun had to be balanced with safety.

Grateful for Sol-e-Mar

The now grown children who stayed at Sol-e-Mar consider themselves fortunate to have had such a caring place to live and heal. They happily show their scars and talk of their treatments. Elsie Lareau Pont suffered from a particularly severe case of osteomyelitis that had spread throughout her body. Her eleventh year was particularly stressful when an operation on one leg was followed by a similar operation on the other two weeks later. When the osteomyelitis spread to Elsie's arm, they decided to give her maggot treatment.

This new approach was discovered after World War I when a soldier was found in Flanders' Field with open wounds covered with maggots. The maggots had cleaned the puss and infection from the wounds. The treatment was attempted in America on osteomyelitis patients. Maggots were put into the open wound in Elsie's arm, with a screen over the wound, so they couldn't crawl out. If the maggots began to eat living tissue, it could be painful but Elsie is proud to have undergone such an innovative treatment.

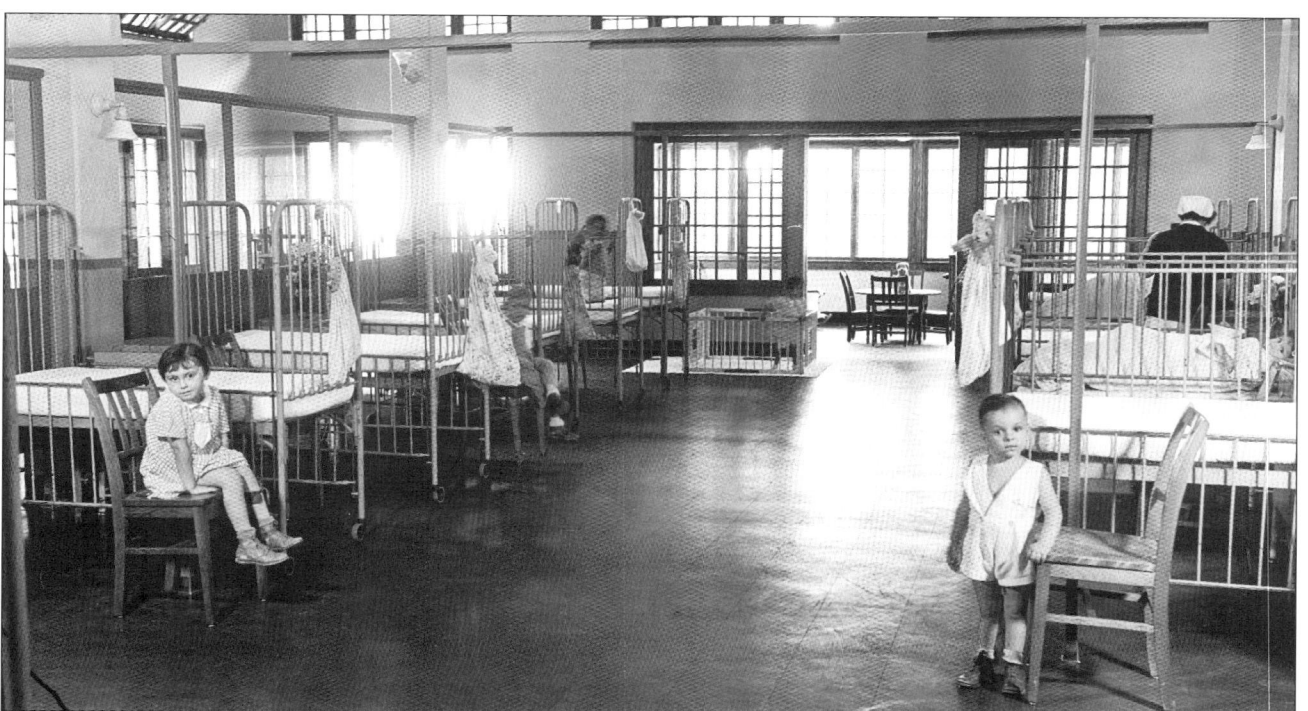

St. Luke's Hospital Medical Library

When Elsie was 27, she received the new penicillin shots which finally rid her of the osteomyelitis infection. She had 104 injections of penicillin, one every four hours.

When Sol-e-Mar shut its doors in 1960, it was for good reason. The discovery of penicillin, new therapies for crippled children and the expansion of St. Luke's Hospital reduced the need for a specialized facility. The hospital couldn't afford to stay open.

Leaving Sol-e-Mar

The children often experienced culture shock upon leaving Sol-e-Mar and going back home. On Sundays, only adult visitors were allowed. Siblings were forbidden because of the danger of spreading germs. Since many children at Sol-e-Mar had been patients for years, some barely knew their brothers and sisters. Then again, other families had no cars so these children rarely saw their parents.

Russell Forand

Cowboy Tom Mix visits Sol-e-Mar. Former patient Russell Forand has many fond memories of life at Sol-e-Mar. "One of my memories is the day Tom Mix came to entertain us with his wonder-horse, Tony. He put on a show lassoing wooden blocks. We were told to yell out the numbers painted on the blocks.

"My year at Sol-e-Mar was a happy one despite the fact I was confined to a contraption known as the frame, which was built with iron piping and covered with flannel and diaper material. I was confined to this frame for six months before I was fitted for a brace.

"I was born with a wry neck twisted towards the right shoulder. Dr. Webster made an incision in my neck at the right clavicle and stretched the tendon. I was placed in a cast with my neck facing my left shoulder. Though the operation was a complete success, eight years in that position made my back very round shouldered, thus I was sent to Sol-e-Mar.

" I enjoyed the sunshine and fresh air, the whirlpool bath and the sunlamp room. I remember us walking down to the beach with broom handles across our backs and our arms draped around them.

"My treatment was a huge success. My back became so straight and strong, I almost cry whenever I think of my time and success at Sol-e-Mar. I want to thank Mrs. Leathia Gallagher for taking care of me during that time."

Those identified in the photograph include Tom Mix, Miss Leach, Mrs. Sale, Helen Allard, Miss Lyman, Marion Phillips, Leathia Roe and Alliette Lafayonaise.

Mayor Charles S. Ashley visits, 1930. Many people visited Sol-e-Mar, including politicians, entertainers and volunteers. Miss Augusta English, a superintendent of the hospital, would say that the prettier the clothes you wear, the more the children will enjoy seeing you.

As chronic illnesses such as polio, tubercular bone and joint diseases, osteomyelitis and rickets became comparatively rare, the need for an 80-bed children's hospital continued to decrease. By 1953 the hospital beds were reduced to 40 and the patient population dropped to 20.

Fourth of July celebration, 1948. *Children bring their July 4th party outdoors.*

Because all the children at Sol-e-Mar were in the same boat, the children never encountered any mocking criticism of their condition. However, when they returned to public schools they learned all about it.

Caroline Medeiros lived at Sol-e-Mar for over three years, so when she went back home she couldn't remember the Portuguese that was spoken in her house. Home was incredibly lonely for Caroline compared to the companionship at Sol-e-Mar.

Day after day, she practiced walking before she left so she wouldn't go home limping. She wanted her family to see how she had healed and to be proud of her. However, when she went to school she was called "Hopalong" because of her big heavy shoe. Caroline's solution was to wear regular shoes, even though they hurt, to avoid the teasing words of the other children.

What those children failed to see was that Caroline wasn't much different from them. She had found herself a boyfriend while at Sol-e-Mar. She had gotten into trouble like any other child her age. (Carrie liked to crawl out of bed and get underneath the other girls' beds to shake their mattresses and scare them until they screamed.) She endured all the same growing pains as any other girl her age and she feels that Sol-e-Mar guided and encouraged her. After returning home, she worked hard so she could get a job and live a normal life.

Caroline, now married and living in South Dartmouth, has led more than a normal life; it has been rich and full. She is still close to both Elsie and Lucille.

Today there is no sign of Sol-e-Mar Hospital. In 1965 the Carmelite Convent of Boston bought Sol-e-Mar and created the Dartmouth branch. The Carmelite nuns were cloistered there until 1987 when their numbers so diminished they could no longer run the convent. The land was sold to a developer who tore down the buildings and constructed a 74 unit condominium complex for the elderly.

Though the woods and beach in South Dartmouth remain beautiful, the modern buildings there disguise the proud history of Sol-e-Mar and all who made this good work possible. Besides its great impact on patients and staff, it was a model of love and caring to the citizens of Greater New Bedford.

Christine Woodhouse is a native of Lakeville, MA and a graduate of Syracuse University. She worked as a freelance writer for Spinner before accepting a job at Simon & Schuster in New York City.

A letter to Santa, 1950s (left) **and watercolor thank you card.** *A simple message conveys a child's appreciation.*

St. Luke's Hospital Medical Library

Carriers brought together by 10-year-old entrepreneur Ned Peirce, 1906. The group of boys and one girl, his sister Helen, were hired by young Ned so he could increase his profits selling the Saturday Evening Post. Peirce is the tall lad in the front row with Helen at his right. Also present are Arthur Hathaway, Mark Leonard, Edwin Babbitt, William Batchelder, Donald Cook, Robert Mein, Milton Carrol, Howard Crowell, John MacPhail, Nicholas Yellenti and Edward Sears.

Judgment Day

MARSHA MCCABE

Edward C. Peirce, a man whose career was marked by extraordinary highs and lows, was elected mayor of New Bedford in 1952. Mr. Peirce made his first million at age 30 as a cotton broker, went bankrupt with the collapse of the textile market, then took out his shovel and worked for the WPA (Works Progress Administration), building sidewalks.

He rose again to become a state senator, then mayor. After serving a year and a half on the job, he was indicted and sent to jail on two charges of protecting gamblers. While in jail, he was diagnosed with liver cancer.

The mayor's daughter, Nancy (then Estelle Wheeler), stood by her father throughout his ordeal. When his illness was diagnosed and he had scant time left, she appealed to Governor Christian Herter to pardon him and was rebuffed. She then threatened to scream "at the top of her lungs on the State House steps"—and get herself arrested—if her father was not released. In response, the governor quickly paroled (but did not pardon) Mayor Peirce, who was taken to New Bedford by ambulance. He died just days later.

Edward Peirce and sister Helen, 1902.

For the next 30 years, Nancy thought about her Dad every day but became so distressed at the memory of his trial and jail sentence, she tried to erase it from her mind. Then 15 years ago, she began to confront that bleak time in her life, immersing herself in her father's history and constructing an elaborate documentary of his life. She believes her father was set up by the gambling interests of the time, precisely because he was trying to end gambling in New Bedford. Her sincere wish is to restore his good name and rightful place in New Bedford's history.

In a day when New Bedford's present mayor, Rosemary Tierney, the City Council and many citizens are campaigning to bring casino gambling to New Bedford, Nancy's story has particular poignancy.

This is a story of a daughter's love for her father, a daughter whose bright happy childhood memories are as alive in her as those final heartbreaking years. Her house is filled with photographs, old campaign literature, detailed, memory-laden scrapbooks and other memorabilia.

"Dad was always honest and would not have thrown away everything he worked so hard for in order to gain $2,000. Dad was an honest and good man. That's just the way he was," she said.

Edward Peirce with mother and Helen, 1905. Ned Peirce kept close ties with his family throughout his life, sending his sister to Smith College and working several jobs during the Depression to provide for the family. Here, they show their Sunday best at home at 320 Cottage Street in New Bedford.

Peirce family, circa 1928. A young Ned Peirce stands with his mother, Estelle Cook Peirce, and his first wife, Inadell. Kneeling is his grandmother Nancy Cook, and his young daughter Nancy.

Peirce Family Collection

Peirce Family Collection

Nancy's Story

When I was six, we lived in South Dartmouth, in the Old Stone House on Smith Neck Road, and we had a chauffeur and a maid. Dad was a cotton broker and made his first million before he was 30. I adored my father. I was an only child and he wanted a boy but he got me. We did boy things like camping and fishing.

The good life did not last long.

The Entrepreneur

Before I go any further, you should know a few things about Dad and his childhood and how special he was. His parents had separated and his family was poor. He wanted to help his mother survive, so when he was about 10, he began a business that ended up attracting national attention.

His mother had sent him to the grocery store and a poster on the wall caught his eye. *The Saturday Evening Post* and *The Ladies Home Journal* were looking for boys to sell magazines. He ran home, got permission from his mother, filled out the forms and got the job.

After several months going door-to-door selling magazines, he said: "This is stupid. If I split my profit and hire more boys to go door to door, I'll make more money." He called up the *Post* and asked them if that would be all right. They said yes.

So he got 25 kids or so to work for him and sell the magazines, including his sister, Helen, the only female in his sales force. *The Saturday Evening Post* was so impressed with his business, they took a picture of the group and published it in the magazine. But they said they didn't want any girls in the picture so my aunt Helen isn't there. Can you believe that?

Peirce Family Collection

Employment poster, 1909. This advertisement, taken from Ned Peirce's scrapbook, is typical of that era when young boys were encouraged to work the city streets selling newspapers and delivering messages. Peirce eagerly responded to sales competitions.

Newsboy Peirce, 1906. Ned with serious demeanor selling his beloved Saturday Post.

Peirce Family Collection

But anyway, you get an idea of how enterprising he was even as a young boy.

He was close to graduating from high school when he took a job at the railway station as a dispatcher. There was a lot of freight coming and going and the faster a dispatcher could get trains in and out, the better it was. Dad was very fast getting them in and out.

A man named Mr. Eaton, a cotton broker, heard about Dad and saw how fast he was moving the trains. He asked him if he'd like a job in his office. Dad wanted to help his sister go to Smith College as well as help his mother, so he really wanted the job.

But he wanted more than money. He said to Mr. Eaton, "If I take the job, I want to learn everything I can about the cotton business." Well, Mr. and Mrs. Eaton took him under their wing.

The company was the go-between for the cotton fields in the South and the textile mills in the North, and he quickly learned everything there was to know. After a couple of years, he entered into partnership with a colleague and formed Peirce, Winsper & Co.

But the times weren't good. The cotton market was changing so fast, the company went into bankruptcy. It took awhile, but Dad paid off every bit of debt. That's the way he was.

Edward Cook Peirce, cotton broker, 1913. Eager to join the business world, Peirce quit high school before getting his diploma. His drive and ambition quickly brought new job opportunities. At 18, he landed work in the brokerage of Ingersoll, Amory & Co., which had offices in New Bedford and Fall River. As a broker, Peirce's work involved buying cotton from southern fields and selling it to the local mills. "If I take the job," he said, "I want to learn everything I can about the cotton business." Two years later, he and his partner started their own cotton brokerage firm, Peirce, Winsper & Co. Near the end of his life, he reflected, "The drive and ambition of one with a goal can be treacherous and catch up with him."

Peirce Family Collection

Peirce Family Collection

Finally, he established the Direct Sales & Finance Company in Fall River. After studying the cotton market, he concluded that if cotton was shipped in larger quantities and stored in a warehouse until the mills needed it, not only could it be bought low, but it would be available immediately when needed.

I would go to his office and sit on a stool and fold paper for envelopes. I loved to hear the click, click, click of the tickertape. He had the latest returns as soon as they were fixed and it gave him the edge on the other brokers by getting the news to him fast.

Unfortunately, the new company was right in the path of the Great Fall River Fire and the business was lost. It was a tragedy, of course, but Dad was only concerned about two things. He wanted to save the two pictures his grandmother had given him when he opened his office—a picture of the Old Stone Fleet and a scenic view of New Bedford harbor. This is the kind of man he was.

The Depression soon followed. Dad went from making his first million at 30 to making $15 a week for the WPA, a government program for unemployed workers. He built sidewalks and went starfishing.

My mother blamed Dad for the Depression. We moved from our beautiful Old Stone House in South Dartmouth to an old house in North Dartmouth. Our chauffeur and maid days were over. You should also know some things about my mother. She was very odd in some ways. She was a beautiful woman, but I think she was jealous of me and she gave me an inferiority complex.

She made me dress in terrible clothes and I was ashamed to go to school. So on my way to school, I would go to my grandmother's house. My grandmother had made me some nice clothes and I'd quickly change into them and go on to school. I had to be tricky about getting to my grandmother's house because my mother would be looking out the window. So I would pretend to go one way, then go another.

Meanwhile, Dad decided to go into the nursery business and he opened Peirce Cottage Gardens at 355 State Road. I was 12 years old. We all had to work in the garden. Dad had me out there weeding all the time. I hated weeds so bad! But the nursery was doing well, and Dad made a miniature golf course around the garden to attract people. We also took in tourists upstairs. That's how we got by.

Peirce Family Collection

Peirce Family Collection

Millionaire Peirce, 1926. In 1925, while with Peirce, Winsper & Co., Peirce experienced the first turbulent public reversal in his life. Accused of juggling cotton sales and deliveries, he went to trial and was found innocent of the charges.

Following this experience, Peirce struck out on his own and formed the Direct Sales Company with offices in New Bedford and Fall River. The company issued common shares of capital stock and Peirce went on to advance the company by learning to play the cotton futures market. He made a tremendous amount of money buying surplus cotton from southern dealers at a low price and filling his warehouses in New Bedford, later selling at market prices. By age 30, almost overnight, the young entrepreneur had amassed a fortune of $1 million.

Ned Peirce in Dixie, 1927 (top left).

Peirce Cottage Gardens, 1952. The Peirce family floral business began with Ned's grandfather William in 1867 and expanded to include several shops in New Bedford, Dartmouth and Fall River. His father Edward, noted for his love of the rose, operated the "Home of the Sweetheart Rose" in New Bedford. The Cottage Gardens was located on Route 6 across from what is now the North Dartmouth Mall.

Peirce Family Collection

Election poster, 1942. *Though Ned Peirce lost his initial bid for Senate in 1942, his aggressive campaigning and persistence won him his first term in 1944 when he defeated attorney Joseph F. Francis. He won three reelections, spanning eight years, and finished out his term while serving as mayor in 1951.*

As Senator, Peirce was active in efforts to improve Old Age Assistance laws, and was instrumental in improving conditions for veterans and workers. In 1951, he favored state legislation to prepare a master plan for shoreline development and earlier had proposed a New Bedford Port Authority.

The Politician

At this time, Dad decided to go into politics. He began as a town meeting member in Dartmouth, then ran for town clerk and treasurer. Though he was defeated, that didn't stop him. He was determined to get into politics. He then ran for state senator from the Third Bristol District and won after a couple of tries, the second Democrat to win the office. He ended up being a state senator longer than anyone had been before, serving eight years on the job.

As a state senator, he did a lot for New Bedford. The city had lost its cotton industry and was trying to come out of the Depression. He believed the city could be saved by good rail service so goods could come and go quickly, and he felt the deep water port could play a role in bringing the city back. He was on a transportation committee and did all he could.

Dad had a real personal touch. He'd come home at night by train from Boston where he'd been working all day. He had an office in our store and there would be lines of people waiting for him. If you needed something and went to him, he was there for you. He got people into veterans' hospitals or helped them with housing or food subsidies. Some wanted him to fix tickets, but he would always go to the police and inquire about what the problem was and make a decision only after he'd talked to them. That's the way Dad was.

My aunt Helen graduated from Smith College and taught Spanish there. She wanted me to go to college too and she said she would pay my tuition. I took the two-year program at UMass Amherst in floriculture and earned my associate's degree. Since I grew up with flowers and always had my hands in dirt, this gave me a scientific background to go with it.

You should know I'm a very strong Democrat, as was my family. I grew up with Roosevelt. We were able to refinance our house through the HOLC program (Home Owners Loan Corporation) and this is how we saved our house. And as I said, when we had no money, my father got a job with the WPA. We also had help getting coal for the winter. If you're poor, you know what a great president he was.

In 1949, Dad decided to run for mayor and didn't make it. The second time he ran, they said he lost, but he called for a recount. The ballots were in blocks of 50. There were many blocks with Harriman's name on top, but they were all Peirce underneath. In the recount, he won by 42 votes. New Bedford could be very crooked.

I was very involved in the campaign and made the first speech of my life before the League of Women Voters. Dad was inaugurated in 1952. He only served one and a half years before things ended in tragedy.

The trouble began almost immediately. First, you should know that Dad hated gambling. He felt that the mob controlled the city through gambling. I can't tell you how against gambling he was. He wanted that element out of the city! It was a brave position to take. Nobody tries to fight the mob today.

He said: "When a city is crooked, progress cannot be made." In his inaugural speech he said, "The invisible government which controlled the city through several administrations would not control City Hall as long as he was in office."

So his first act as mayor was bold. He set the state police up to raid various gambling places. He decided to work with the state police because he didn't trust the New Bedford police.

He set up a special squad to investigate rackets and he put Alfred Figueira, a recently retired police lieutenant, in charge. The day before his inauguration, the special vice squad led a raid on the Depot Social Club and 33 persons were arrested on gambling charges.

The police had to climb ladders to get to the second floor where the gambling took place. They found some cash, 280 pairs of dice, 12 packs of playing cards, two loaded revolvers and one loaded shotgun.

Putting Alfred Figueira in charge might have been Dad's first mistake. In the end, he may have gone over to the other side— the side that was trying to set up Dad.

Anyway, one day Dad got a call from a man named Mr. Angell, a businessman who owned a fleet of boats. He said he wanted to make a campaign contribution of $2,000 and asked where he could meet him. The call came to WNBH where Dad ran a talk show, another thing he did as mayor.

They all agreed to meet on Popes Island. Now, there is nothing wrong with accepting campaign contributions. All politicians have to accept such contributions in order to run for reelection. So Dad met them and two people got in his car, Mr. Angell in front and a contact in back. No money was passed that night but Dad got bad vibes. He asked around about Mr. Angell and discovered he had a bad reputation so he wanted nothing to do with the money.

I remember Dad calling me on the phone and saying, "They're out to get me. I don't want any dirty money. If anyone gives you even so much as 50 cents, don't take it."

Meanwhile, Mr. Angell called my father's wife, Alma, who was working at the store. "We'll meet you in back of the store and give you the money."

Alma said OK. You have to remember we were back in hard times and money was in short supply, so Alma went out back and took $500. Dad didn't know about it. A couple of days later, Dad got a phone call and a man said Alma took $500.

When Dad confronted her, she admitted it and said, "I put it in the store. The store needed money."

Well, as you can imagine, this was an emergency. At the time, I lived with my first husband in New Bedford and was known as Estelle Wheeler. We met with two lawyers at Dad's house in Westport, where he and Alma lived. He said to Alma: "Do you know you've doomed me?" Those words I'll remember for the rest of my life.

While all this was going on, Dad was also busy being mayor. The vice squad was reporting directly to him and they made over 130 arrests and convictions. He was also trying to get diversified industry to come in. He was in Washington lobbying to get a nuclear blast plant in New Bedford. On his way back from that trip, in Akron, Ohio he got word that he was going to be indicted. He made a public statement from there.

The Indictment

According to newspaper accounts, Mayor Peirce said: 'There is no basis for an indictment against me. Like prohibition, gambling will exist in some form as long as the great majority of people desire to gamble. In my inaugural, I clearly stated that while I was not going to conduct a crusade, I would stop open violations of the law and maintain, as far as I could, an orderly city.'

He went on to say that his policies met favor among workers but not with those who have controlled the political and economic life of the city and maintained a pool of unemployed workers that would be to their advantage.

The district attorney, Maurice M. Lyons, indicted eight people on conspiracy to hinder gambling violators and to induce the New Bedford police vice squad to abstain from and neglect its duties. (Also indicted were:

The Standard-Times

Mayor Peirce addresses the public, 1951. *Mayor Peirce kept in touch with his constituents through his weekly radio talk show and by holding open press conferences in his City Hall office. He loved debate and would go without his meals to engage in discourse on a subject close to his heart. "Peirce spoke rapidly, the words spilling out in a fashion that sometimes gave the impression his mind was moving faster than it was physically possible to give expression to his thoughts."* [Standard-Times, 2/1/55]

The Standard-Times

Scene of the crime, August 1952. *The bad blood between District Attorney Lyons and Mayor Peirce came to a boil over an alleged incident in this building at Purchase and Linden Street—a popular club for card playing, pool and pinball. Lyons' office claimed that an $11,000 dice game holdup took place here and was reported to his office by two gaming victims. An outraged Mayor Peirce called the incident "a hoax to bring discredit to the vice squad."*

Investigating city officials found nothing. There were discrepancies as to which robbers held guns, and the vice squad found no evidence of reported gunfire. When police questioned club members, no one would confirm that a robbery took place. The idea of reporting a robbery at a dice game amused the mayor. "A man couldn't be convicted of shooting dice if he reported he was being robbed…They could have been talking politics."

Responding to Lyon's statement that gambling activities in the city ran rampant, the mayor said he was disinclined to stop pinball or gaming machines in small establishments while allowing them to operate full scale in large organizations. "We have tried to control such activity and a certain element remains. But if held under control it is not a damaging influence. If discrediting attempts of this sort continue I might give him (Lyons) exactly what he doesn't want and shut down everything completely. If we do that, we deprive ourselves of a source of information that enables us to keep gaming in check…and next will be faced with something boiling up from underneath."

Leonard Healy, 38, president, New Bedford City Council; Alfred Figueira, 57, recently retired police lieutenant who was the mayor's appointee as head of the vice squad; Arthur Dufresne, 52, retired police detective; Antone Thomas, 49, of New Bedford, an ex-boxer and John Doe and Richard Lee.)

"I was shocked and surprised to learn of the indictment," said the mayor in newspaper accounts, "and will return to New Bedford promptly to meet any charges because there can be no basis for any charges of wrongdoing and I have done nothing wrong."

District Attorney Lyons said: "State police for several months have been investigating reports of gambling in New Bedford and what part city officials have had in interfering with the duties of police officers." Reports that gambling had been wide open with bets being placed on street corners and in taverns, in open sight of everyone, were ridiculed by Mayor Peirce.

Mr. Angell and Mr. Thomas were alleged to have been the operators of the game in the Depot Social Club on Purchase Street, which was held up August 16. There had been reports that a shot was fired but police found no evidence in the first search. Two days later, in a general search at the mayor's request, members of Figueira's squad found a bullet hole in the ceiling. The Mayor said the reports of the stickup were a hoax to discredit the vice squad.

Dad's original lawyers were Harry Lider and Louis Perras, but he was worried they were too local and didn't have the experience to handle the case. Some people told him he should get a "Boston lawyer" and they sent a highly-recommended man to him, a Mr. Francis Juggens. This proved to be bad advice.

The trouble was that after Dad hired Mr. Juggens, he couldn't get in touch with him. Imagine that! His own lawyer wouldn't speak to him. Does that sound like a set up? At the trial, Mr. Juggens didn't do well. Two trials were held, one immediately following the other. Everyone but Dad pleaded guilty and turned state's evidence. The four defendants in the first trial were William Angell, Antone Thomas, Alfred Figueira and Dad.

The case was heard in Fall River Superior Court in front of Judge Daniel O'Brien. According to newspaper reports, the first trial was highlighted by testimony of Mr. Angell who, along with Alfred Figueira, became a witness for the state. He testified that he operated a dice game after giving Mayor Peirce $2,000 in "political contributions." All of the money was intended for the mayor and was paid between August 1951 and the city primary in September. Mr. Angell described the payments as a "political contribution for operation of a club" and said when they were made, he had in mind the "running of a dice game."

He said he paid Mayor Peirce $500 directly, in the presence of Mr. Figueira, in a car on Popes Island, $500 directly to Mayor Peirce in his flower shop at 1360 Acushnet Avenue, $500 to the mayor's wife in the back room of Peirce's flower shop and $500 to Mr. Figueira for the mayor.

Under cross examination, Mr. Angell admitted the mayor had said nothing about "protection" for the proposed club during the auto parley.

A guilty verdict was returned for the mayor.

The second trial immediately followed the first trial. Mr. John McIntyre, the assistant DA, declared the evidence would show that the mayor had given bookies, in the employ of a Mr. Sullivan, protection. After Mayor Peirce named Alfred Figueira as head of the vice squad, McIntyre said, Figueira made the mayor's office his headquarters and Mayor Peirce made it clear that the vice squad should report directly to him, the mayor.

"A favored group was given permission to operate a dice game without fear of prosecution as far as the vice squad was concerned," said the prosecutor in his opening statement.

He said the evidence would show a bookie named Lejeunesse operated a scandalous establishment in the center of New Bedford, that the vice squad asked permission to pick them up, but that Mayor Peirce told Mr. Figueira that Mr. Lajeunesse was not to be arrested unless his operation became so obvious that an officer could not fail to arrest him without causing a public scandal.

The Trial

Nancy was 35 years old when the trial began on May 18, 1953.

I drove to the Fall River Superior Court every day of the trials. I took my grandmother at the beginning too but she couldn't keep it up. There was no doubt in either Dad's mind or our minds that he would walk out of there.

It turned out that three policemen were witnesses for the state. I saw the prosecuting attorneys hand them papers and then they were asked: "Does this refresh your memory?" They were simply told what to say. When they started to tell lies, Dad's lawyer would challenge some of their contradictions, and sometimes not.

Dad was declared guilty of conspiracy. At the second trial, it was the same thing—Guilty of conspiracy. He was shocked and we were shocked.

On May 26, 1953, Mayor Peirce was sentenced to four years in jail. He issued two statements prior to his sentencing. In both, he protested his innocence and said he would continue to fight to make New Bedford a prosperous and happy place. "I am going to jail today because I will not desert the people who elected me. I am taking punishment for a crime which I never committed…

"I am still the mayor of New Bedford and will never willingly give up the office I was elected to by the people and which I swore to fill honestly and faithfully."

True to his word, Mayor Peirce did not relinquish his office. Until the end of his term in 1954, he collected his weekly salary as the city's chief executive. City Council President, Francis L. Lawler, was named temporary mayor and both he and Mayor Peirce were paid the weekly salary of $124.60.

Central Cafe, where bookies operated, September 1952. *Raided by state investigators under District Attorney Lyons was this well-known club on Purchase and High Streets. Soon after Peirce took office, Lyons sent statements to the mayor alerting city officials about known gaming establishments and threatened to take action. At trial, vice squad Lt. Alfred Figueira said the mayor ordered him to ignore going after many of New Bedford's gaming kingpins.*

Assistant District Attorneys were Jack London and John W. McIntyre. Their indictment charge claimed that Peirce "did conspire to cause the Vice Squad of the New Bedford Police Department to abstain from and neglect performance of their duties respecting the taking due notice and prosecution of all violations of law concerning gaming." [Standard-Times 5/22/53]

The Standard-Times

The Standard-Times

Mayor Peirce outside Fall River court, May 25, 1953. *This is the last press photograph of the mayor before he was sent to prison on May 26.*

During the trial, the most damaging evidence came from vice squad sergeant Alfred Figueira, who said Mayor Peirce told him not to bother with bookies Lariviere, Mello, Pertras, Simon, Altman, Abrams and Sullivan. He was ordered to arrest only those bookies who were seen by him or other members of the vice squad in the open act of placing bets. Figueira said he was required to check with the mayor when reports of gaming came to his attention. The mayor instructed him: "Never mind bothering the lottery slip boys. All right on the horses." The number slips were the Sullivans, the horse bets were not, Figueira said.

Figueira quoted the mayor as saying, "If they book in your presence, then they deserve to be arrested." When he complained of the bookie operations of a man named Gilly Tavares, the mayor first told him to "Wait." Then he said to "Knock him off," and later added, "Either he'll book for the right man or not at all."

[Standard Times 5/22/53]

I only had the chance to go to his office and get some papers before he was taken to the House of Correction. The next morning he was taken to the Norfolk County House of Correction in Dedham and put in solitary confinement for a week. We had no contact with him.

After a week, he came out of solitary confinement and could have two visitors a week. He was only allowed to send out two letters a week. They were very, very strict about everything. I had to leave my purse and everything at the front desk. I remember the doors opening and closing, opening and closing, and the guards looking down. It was a scary place. We had to meet in a visitors' room and I would go to throw my arms around Dad and a guard would step between us.

He was in the Dedham prison for two years. We were devastated but he was a very optimistic person, even in the worst of times. That's the way Dad was. He got a job in the laundry at the prison, then was transferred to kitchen detail and he cooked and served food. He took the work seriously and did the best he could.

He was always looking out for the other prisoners. He got the authorities to agree to add condiments to the prison food. Prior to this, the prisoners had no salt, no spices, nothing. At Christmas time, he had me make candy packages for the prisoners who had no one to give them any gifts.

He had a very small cell with nothing but a bed and pail in there, but he got a couple of orange crates and made tables and chairs. Then he could do his writing. He was working hard to get a pardon. He always suffered from claustrophobia. He couldn't even handle an elevator, but he got used to the small space in jail. After the first year, the guards began leaving the door unlocked.

On January 21, 1954, Mayor Peirce received a letter from Charles A. Blanchett, an old friend who decided he could not come to his aid. The letter read:

"In regard to your liberation, fear of possible revenge against me has made my wife ill. The jailing of Peirce hangs like a specter and a pall, a smog over the New Bedford skies. The longer he remains in jail, the worse it will become. His release would relieve the tense atmosphere which has terrified the population into silence and fear for their own safety."

I used to take fruit to Dad in jail and he really liked that. He would eat every bit of it because there was no fruit on the jail's menu. At one point, however, I was curtailed from bringing him fruit. I always thought this was his downfall.

After that, he began getting pains in his stomach. He was really hurting and needed to see a doctor. They took him to Walpole, (the Norfolk Prison Colony Hospital), where they had a good medical facility. Dad told me he was going in for an exploratory operation.

When Dad was at Walpole, I could see him every day. There were no restrictions on visitors. After the exploratory operation, the doctors told me he had something very serious but they wouldn't tell me what it was.

The doctor who did the surgery had an office in Foxboro and I went to talk to him. He told me Dad had cancer of the liver and it was inoperable. I didn't tell Dad the terrible news. He would have lost all hope.

I wanted Dad pardoned and out of jail and I called the governor's office, Christian Herter. I talked to a secretary about four offices removed from the governor, which means I wasn't close to making the important contact. They said they knew nothing about the case or about Dad anyway, which wasn't true.

I drove to Boston, went to the State House and walked up the stairs to the governor's office. I had a letter from the doctors that said how serious my father's condition was. I also arrived with petitions, thousands of names of New Bedford people who supported a pardon for Dad. At the Memorial Day Parade, we went from one person to another. The people were sympathetic, but of course the mob wasn't.

I walked into that secretary's office with the doctor's report and all those petitions and said I'd like to speak to the governor about a pardon. They said to go home and write a letter. Imagine! I said I had already written letters to everybody in the State House. I wrote them on a typewriter and I didn't even type.

But this time, I didn't have time for these ridiculous delays because Dad would probably die in a week. They knew I was desperate. But they said they were sorry, there was nothing they could do. Just at that moment, Governor Herter, who's a Republican, walked in. I ran up to him. 'My father is dying,' I said. 'I want one minute of your time.' He shrugged me off.

I was irate. I said to the secretary: Convey the following to the governor. Tomorrow morning, when the State House opens, I'm going to be here and scream at the top of my lungs and I will be arrested.

Well, they must have given the governor the message because the next morning, Dad was released. I went down to Post 1 in New Bedford to beg for an ambulance and they got me one. I went to Walpole in the ambulance and when we arrived, the authorities said to go around to the back, that's where I could pick Dad up. Well, that's where the corpses come out.

Dad came out in a gurney and it was a very happy moment of his life. He thought he had been pardoned—he was only paroled—but I didn't tell him. Before we took him to the Union Convalescent and Nursing Home in downtown New Bedford, we stopped for ice cream and we went to see the flower store at 1360 Acushnet Avenue, the one that burned down several years ago and we rebuilt.

He was in the nursing home for five days and I went everyday to see him. He was so sure he was going to be leaving there, he was measured for a suit he was going to wear on his way out. Instead, he died. It was January 31 and he was 59 years-old.

Dad's wife Alma was in charge of the funeral and I tried to stay out of the way while preparations were going on. I just continued working in the store. Then at the end of the evening, I sat with him in the Wilson Funeral Home for over an hour.

He was buried in Rural Cemetery. The day before the actual funeral, we had one of the biggest snowfalls we've ever had. The city came in and plowed the route from the funeral home to the cemetery. A lot of people were at the funeral but the snow cut into the attendance. There were over a hundred wreaths and flower baskets.

I haven't been able to face any of this until the past 15 years. I would read something and just get so emotional. Not a day goes by that someone doesn't mention him, even today. I still think about him all the time. And I ask you, how could a man lead two lives when nothing in his history shows his dark side? That's what I want to know. Dad was always honest and would not have thrown away everything he worked so hard for to gain $2,000. Dad was an honest man. That's just the way he was.

The Standard-Times

Mayor Peirce, July 1952. Edward Peirce's term as mayor unsettled the patterns of many years, and his force was felt in many municipal departments. He ordered a gambling raid seven hours before he was officially sworn into office. "Tell me where there is a crap game going on and they won't be operating 24 hours later. Big money for gambling brings in bad influences. We don't want them here. I don't want to see any dice games, they bring in riffraff." (Peirce's response when told of the $11,000 dice game holdup in the North End)

He promoted more ranking officers in the New Bedford Police and Fire Departments than any mayor in history over a comparative period. He broke precedent by conducting a "quiz" of police officers in the mayor's office, interrogating the officers on their knowledge of gaming in the city and administrative practices in the department, and whether they had been interfered with in the performance of their duties.

Epilogue

Nancy's Notes During Trial, 5/18/53

Dad's mother, Estelle C. Peirce, and I entered the courtroom and took seats near the front. Many friends of Dad's occupied other positions as well as those that wished to see him convicted. When people were asked to stand and the judge entered, the silence was almost ominous and that mood continued throughout the two trials.

Nana and I held hands, feeling in our hearts it had to go favorably. Each generation had been brought up God fearing and Dad had been an inspiration to me all my growing up years. It was comforting to see friendly faces all around us.

When the indictments were read, they were most vague and did not specifically convey the terms of the conspiracy. To make it more complicated, a John Doe and Richard Roe were added to the group of named conspirators. However, they were later dropped and certainly never identified…

Mayor Peirce leaving City Hall, election night 1951. At the mayor's side, during good and bad times, was his wife, Alma P. (Plante) Peirce, and his mother, Estelle (Cook) Peirce.

Peirce Family Collection

There were two trials, one right after the other. When the first jurors returned with a verdict, the second group of jurors had been chosen and were seated when the guilty verdict was given. A definite moan could be heard over the courtroom while it was being read.

As the trial went on, I was alone. We agreed it was putting too much of a strain on Nana and she was very tired. Dad turned very pale and held to the rail when the verdict was read. Later when we met in the hall, all he could say was how could they do this to me. I have always tried to live an honest life…

Letters From Prison

From jail, Mayor Peirce ran in the primary election that fall. The acting mayor, Francis Lawler, topped the list of seven candidates for the office. Yet Mr. Lawler lost the general election to Arthur N. Harriman (whom Mr. Peirce defeated in 1951). Mr. Lawler returned to win the election two years later.

July 28, 1954:

Mother Dear,

As I sit here talking to Mr. Brown, I wonder where I would have been if I had won my fight with Lyons. Mr. Brown runs the kitchen (of the jail) and is a very pleasant man and easy to get along with.

Have finished up the morning work, had a good shave and in about half an hour will go outdoors for recreation. Feel perfect and as I read the papers, (I received the one you sent), I realize that no one seems to have just what they wish. It is not pleasant to be away from home and I certainly did not like getting licked by the Duff-Lyons outfit but today I would not change places with any of them. The good this has done me far offsets the bad and I find it hard to believe that I can feel so good. When I wash in the morning at 6:00AM, I feel perfect, which is something I could never say at home.

Estelle brought Charles in Monday and as you say, he is passing through a period of "know it all," but it is not serious. He looks a great deal like I did at his age and I guess he has some of my faults as well but he's a normal boy and seems to be contented. Like all children he is using any home trouble to his advantage and it is not seriously upsetting him. We think of him as a baby, but I was selling extra editions on election nights when I was his age and going everywhere. It is hard to realize how soon children grow up. I look forward to enjoying a lot of time with him.

All my life, good times have followed bad. I have complete confidence that will happen again. As long as you don't worry and take care of yourself, everything is O.K. with me. Enjoy yourself and I think you will be satisfied when you see me that I am all right.

Love to you and Helen

October 6, 1953. Running for mayor from prison.

Dear Estelle,

It is after dinner on primary day and I am wondering what everyone is doing and trying to decide in my own mind what I want to happen…The natural feeling is a desire to win and prove that I was right. It would mean a tough battle but I think I could win it.

Then I wonder if it is worth the effort and even if I go back to political life later if it would not be better now to lose and get other things straightened out. As I promised, I have been a candidate. I offered leadership which is badly needed, but if for any reason it is not accepted, I cannot be Blamed for the result.

Unless the new mayor can do a good job, he will have a very tough time the next few years, particularly after following a fool like Lawler.

While I am interested in the final returns, I have no great interest that will interfere with my sleep tonight. Whatever the answer, I will probably know it tomorrow and immediately start to adjust to whatever conditions exist…

Today is the climax of something that has been building for a long time. Once I started in politics, I could not stop and last year, I had to win for mayor to get a chance to straighten out. Once I took office I had to back the group that ran the city and if I had not done so, I would have been defeated this year.

As I sit here writing under none of the strain of the past, I wonder if it has not been for the best. If there had been no trial, I still would have faced a bitter fight for mayor and all the pressure that is now on would have been against me. It would have been impossible to get campaign contributions and, win or lose, I would come out of the campaign broke and in debt.

If I had been acquitted, the same conditions would have existed. If I had resigned and given up office at the time of the trial, everyone would have felt sorry for me but had no respect. It would have been impossible to straighten out the business and I have been able to do much more here along those lines in the past four months than I could have done outside.

Now, win or lose, I will not be in debt, the business is in good shape and will get better and my health is certainly improved. Down deep when I forget the pride angle, I think going back to the business would right now satisfy me more than anything else. There is so much started and so much that can be done that I would enjoy coordinating everything and doing a regular day's work.

By this time tomorrow, we will have some of the answers and I wonder how I will feel when the returns show what I face in the immediate future. Today may culminate what I started 12 years ago when I decided to run for the Senate. I have always been under the strain of those who are going ahead politically. Even if I win, the urgency has gone. The fear of losing and the necessity to win. As I look back, I have enjoyed it, even the worst. I have been able to do a lot of good and leave a mark on legislation which means much to the workers and needy.

But it has not been a normal life. Here in four months, I have gotten back to normal thinking and, strange as it may

Peirce Family Collection

Mayor Peirce outside City Hall, 1952. A man on the move, Peirce made repeated trips to Washington and Chicago in an effort to obtain new industries for the city. He recognized that the textile industry would not maintain its strength and sought economic diversity. Firestone (later Chamberlain Mfg.) officials said his efforts aided their plans to open their shell manufacturing facility in New Bedford. His offices in City Hall were a hubbub of activity.

After his incarceration, Peirce refused to relinquish his title as mayor and continued to draw his weekly salary as the city's chief executive.

Peirce was constantly battling for working people. In a Boston Post interview, November 1952, the mayor blamed "short sighted industrialists who feel I am breaking up their pool of unemployed, which they can recruit for low wages, by bringing new diversified interests into New Bedford, for instigating this thing…A major industry, long barred from New Bedford, may locate here within a relatively short time unless the efforts to stop it and discredit the city and this administration are successful.

"This new industry should be popular with the worker and small merchant who does not meet with favor from those who for many years have controlled the political and economic life of this city and maintained a pool of unemployed workers which would work to their advantage."

Peirce the Florist, 1949. From prison, Ned Peirce dreamed of the day when he could return to his beloved floral business.

seem, more normal living here than I did outside. I realize that what happens to me is not as important I may have thought in the past. Whether I win or lose will make little difference to the people who are really friendly. I would have liked to finish the work I started, but I tried and if it was more than I could handle certainly no one can blame me…

Love to you all, Dad.

November 25, 1954

Dear Mother,

We have finished up a busy day and are waiting for the boys (inmates) to come down to supper which will be two large pieces of pie and all the milk they can drink. The dinner table looked very attractive. On every plate there was nearly a pound of turkey, excellent dressing, onions, squash, mashed potatoes and giblet gravy…

Harold Gorham, the cook, worked all night and everything was done well and served good and hot. As soon as they started to eat, there were seconds on everything including cranberry sauce. Both Harold and I enjoyed putting the dinner out and the boys seemed to really enjoy it. I ate the edge of the dressing in the pan while I was serving and picked on the turkey meat and enjoyed it but did not overeat and feel fine tonight, better than in many previous years.

Would have liked to be with you but have spent the day really thanking God for what I have. First, I have you. I have Estelle, Alma and the boys…

Lots of love, Ned

January 7, 1955: Ned Peirce's last letter. He died 14 days later.

Dear Mother,

I may be transferred to the hospital at Norfolk at any time now and I am writing you as I may not have much time when the notice comes through. The guards and several men who have been there say it is a very good hospital and that some of the very best doctors come out there. It is a modern and top grade hospital and I think it will do me good.

I have been worried about you and things at home. Sometimes we forget we are all in God's hands and think that there is some better answer to our problems and troubles than trust in God. When we are smart enough to realize that His way is always the best way, we have the answer to our problems.

I know this and it has been proven to me in many ways, but I have my weak moments and it is for them that I am suffering now. All that is fundamentally wrong with me is nerves and they have brought on these things that have given me a rather rough two weeks. I feel confident that the doctors at the hospital will know the answers and get me straightened out quickly.

In fact it may turn out for the best and I can get a general check up which I have not had in years. As I think, and recently I have had plenty of time to think, I have never once wished I had won my fight against Lyons. Whatever life may hold for me, I am very confident it will not be a life of wealth and power.

In the past couple of months, I have seen even more clearly what ambition does to a man. I think that is what upset me. To see big men crawl and hedge to gain or hold power, has made me realize the price is higher than I would want to pay.

I honestly think I have won the fight against nerves and that I feel better than I have for several weeks. Everyone here has been very good to me and extremely considerate. It is just that the facilities are too limited, that I was willing to be transferred.

Life is funny but I have found that after a period when everything seems discouraging there is always a good period…

Take care of yourself and don't worry about me.
Lots of love,
Ned

Interview from Prison

This excerpt is from Mayor Peirce's last meeting with the *Standard Times* press. Published May 23, 1954, it was written by Edward B. Simmons who found Mayor Peirce a remarkably changed man.

"Oh, Ned Peirce…Ned Peirce," the man called from the doorway. His voice carried across a sunlit courtyard but met a steady babble from the adjacent playing field. Somebody relayed the words onward. A few moments later, a clean-shaven, slim figure in blue denim, the shirt with the white pinstripe, came through the doorway into the somber central hall of the Norfolk County House of Correction.

He waved at the two persons awaiting him on one of the polished wooden benches and disappeared briefly down a long corridor fanning out from one of the many-sided halls.

Reappearing with several papers and letters, he hurried over, kissed his wife, Mrs. Alma P. Peirce, and greeted the reporter, whose last view of the former mayor of New Bedford had been in a tense Fall River court room a year before…

Absence of the mustache made a difference, of course. But there were striking changes. The glasses were gone. Facial lines had disappeared, though he obviously was much thinner. The hands that nervously toyed with two matchboxes every minute of the trial were reposed. Telltale signs of chain smoking were no longer visible on the fingers. He smokes one cigarette for every six he used to. Only an occasional filament of gray interrupted his brown hair. He was sunburned, May's overcast notwithstanding. "I've been umpiring a baseball game," he explained…

"Oh, the mustache? I took that off shortly after I came in…wasn't it, Alma? Anyway, it's so long ago, I've forgotten it. As a matter of fact, I find I don't need any glasses except when I am reading book type. Been wearing them constantly for 12 or 13 years too."

He was told he seemed temperamentally different, also. Much more relaxed. "Funny thing," he rejoined. "Did you know very few people die in jail? My nerves are perfect. It's the first time in 15 years I have had an opportunity to relax and meditate. It would be good for most of us. There are no distractions, except reading, if you call that one. I read reasonably serious stuff four hours a day.

"Jail brings out the best in one. Just like one of the fellows said to me the other day, 'I wish I could be the same on the "outside" as I am on the "inside."'"

"We're out at 8 in the morning, and stay out 'til 4:30, except for an hour after lunch. The food here is very good. They are strict, but there's a difference between strictness and meanness. If we vary, we are snapped up; disciplined, but in a very human way.

"When we're not working at jobs, we have an hour in the morning and an hour in the afternoon when we're free for anything except to 'go over the wall.' That softball is a good, live game here. Everybody enjoys it. Funny thing, for eight years in the Legislature, I had a pass to the Major League games in Boston. I never went once. I would have considered it a foolish waste of time, I suppose. My friends will find it hard to understand the change."

During a pause, the former New Bedford chief executive was queried as to his expectations as to getting out of jail, to which he was sentenced for conspiracy to permit gambling in the city.

"Let's see. Approximately eight months ago, he (the judge) took under advisement a request for cutting the sentences. Several times he has said he is going to give me an answer but there has been none. I still have rights to appeal on several counts, but that's in the hands of my lawyers…"

At this point in the interview the former mayor showed more of an inclination to discuss future plans.

"My political life? I'm going in for meditation and relaxation now. I can't relax, and think of an indefinite date-

Peirce Family Collection

Photo-op with young intern, 1952. Mayor Peirce tried to make himself available to everyone. A close associate once said, "It doesn't make any difference if a constituent wears tails or overalls when they come to Ned. They get the same consideration and help." A prolific writer, Peirce kept three secretaries busy. He often reported to his office by 7am and worked late.

Peirce Family Collection

On the lecture circuit at New Bedford Textile School, 1951. Mayor Peirce performed regularly before students and civic groups. After one-and-a-half years in prison he reflected: "I think I've gained more years of life by being here than I lost, so to speak. I had been under a strain for years. I worked hard at many things. When I came here I was tired. It took me four months here to slow down."

when I might get out... I think I've gained more years of life by being here than I lost, so to speak. I had been under a strain for years. I worked hard at many things. When I came here I was tired. It took me four months here to slow down.

"I never had more confidence in the future than I have right now, but what that future will be I do not know. Lots of people are wondering what I want to do. I got more letters last month than ever before. Many of them feel I've been here too long already.

"From what I hear, conditions in New Bedford are not so good. They can deny it, but certainly some of it is due to the policy I always fought—of limiting industrial diversification. There's no doubt in my mind, we're going to see the greatest economic boom ever in this country. It will be a peace boom, not based on war, a period of peace, period of boom. New Bedford is going to make a mistake if it doesn't readjust before that happens."

The former mayor suddenly seemed to realize he was leaning forward on the bench, permitting matters over which he could have no control to intrude into his calmness of mind. He sat back and abruptly changed the subject.

"I can't be mad at anybody," he said. "I've learned a lot in here. My religious reading has taught me something, especially about money. There are two things you cannot buy. You can find satisfaction, perhaps with money, but you can't be sure of contentment or happiness. Ask anybody with money and power if he has contentment.

"That story in Life magazine about Eastman was a perfect example of what I mean. He had money and success; yet, he shot himself. The failure of money to bring contentment runs all through the New Testament.

"I have a feeling that whatever my punishment is for—it was not for criminal actions, that is another fight. But the drive and ambition of one with a goal can be treacherous and can catch up with him. What time do you have to think clearly on the outside, to really meditate? You think you're pretty smart. I did. But you're really thinking in one track and see only what's in front of you.

"Yes, my plans for the future are not concerned with how am I going to make a dollar, but with how–with what outlook–will I live. Look at me. I don't know what it was, luck, brilliance, the help of the Good Lord, maybe, or what it is. But I had $1 million before I was 30. Yet, a few years later, in 1936, I was working on the WPA. And within eight years of that, I was in the Massachusetts Senate.

"With that drive, people must have figured that I was reaching my objective. But I have no desire to go through it again. If someone said he knew where I could make a million again, I wouldn't be interested. You learn not to be so foolish about material gain here. They don't worry you and you learn to appreciate small things. It reminds me of the extent to which the extra pancakes on Sunday morning are appreciated. You'd be surprised at how good they taste.

"You don't take anything out of this world. Who wouldn't change his place for a contented mind and good health? I've learned that here, and it's worth whatever it has cost me. From a material standpoint, I could be sad about my personal affairs. But I couldn't buy the things I think I can have now."

Once more relaxed, the former mayor permitted his thoughts to travel outside again.

He is quite certain the New Bedford tax rate will rise a total of $8 between 1953-1955.

I am not at all hopeless about the future. The odds are better all the time. The fact I have served a year may cause many more persons to think I've been here too long. I have never regretted coming in here. As you probably know, I could have resigned and there would have been no jail sentence. But I never duck a fight. They licked me. But I believe none of those who put me here are as happy as I am. I am positive they are not as healthy. Why, I can do ten pushups..."

On February 1, 1955, at the age of 59, Edward Cook Peirce died of lung and liver cancer.

Obituary of Edward C. Peirce

The passing of Edward C. Peirce brought to an end a career of one of the most striking political and business figures in New Bedford's long history.

His meteoric rise to the heights in both public and private life, from a modest beginning as a $4 a week office boy 44 years ago, has few parallels. How he rebounded from crushing economic reversals to become a State Senator and Mayor, a Democratic Party leader and a prominent city businessman is a dramatic story.

Gifted with seemingly boundless energy, Mr. Peirce worked tirelessly. He was proud of New Bedford's glorious past and envisioned an even more abundant future with an economy based on industrial diversification.

He was dynamic, but his kindly ways were apparent to those who knew him. Helping others in time of need, easing the burden of men less fortunate, were traits characteristic of Ned Peirce, as he was popularly known.

However grievous his sins may have been, Peirce paid his debt to society in full, if not indeed, in excessive measure. Although others shared his guilt equally, they did not share his punishment.

Paroled but not pardoned, at last, Mr. Peirce was permitted only a few uneasy days with family and friends before his death. There may be some small measure of consolation to them in the knowledge he died a free man in the city where he was born.

Editors' Note:

Two issues are at the forefront of public opinion as to why Peirce was brought down. First, he made bitter enemies with New Bedford tycoons/power brokers John and Mark Duff. One of his first acts as mayor was to take the heating contract for all municipal buildings away from the more expensive David Duff and Sons Coal Co. and award it to the cheaper Pacific Coal Co.

This was an enormous contract that included the city's many schools, garages, fire stations, etc. It was a huge rebuff to the Duffs, whose economic interests in New Bedford included bank presidencies and ownership of textile mills, the Union Street Railway and the New Bedford Hotel. The Duffs had great political influence in Massachusetts. Mark Duff was a major player in the state GOP. District attorney Maurice Lyons was a close friend of the Duffs and had his office in the Duff Building. Peirce often referred to his courtroom nemesis as the "Duff/Lyons outfit." With this formidable opponent, many people feel the mayor's fate was sealed.

The second obstacle Peirce faced was the gaming cartel. While he appeared to be a staunch foe of gambling, evidence brought out in the trial showed that Peirce had a hands-off policy toward some bookies, while cracking down on others. This duplicity made him an easy target for plea-bargaining stoolies and a zealous district attorney crusading against illegal gambling.

Nancy Peirce Carvalho started working in the Peirce flower business (then on State Rd.) at age 10 and never stopped. She ran the business (now on Acushnet Avenue) for 25 years, then turned it over to her son, Charles, for whom she now works. The original Peirce the Florist was founded in downtown New Bedford in 1867 by her grandfather and uncle.

At 78, she still puts in a five-day work week. She also does historical research on local towns and is trying to put her Dad's life into book form.

Marsha McCabe is a writer and senior editor at Spinner Publications.

The Standard-Times

Edward C. Peirce, outside Fall River court, May 1953. *Once Peirce immersed himself in politics, he never got it out of his blood. He had a keen sense of history and tried to steer New Bedford away from economic ruin. "From what I hear, conditions in New Bedford are not so good," he told a reporter while in prison in 1953. "They can deny it, but certainly some of it is due to the policy I always fought—of limiting industrial diversification. There's no doubt in my mind, we're going to see the greatest economic boom ever in this country. It will be a peace boom, not based on war, a period of peace, period of boom. New Bedford is going to make a mistake if it doesn't readjust before that happens."*

*The **Helen**, aground on Martha's Vineyard, 1940s.* According to a television news report by Mike Taibbi, the Helen is said to be the same boat as the Black Duck. The story goes that the Black Duck ran aground on Martha's Vineyard, despite tales that it was sunk by the Coast Guard. Evidence suggests that the boat was seized one night while landing in Rhode Island and was eventually sold into private hands. It was serving as a launch under the name Helen when this picture was taken in the 1940s. Note the long, flat expanse of deck, ideal for stacking the boxes of liquor.

Westport Rum Runners

Davison Paull

Westport Point became one of the most active rumrunning centers on the Atlantic coast during the wicked, wild days of Prohibition. Fueled by the Temperance Movement, the Eighteenth Amendment was passed in 1919. It prohibited the manufacture, transportation and sale of beverage alcohol in the United States.

The Point was ideal for illicit activities as the harbor and river are treacherous for those unfamiliar with the area. Named the devil's pocket by British sailors during the Revolutionary War, the harbor mouth's overlapping jaws make boats seemingly disappear as they enter the river.

Westport was also far enough away from federal authorities in Boston and New York to allow the bootleggers to carry on, yet close enough to the northeastern cities to insure reasonably swift delivery of liquor to major markets. Directed by organized crime, loosely referred to as The Syndicate, with labor provided locally, rumrunning thrived in Westport.

Nightly, small speedy boats left the harbor to rendezvous with large boats and their liquid cargo waiting in international waters. Loaded to the gills with whiskey—for it was whiskey and not rum that fueled the speakeasies—the smaller boats would slip back to unload before the dawn could break. Most of the time, it was easy money.

Davison Paull Collection

The following excerpts are from *Images of a Westport Past*, a collection of oral accounts that tell the story of Westport Point. Interviewees include:

Richard Paull, who first came to Westport as a child recovering from polio and stayed all his life, becoming a lawyer and local historian; **Carlton Manchester Sr.,** *Westport native and Navy veteran, who observed the spoils of rum running as a boy;* **Ab Palmer,** *the shellfish warden in Westport for many years, retiring in 1980;* **Archer Tripp,** *born and raised in Westport, and interviewed by Mary Giles in 1976 in celebration of Westport's Bicentennial; and* **Janet Grindley,** *the author of two books,* With a Merry Heart *and* A Joyful Noise, *about her childhood summers in Westport (she writes under the name Janet Gillespie).*

Bootlegging was an open secret in Westport and many knew who the rumrunners were. Those who might have voiced opposition were kept quiet through the unspoken threat of retribution. It was a major, illegal operation with high stakes and lots of money involved, and whatever one felt about it, it was very serious business.

Many Westport townspeople noticed strange doings on land and sea in those rumrunning days.

Richard Paull

Way down at the end of Westport Point, on the west side, there was a building called the Liar's Club. In front of it, at the first pier, was a long boat that appeared to be designed for speed and not for cargo. I was maybe eight or ten at the time. Captain Eli Allen,

Westport Point, 1934. *A quiet and quaint New England village peninsula by day, becomes a haven for contraband and stealth by night.*

The Standard-Times

a Spanish-American War veteran, was aware much more than I as to the illegality and notoriety of rumrunning, and also of the danger of that activity. He addressed me once: 'If you're a sensible boy, you'll keep your goddamn mouth shut.' I got the hint that it was better if I didn't say anything about what I saw.

Carlton Manchester

Behind the Village Store we had a converted barn we used as a garage for trucks and pleasure cars. One of my duties was to open the big door of the garage as soon as I arrived at work at 7:00AM. I opened the door one morning and almost instantly heard a thump on the old mow floor above me. Startled, I picked up a baseball bat and quietly ascended the stairs. Slowly I peeked up over the floor level. The morning light shown in one window, directly on a huge pile of new burlap bags. I saw the form of a big person lying there.

He appeared to be asleep; slowly I stepped closer. It was a man I recognized. He wore a big overcoat, open with the front half laying back. I saw a billfold lying on the coat, knelt down and saw currency showing—a hundred dollar bill, no, a thousand. I couldn't believe my eyes. Thousand dollar bills were not that familiar to me.

I raised up and touched his foot very gently. He stirred and I spoke, called him by name and suggested he take care of his money; someone else might come along and have ideas of their own. He said the money was marked by the bank, no one could cash one of those bills without his signature, but thanks just the

Ruth Edwards

The Standard-Times

Westport Point, 1947. *The Point's remoteness, shallow waters and spacious waterways made it ideal for rumrunning. The old Westport Point bridge, spanning the mouth of the East Branch of the Westport River, connected the Point with Horseneck.*

Well, the barn was a place where they could store it, but if they weren't being harassed they'd come right into the town wharf and unload into the trucks, which would immediately go back to The Syndicate, either in New York or Chicago. The boats would tie up at the wharf with the other fishing boats during the day.

There were very few people who complained about the rumrunners and there was very little talk. They were afraid they'd get retaliation if they squealed. People just accepted it as being here, and probably hoped it would go away sometime.

We know that Everett Coggeshall (the town constable) asked for help several times from federal authorities when he knew the liquor was in, and he never got it. By the time the authorities got here, it would all be out of sight so they got tired of coming down here and not finding anything. Everett couldn't do this alone. If he went in and tried to arrest them while they were unloading, they'd have hog-tied him and taken him out and forgotten him.

If the feds had been available out of New Bedford or Fall River, and could have been here in half an hour, it would have been a different story. So Everett worked alone, and I don't think he did much good but he did the best he could. He was a pain in the side to the rumrunners and they were a headache for him.

You only needed two people on the small boats when they went out, but when they came in, they needed men right there to load the trucks, so they had a shore crew of fifteen or twenty people and they'd use the chain method, one passing it to the next and the next and so on. Everything was done by hand.

I don't think they would shoot back at the Coast Guard, but they had side arms for their own protection. If the Coast Guard was after them they'd try to get away. They didn't stay there and have a pitched battle. They didn't want to get caught and they didn't want to fight. They were in the rum business, not the fighting business. They would go out before dark, and start loading after dark and everything would be cleaned up by daybreak. Maybe the big boat would stay out there for a few nights, but it was safe beyond the three mile limit.

There was money in it because the only place you could buy liquor was in the speakeasies which The Syndicate controlled. They named them speakeasies because it was a place where you could go in and have drinks but you had to keep your voice down. There'd be no hootin' or hollerin' or anything boisterous. Everything would be kept on a very low level. It was a regular bar like today, only they were in areas where they didn't want people to know where they were.

Rum Trail, 1932. Reed Road, generally deserted by day, was a busy rum trail after dark. The road was reported to be the main artery of the liquor traffic in southeastern Massachusetts. The small building on the left is the town's police station.

The Standard-Times

Ruth Edwards

There was nothing around here, but I'm sure that somewhere along the line some of the workers would steal it and sell it to Tom, Dick, and Harry. I'm sure it was available around here, but not in speakeasies. There was big money in it—to get people like Capone into it there had to be. And the fishermen made good money, and I guess they'd want to for taking a risk like that. For getting shot at they'd want good money.

Archer Tripp

I don't think I should tell. An awful lot of people were involved directly. They might rent their barn or their cellar so the liquor could be stored there and they got paid for that—so much for a case. During those days the only thing that kept the people going around here was the rumrunning. Only a few got arrested. They never had to serve time or anything, they had to pay a fine.

The Syndicate would have a man there to receive the liquor, and they would hire a man to be there when the liquor came in. After it was unloaded, the men would get paid right then for the work. After it was stored, if they had to leave it a certain length of time, he would pay for the storage and it would all come right down the chain.

When all this was going on I was nineteen years old and working for the Westport and Dartmouth Lobster Company in Padanaram and Westport Point. I used to have to take the lobsters to Boston. So one morning I came with a truck to come pick up the lobsters and when I drove down on the dock this fellow came out with a light and a revolver which he stuck right into my stomach and said, "Hold it right there." Then he looked and said, "Oh, they're lobsters. Pull over here 'til we get this settled."

Richard Paull

Rumrunning was the principal occupation of a good many Westporters, including some otherwise respectable citizens. The rumrunners, though they were pretty well known by those in town, weren't exhibitionists in any way. I remember there were some reports of boats that had come in riddled by Coast Guard machine gun fire. It was rough business.

The town treasurer of Westport in 1927 got involved in rumrunning in such a way that the town funds were put into a cargo of liquor which got hijacked, and then just by coincidence there was a store that caught fire that had all the records—so they couldn't show what had happened. The rumrunning had permeated the town.

In 1927 there was a long grey boat up alongside the huge Coast Guard vessel. It had two Liberty motors, which were World War I motors, and I could not understand how this boat could continue in the business and not be hauled away somewhere. There wasn't any question that it was in rumrunning activities and it was hard to realize how anything illegal was tolerated.

Westport Point, 1947.

The Standard-Times

Over the years I've come to realize more and more what did take place. I can remember well when Prohibition was erased in 1933. A great many of those who had been in the rumrunning were working on the WPA, building the sidewalks up and down the street. Their means of support had been suddenly taken away from them.

Janet Grindley

My grandmother and Aunt K used to see the lights in winter. Someone on the sea would flash to someone on the land. Then they'd come in and they'd land down at the wharf or at Cape Bial. This was at night, of course, and then they'd drive up through the village in trucks full of tinkling bottles.

Near the mouth of the Westport River, 1938. This view, looking west across the entrance to Westport Harbor, shows Cherry & Webb beach in the foreground and the old Cherry cottage nestled in the dunes. Rumrunners took advantage of the waterway's remote and shallow shores to slip in and out of port unnoticed. From here, passage to either branch of the river and to the Westport Harbor can be made.

Many of the tales from the rumrunning days have become part of Westport folklore. Three tales in particular are now local legends—the wicked adventures and sudden demise of the *Black Duck,* the daring escapes of runners beneath the old Point bridge, especially the wild ride of a "mysterious boat" whose bulletproof windshield was sheared off and, of course, the visit of the notorious gangster, Al Capone.

Ab Palmer

Well, the *Black Duck* was built primarily for rum running, and whatever she needed was put into her. Someone said she had smokescreens and I don't know about that, but whatever it needed for rumrunning it had. I don't think that thing ever fished. It would come in after dark and leave before dawn, and it would go wherever they needed it.

It was fast enough to go down to Long Island if they needed to unload down there, and they used the *Black Duck* wherever they could. That was all she was built for and all she was used for. I think they picked her up around the islands out here, and that's where they sunk her. I don't know what she was doing out there. Maybe trying to escape the Coast Guard by hiding in the islands, or making a run for Westport or Sakonnet, but she was sunk.

Carlton Manchester Sr.

The *Black Duck* was certainly in the news those days—late twenties especially. I saw her alongside the dock a couple of times, she had unloaded her cargo at night and decided to stay put. On a dark night she would cut her engines, come in by the harbor rock with the rising tide, and continue to drift toward the turn of the channel. This with the Coast Guard tied up at Charlton's dock, on her port side. I heard there was only one Coast Guard commander who could not be bought off by 'the Gang.' It was then I began to understand how so many successful trips were made by the *Duck*, the *I'm Alone*, and others.

The *Duck* operated out of Scunnet River and Tiverton. A man by the name of Red controlled that local gang. He had an agreement with the Point gang that he could unload at the Point if he was pressed by the CG in his area. Likewise, the Point runners could go to Red's area if necessary. There was another gang operating out of South Dartmouth that had the same agreement with the Point and Red.

One morning we heard that the Coast Guard had fired point blank into the *Black Duck* after they had 'heaved to' dead in the water. Some of the boys were killed—murdered, as the survivor called it. Herb took five slugs through the body and survived. He pressed the issue with the authorities, there was hell to pay for a long time.

In later years, Herb had a float stage tied along the east shore bank of the Nanaquacket pond in Tiverton, about a mile or so south of Stone Bridge. Some man named Almy was in a running feud with Herb, and he walked down on the float and shot Herb five times in the gut. Herb survived that also. I understand he died of natural causes. He was tough.

Ruth Edwards

Rum runners barn. *This Westport shack was said to have been a liquor storage area for local bootleggers.*

The Chantegulf, circa 1920. *Parading through New Bedford Harbor is this government speedster, with machine gun mounted on her deck. She was typical of boats used by the Coast Guard in pursuit of bootleggers.*

Spinner Collection

The Standard-Times

Rum runner Mary Langdon, under tow, 1925. *The Coast Guard Cutter* Acushnet *enters New Bedford Harbor with the* Mary Langdon, *seized in Vineyard Haven after it was discovered that she was carrying a cargo of more than 3,000 cases of liquor. The contraband was concealed beneath a load of lumber to give her the appearance of a vessel in the coastwise lumber trade. While speedboats were popular rum runners in the latter days of prohibition, old schooners, barges and packets also ran successful clandestine operations.*

Alcohol unloaded at Woods Hole, 1935. *State Police and Coast Guardsmen transfer liquor found in South Dartmouth and suspected to have been smuggled in by the Canadian ship* Accuracy *during the early dawn. Though no contraband was found on the ship, and despite protests from the Canadian government, the Coast Guard seized* Accuracy *and arrested her nine crew members for conspiracy to violate the tariff act through smuggling alcohol.*

The fate suffered by the Duck *was shared by many other boats over the years, and the encounters with the Coast Guard could turn deadly. Some chose to better their odds, others to get away at any cost. One boat, it seems, did both.*

Ab Palmer

The Coast Guard was capable of making it rough for the boats and crews with their thirty-caliber machine guns. One day the boss and I drove down onto the main dock at the Point. A strange boat was tied up at the very end, and an out of state paneled truck was parked nearby. The only familiar thing in sight was one of our seafaring men. He seemed to be arguing with a well dressed man. My boss said 'Let's stick around, maybe we can be of help to our friend.'

About then the stranger pulled out a .45 caliber and said 'all right, go below and we will find out if it is as good as the guarantee.' Our friend said 'Not me, you go down and let me pull the trigger,' so the stranger passed our friend the gun. We were dumbfounded as to what was going on.

The stranger jumped aboard the vessel and stood behind what appeared to be a newly installed pilot house with a thick glass windshield. He said to our friend 'Shoot.' The fisherman said 'I cannot, get out from behind and I will.' He walked forward a few feet, turned, and fired. There was quite a racket and a loud THWACK. Lead flattened out against the glass. We had just seen a bulletproof windshield tested out. The installer was sure it would stop a .45.

A few nights later that same boat was tied up in the same spot with a few hundred cases of booze aboard. A lookout gave the word that a thirty-six footer (*Coast Guard patrol boat*) was closing in on them. A rising tide was bringing it to them, silently.

The Standard-Times

Two small lines held the rumrunner to the dock, and there was no time to cast off. The engineer got the word, "Full speed ahead." The lines snapped, and the pilot swung the boat hard-a-starboard for a hundred yards and then east, toward the old wooden bridge. The tide was nearly high—not enough clearance for her to pass under. The pilot headed her straight for the bridge and increased speed, told the deck-hand to 'lay flat.'

With a tearing, shearing sound the boat came out the east side of the Point Bridge minus a bullet proof windshield. The skipper and deck-hand were spared. The Coast Guard boat could not go under the bridge and they could not wake John Kenny, the bridge tender, a sound sleeper!

The next day we were told where the remaining cargo had been unloaded, on the shore of the property where I was born eighteen years before, a stone's throw north of Masquesatch and Ship Rock.

In the coastal towns involved with rumrunning, the classic New England myth, "George Washington slept here," has a companion: "Al Capone came here." Westport seems to have missed out on George Washington, but Al Capone did stop by.

Carlton Manchester Sr.

I delivered orders to homes through the village on Saturdays for Johnny Fish who ran the Point Store. I had an order for the man who headed The Point rumrunners for two men from Attleboro. The big boy was called Attleboro Sam. This Saturday, when I drove in with the order, I noticed a big, black, seven-passenger sedan with Illinois plates.

When I entered the house with the order, my uncle—right-hand man for the man in charge—gave me a wink and raised one finger and nodded to the next room. I got the message. Later that day my uncle told me that Al Capone was there. I laughed in his face. He said, "You saw that Illinois car out there. Who do you think was in it, President Hoover? Don't advertise it around town." At that age (seventeen) I knew enough to keep my mouth shut.

The only word I heard of that visit was "I have no plans for this part of the country, just driving through," says Mr. Capone. My older brother, now deceased, met Al.

I did not realize fully what was going on. I had heard of Al same as everyone else, but it cut no ice with me that he 'must' be part of rumrunning. I couldn't care less, long as I got my 25 cents an hour. I guess Al kept his word, as I was around there for the next ten years and saw no sign of Al.

Rumrunning continued in Westport until 1933, when the Twenty-first Amendment repealed prohibition. Prohibition failed because the flow of liquor through this country was largely unstoppable. Although Westport was exceptional in the amount of liquor that came through the town, its experience with the law enforcement of the era was typical. There were simply too many people who wanted to bring the liquor in and too few paid to keep it out.

Author Davison Paull grew up in Westport, graduated from UMass Amherst and works for New Video Group in New York City. "My grandfather first awakened me to the story behind my town," he says, "and inspired me to write an oral history, Images From a Westport Past.*" Davison Paull is also indebted to Mary Giles who taped the stories of more than 40 Westporters during the town's Bicentennial.*

Ruth Edwards

"This is that famed shot I took of the Argo Merchant, sinking in Nantucket waters, in December 1976. The plane's window was frozen shut. I got it open and told the pilot to go low enough to get spray on the windshield…and he did." The Liberian tanker ran aground on Nantucket Shoals and eventually broke apart, leaving a trail of 7.5 million gallons of light crude oil.

Milton Silvia: "As I Saw It"

MARSHA MCCABE

"A great moment caught on film has a clarity that's magic, an arrested moment in time," says photographer Milton Silvia, at home in New Bedford. "It delights the eye and pleases the brain. It stirs emotion. It becomes an old friend with each successive viewing." Milton Silvia has chosen some of these old friends to exhibit in *Spinner*.

Milt is a photographer who never played it safe. In over a half-century of work, including a 30-year career at the *Standard-Times*, he has captured on film most of the people, events and charm that has made its way through southeastern Massachusetts: from blazing fires to sinking ships; from the hands of old men in prison to children smelling flowers. Milton's work is a vibrant and comprehensive record of our time—as much a treasure of our heritage as any collection of written documents or masterpiece paintings.

John Durant, 1964. "John Durant is up in his sail loft making sails for the whaleship *Charles W. Morgan, now berthed in Mystic.*" The Durant Sail Loft was on the top floor of the Bourne Counting House on Merrill's Wharf.

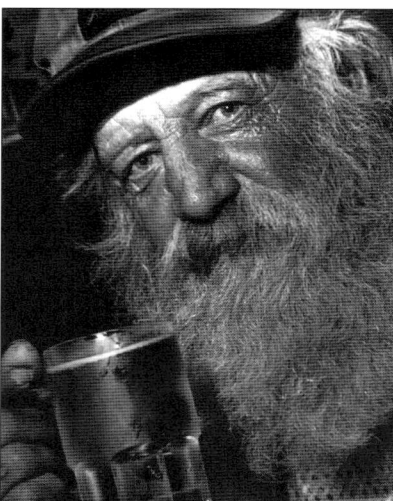

Captain Quahog, 1964. "I was always intrigued by the face of this old salt, downing a brew at a waterfront pub. He lived on the Cape and dug quahogs. He'd hitchhike to New Bedford, carrying two buckets, selling quahogs along the way."

Joe Ainsley, superintendent of Men's Mission, 1960. "I always search for camera angles or lighting that make the picture more compelling to the eye and more powerful in its meaning." The mission was founded in the 1880s to "rally young toughs and old drunkards...to abandon their wicked ways and walk upright as Christians."

Adoption at the Animal Rescue League, 1979. "My all-time favorite photo: A little mother and her puppy await adoption. The thing that grabbed me was their hopelessness...a symbol of the meanness in the world. This prizewinner was the official picture of the New Bedford Animal Rescue League for many years. And yes, the dogs were adopted.

"I'm from the documentary school," says Milt. "I like to film back streets, backstage at the burlesque, the seamy side of life. Being a news photographer fit my personality better than anything else I might have chosen. Being loose, flying around, that's me. I'm from the days of the photo essay. I tell the story in pictures.

"You get a camera in your hand and suddenly you're ten feet tall. When they were building the Braga Bridge in Fall River, I climbed to the top of the steel with my camera equipment and shot the work in progress. I was an ego-jerk, I guess. You do most anything to get a picture.

"No one could meet deadlines with finer pictures in less time than Milt," wrote John Ackerman in the Standard-Times, May 4, 1980, in a full-page tribute to Mr. Silvia on his retirement. "On assignment he was never still and his camera viewfinder was glued to his eye...moving, shooting, moving, shooting, politely asking men, women and children to turn, to look, to move, to stand...and winning their bemused consent because they knew he wanted to show them at their best.

"He had the ability to sum up a situation," Mr. Ackerman continued, "for instance, the gas explosion that damaged New Bedford so heavily, in January of 1977, caught at its raging height in a color photograph.

"But he could sum up more complex affairs in one picture, too...the old man, worn out and alone...John F. Kennedy, his wife and his child caught during that brief moment when Camelot glistened in the sun; the listing broken ship vomiting oil into the seas of Nantucket...

"For 30 years, Milt Silvia has given his best to The Standard-Times, giving it a quality, an outreach many dailies never attain."

Over a long career, Milt has some moments that stay in the memory:

"The drama of the Argo Merchant going down in Nantucket waters, I'll remember always. From the plane I could only see a spot through the clouds. I told my pilot, Norm Gingras, to go in so close, we would get spray on the windshield. He did and we got a spectacular picture. The wire services ran it big.

"I vividly remember the Andrea-Doria/Stockholm sinking and collision. I flew out to the collision site just as dawn was breaking. Through an opening in the clouds, we could see a dramatic tableau on the water below. One ship was cut in half and people were in the lifeboats with their orange life preservers brightly visible.

"Another great memory was being on the movie set when Walter Huston was filming a scene from *The Cardinal* in a rock quarry in Quincy. Huston had been in New Bedford for the world premier of *Moby Dick*, he liked the city and, as it turned out, he remembered me.

"Off I went to the location and the adrenaline was really pumping. Otto Preminger, the director, was rumored to be a tough guy and a tyrant on the set. Huston introduced me to Preminger and they agreed to give me five minutes to shoot pictures after they finished the scene.

"There was a guy there from *Life Magazine* with three or four cameras around his neck and shoulders and they clacked together, making a lot of noise as he moved. They were filming a scene in a boudoir with the actors in bed and our man from *Life* was trying to get in tight with a wide-angle lens. Preminger turned purple and in a very loud voice with dramatic gestures pointed at the door: 'OUD—OUD ALL STILL PHOTOGRAPHERS, OUD,' he shouted. I tried to disappear into the woodwork, then looked over at Huston and he said, 'Stay.' So out went the guy from *Life* and I stayed and got the pictures!"

Milt also remembers the pictures that didn't happen:

"I was trying to photograph Harry Truman in Fall River and my bulb exploded. His body guards had me in a strangle hold in seconds.

"I was sent on assignment to Nantucket with a reporter to photograph a murder scene. When we got to the island, we discovered it was a suicide and the newspaper didn't cover suicides. Since no planes were going back until the next day, we spent the night riding bikes around the island.

"And I missed, no, almost missed, my chance to photograph the great Marlon Brando! I went off to the Circus Tent in Hyannis, all excited, to take pictures of Brando and Wally Cox. But these two wanted nothing to do with photographers. They covered their famous faces with their hands and I shot them sitting on the steps like that.

Noelie Houle, "goat lady" of Dartmouth, circa 1970. "A local legend, she came here from way north of Quebec and we jabbered away in French—I grew up in a French-speaking family. As for this picture, I always like the people and animal relationship. How Mrs. Houle loved those goats!"

Images of the Azores. Milt made two trips to the Azores. He got along by learning one basic Portuguese expression: "Can I take your picture?"

Opposite page, clockwise:

Old man and a boy at the water faucet in San Miguel, 1968. "Dignity has no boundaries."

"In the Azores, life is hard. People are surrounded by the sea and the men have to drag these fishing boats through the surf. As you can see, they make it a team effort."

On the island of Fayal, 1988, "the old woman chops brush, probably for cooking or heating."

Sturdy, hard-working oxen plow through fields, 1988. "When I was taking the picture, the man said, ''No, wait. Come back next month when I get my new tractor.'"

Wash day in the country, 1968: "When I visited San Miguel, I got to see laundry done the old-fashioned way: The women beating the laundry on the rocks, then carrying it home in baskets. I like the composition of the photograph, with the line of the road leading into the infinite distance. The timelessness of the subject pervades over the photograph: the drizzly day, the women working, so shall it ever be."

"But the biggest, most frustrating miss I experienced in my career was the one in Pennsylvania with the coal miners. A number of miners were trapped in a coal mine disaster for several days, and rescuers, who could hear them tapping, were drilling a hole next to the shaft to get down to where they were.

"Dozens of photographers were on the scene with their motorcycle runners, the guys who take the film back to their papers. Like everybody else, I was trying to position myself to get a good shot of the miners as they popped out of the hole, and I didn't dare leave the area for fear of missing something. Donuts and coffee were brought to us. That's what we ate.

"Finally, after several days of hunkering down on the coal-dust covered ground, word came that the miners would be brought out. That started the scramble for position. The State Police had cordoned off an area to keep us back; it was like keeping wild animals at bay. At night, you'd crouch there in the coal dust, check the flash bulb and make sure the shutter was cocked, knowing you have only ONE chance to catch the first man coming out of the hole.

"Suddenly, I heard a voice shout, 'They're coming out!' At that very moment, the biggest state trooper in Pennsylvania stood up in front of me and blocked my shot. You can't imagine the lost, empty, angry feeling I had after days of waiting. I could have killed him."

How did Milton Silvia, a New Bedford native, become an award-winning photographer? Milt points to many influences, but the most important were his mother, a teacher and an uncle. "My mother encouraged me in the arts. She was always buying me paint sets, and I spent lots of time playing around in color. I also took violin lessons.

"And I must credit one of my teachers at the Thomas A. Rodman grammar school. Mr. Paul Vancini, a visiting art teacher in the school department, helped me with composition. He made me think about the arrangement of things. I remember we did a project called the House Book. We drew our own houses with doors and window sills, keeping in mind perspective and arrangement. I never forgot Mr. Vancini. Then I continued in high school, always taking elective courses in drawing and art appreciation. People told me I was talented and, of course, that helped.

"Meanwhile, my uncle was an amateur photographer in New York, and I began meeting people from the New York Camera Club and taking

The great escape, circa 1964. "I took this picture from the little house on top of the Fairhaven bridge. It shows what traffic was like on a typical summer day before I-195 was built. This was when Cape traffic came right through the center of the cities."

Christmas season, downtown New Bedford, circa 1961 (opposite page). "Purchase Street used to look like this on a snowy night before Christmas, all lit up, bustling with shoppers." Note the carriage seeking donations for St. Mary's Home.

Goodyear Manufacturing, 1965. "Industry was off and running then. This composition frames the scene and holds the eye on the worker."

Pete Cullen, Concordia boatbuilder, 1960s. "He is a real craftsman. I love his absorption in his work; totally at home making boats."

my own pictures. It was the middle of the Depression and I was influenced by the photographic style of the Farm Security Administration photographers. They documented the lives and hardships of Americans during the Depression years. Remember the Dust Bowl pictures?

"In those years, I did commercial work like calendar art and, at night, I played the saxophone on boats and in nightclubs. I also joined a camera club that met at the Swain School where I got introduced to salon photography.

"Officially I joined *The Standard-Times* in 1950 and stayed for the next 30 years. These were the best years of my life. A news photographer must work at speed in some difficult situations and still get that good composition with each subject. The challenge is to produce pictures that demand to be looked at—rich, meditative pictures."

In his long career, Milton Silvia had many opportunities to leave the area and go with big newspapers in New York and Boston, but his family was here and the pull was strong. "I love the New Bedford area," he said. "Once you have the sea in you, it's hard to let it go."

Many of the photographs shown here are life's more ordinary moments: puppies at the Humane Society waiting to be adopted, a man playing bass, people at work. They are poetry and composition. And they are love.

Fish lumping, a man's work, 1960. "These fishermen prepare to 'lump' their catch from the ship's hold to the dock. They'll pull the fish out one bucket at a time. Notice how much fish is in this boat. There was a time when our big trawlers filled their pens to the top with cod and haddock."

"The Woods of Dartmouth," May 1971 (opposite page). "Here was our own small version of Woodstock, and the weather was about the same too. This tent city sprung up in the woods on the campus of Southeastern Massachusetts University, now UMass Dartmouth. At a rock concert, you see it all, from the sublime to the ridiculous."

Room with a view, 1965. "I went up the stairs of a nearby hotel, knocked on this man's door and asked him if I could take a picture of the construction of the Kerwin garage from his window. Bill, who was not expecting company, was neatly dressed in tie and shirt, and he touched my imagination with his dignity and gentleness. He represents all the aged people who live alone in small rooms but make the best of it in their own way. He liked his little room that contained all his worldly possessions and looked out over New Bedford harbor. 'From here,' he said, 'a man can look across the river.'"

Flag Day, 1979 (right). "I was enthralled with the mixture of races in a Dartmouth school. They are Americans first, beautiful kids. This was an AP winner."

The Age of Innocence, 1968. "It's a special moment when young girls take time out to smell the flowers in Buttonwood Park. I was interested in the light and this picture has a full range of tone."

Renaissance man, 1965. "The return of burlesque to downtown New Bedford brings smiles, backstage at the Empire Theater."

The summer of '69 (left). "Watermelon has no bones!"

Look what I found! 1970. "The boy catching pollywogs in Buttonwood Pond is framed in rings of bright water. I call it The Age of Discovery."

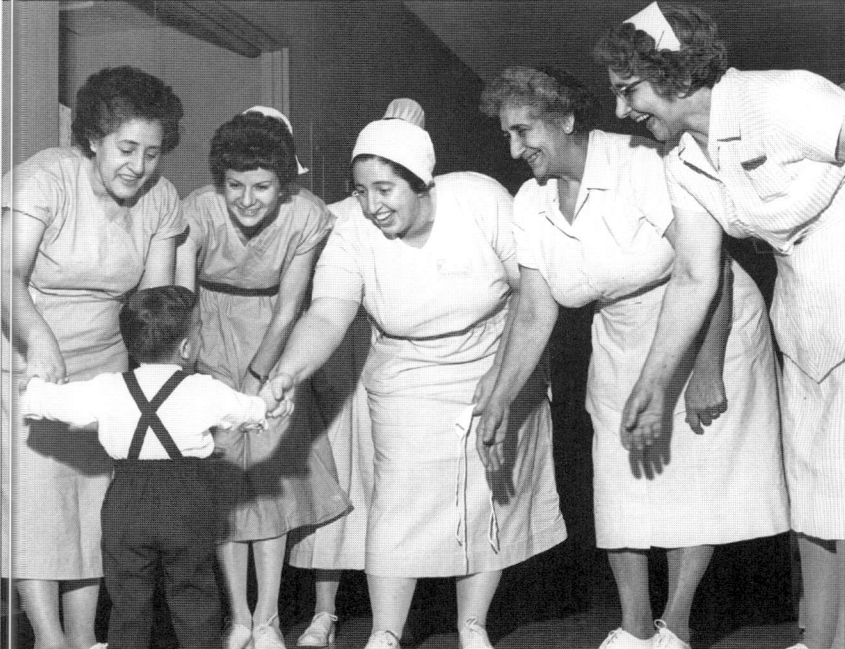

Tiny Tim, released, 1950s. "A joyful scene at St. Luke's Hospital, welcoming the return of little Tim Silvia, a preemie who spent much of his infancy in the care of these nurses. Though Tim's back is to us, you can hear him saying—'I made it!' Which absolutely delights his caregivers."

Challenge to "The Kid," circa 1964. "Here at Ted Williams' baseball camp, the kids said to the genial slugger himself: 'You can hit a ball. Let's hear you play the trumpet.' I look for expressions on people's faces and these faces are great!"

First Communion, 1966. *A young Cynthia Kaye Chamberlain receives communion from Reverend Constantine Bebis in the Greek Orthodox Church in New Bedford's North End. "The solemnity of the occasion, the spirituality, is brought out by the lighting of the window. I photograph the light and that becomes the picture."*

Introducing Nona Smith, Miss Massachusetts. *"I don't know the year but judging from the bathing suit, I'd say a long time ago. A photographer should be totally fascinated with everything that is around him. That's one of my guiding principles. And make it look as though it happened without you being there with a camera."*

Goodbye for now, 1968. "A soldier off to the Vietnam War says goodbye to his girlfriend from the window of a bus before leaving the terminal."

Young organ makers, circa 1970. "In this hands-on picture, Albert Wobecky at the old New Bedford Vocational High School, helps students build an organ."

Bishop Grace funeral, 1960. *A scene at the funeral of self-styled bishop Charles Manuel "Sweet Daddy" Grace at his House of Prayer church on Kempton Street. "His passing left a deep emotional hole in his followers."*

Landau the tailor, circa 1965. *"A pensive Abraham Landau looks out from his tailor shop on Sixth Street in downtown New Bedford."*

Krantzler's Antiques, circa 1965. *"A man in his metier: William Krantzler, the number one antique dealer in New Bedford, poses among his treasures."*

Bill Britto on bass fiddle. *"Bill was one of the best musicians around, a great gentleman and a classy guy. He played with some of the big bands and was always highly regarded. I must have taken this picture about 50 years ago."*

Fresh Air Kids, circa 1967. "The Standard-Times was doing a series on the 'Fresh Air Kids' who would come to New Bedford in the summer as part of a program designed to get kids away from the city and show them mountains and the seashore. I went to New York City to see who these kids were and where they lived. The picture says it all."

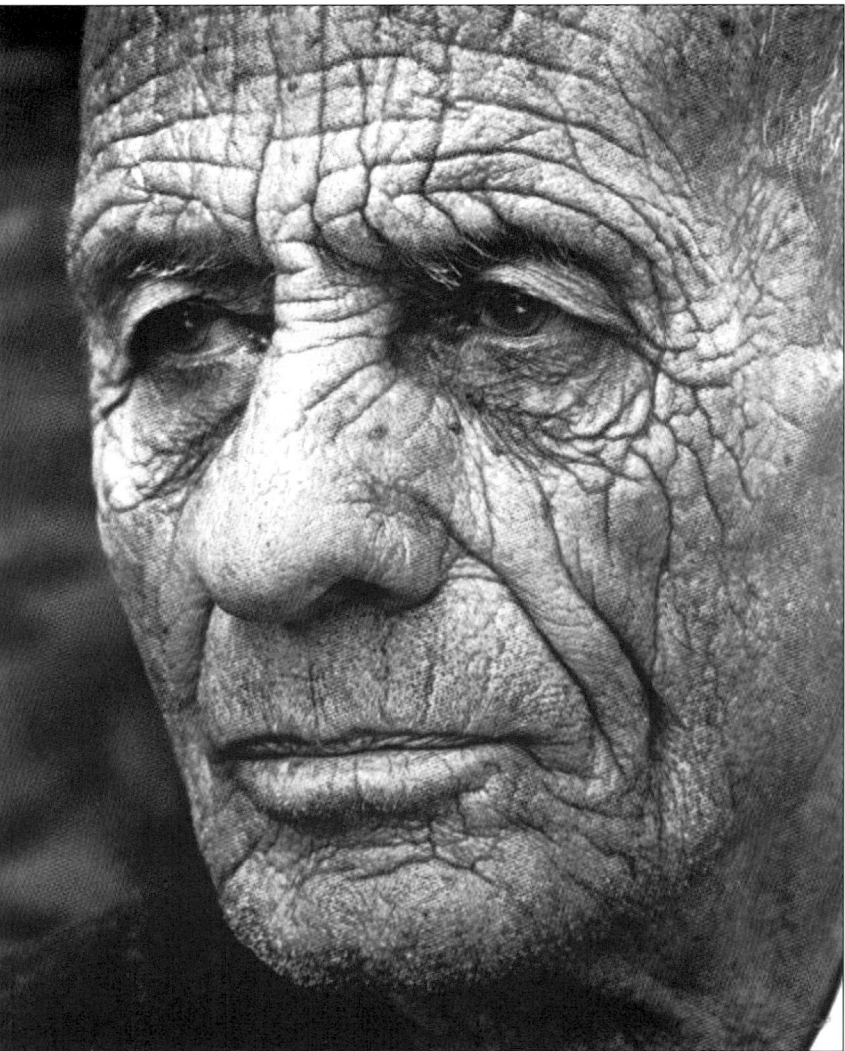

The Poet of Cape Verde. "This man was called the Poet of Cape Verde and he was visiting here from the Islands. I met him down in Bay Village and we couldn't speak the same language but we communicated. That's an extraordinary face. It tells the story of dry arid land off the coast of Africa and hard times. I like the cropping of just his face, nothing else. You can look into his eyes and see a depth of suffering and sorrow as he reflects on the past and future of Cape Verdeans."

Glass factory meltdown, 1965. "This shows the drama and horrific cost of fire, a ghostly photo. It's the old Pairpoint factory going down, part of the city's heritage."

Wrecker's waltz, So. Water Street, 1975. "When you're tearing down Water Street to make way for a highway, it's first things first."

United in song, ***1972.*** *"Pete Seeger sings his heart out at Southeastern Massachusetts University, now UMass Dartmouth."*

New shoes, late 1960s *(center). "This young man at the Schwartz Rehabilitation Center has just put on his first pair of new shoes."*

Love at first sight *(right). "This little girl has found something that's hers, a kitten. I like the emotion, the expression on her face. She is learning to like animals at an early age, beings that are smaller and weaker than she. This is important learning."*

Senator Kennedy charms the local teens, early 1960s. *"A young Ted Kennedy smiles back at his adoring fans."*

At the world premier of Moby Dick, 1956 *"Actor Gregory Peck relaxes on the New Bedford waterfront and absorbs some of the wisdom of the sailing captain at Tabor Academy."*

Reviewing the troops, 1970. *Governor Francis Sargent joins Lorenzo Jeffers, chief sachem of the Wampanoag Nation, at a celebration on Gay Head, Martha's Vineyard.*

Tired hands, 1959 *(left). "Here we have the hands of a prisoner who has been incarcerated for so many years. They couldn't let him out. His only anchor to life is his food bowl."*

City under siege, July 1970. *Senator Edward Brooke tours a grim, burned-out Kempton Street neighborhood in an effort to calm tempers when riots broke out in the West End. In background is the Masonic Temple, which burned at the height of troubles two nights earlier.*

President Kennedy at leisure, 1962. *"In Hyannisport, the New York press corps hired a boat to catch the Kennedy's in their boat, and I was not invited. Instead, I hid behind the door of the post office and photographed the family on the way to the candy store."*

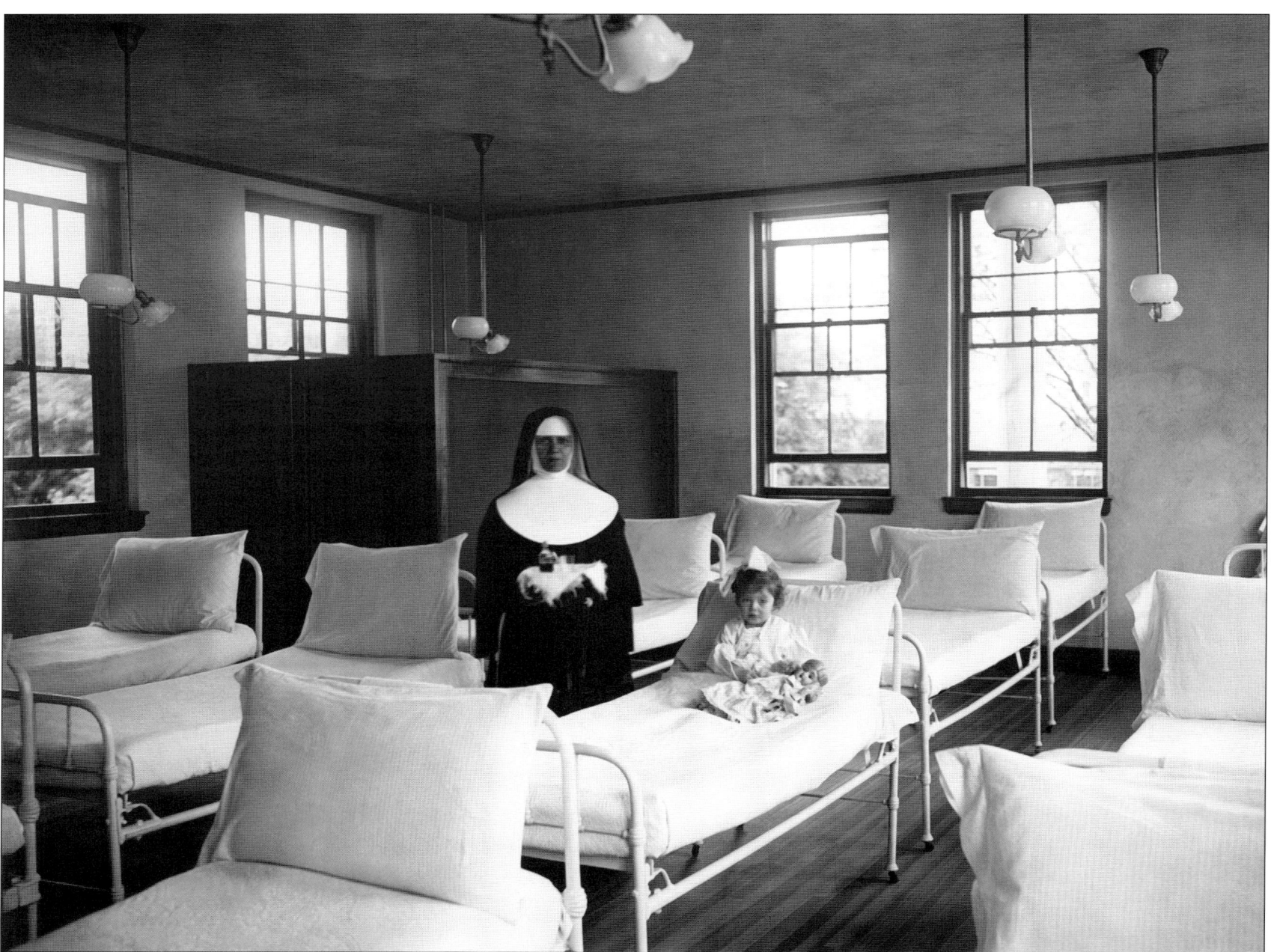

Sister Judith tends to a young resident in the dormitory of Saint Mary's Home for Children.

At St. Mary's Doorstep

RAYMOND RIVARD

Kempton Street entrance.

At 13, Raymond Rivard's world came apart when his parents separated. He and a brother and sister were taken to St. Mary's Children's Home in New Bedford where they lived for four years. Mr. Rivard looks back on those years at St. Mary's, where life was strictly regimented and obedience was the rule. In spite of a sometimes harsh environment, he found love there and a place to belong.

At 22, Mr. Rivard returned to St. Mary's to work as its custodian, a job he held for over 29 years. He is grateful to St. Mary's for giving him lifelong values and a strong work ethic; it helped make him the thoughtful, caring person he is today. "St. Mary's means a lot to me," he says, "because if it was not there, I would have been living in the street."

I came from a family of eight children, five boys and three girls, and we lived in Presidential Heights in New Bedford. Originally, there were nine children but a baby boy died from crib death. Times between my mother and father were rough. I didn't know the great trouble my mother had. Hey, with all those kids, we really didn't mingle in it.

The year was 1948. When I was 13, I was out caddying at the New Bedford Country Club on the fifteenth hole, when my older sister, Audrey, came and told me I had to go with her. The next thing I knew, I was walking through the front doors of St. Mary's Children's Home.

I was shocked at losing my parents and being put in a Home. I later learned that when my parents separated, we all got separated. We lost track of my mother and eventually heard she'd moved to California to live with one of her sisters. The older children went to live on their own, and three of us ended up with my father—me, my five-year-old brother, Bobby, and my seven-year-old sister, Patricia. He took us right to St. Mary's Children's Home.

My father was a sewing machine repair man and went to all the mills to repair the machinery. He had a good job but he had drinking problems. I only saw my father twice after going to St. Mary's. Years later, we learned he had died when the funeral home called and asked who would be making the arrangements.

At St. Mary's Home, my sister had it rougher than my brother and I. She was so small, she took a lot of abuse from the other children. The girls were isolated from the boys so we weren't allowed to see her. I could see her but I couldn't talk to her long enough. We would talk in school 'cause we were in the same classroom, but that was about it.

At the time, there were 110 kids who lived at St. Mary's, many more girls than boys. We had like an imaginary line out in the playground, the girls on one side and the boys on the other. I think they had to separate us because there were a lot of 16 and 17-year-old boys and they were rough. I had to make sure I was their equal so we had fights constantly.

The second week I was there, I got the chance to prove myself 'cause the biggest kids were supposed to be the toughest. I was tall for my age. Well, there happened to be a kid who kept pushing me but I never retaliated back. When I did hit him back, there was a Sister standing in the doorway. She hadn't seen him hit me. She told me to stop hitting the little children and she gave me a left hook. The next thing I knew, I was down on the ground. After that, I realized what the Sisters wanted, obedience—and I just kept out of their way.

Raymond Rivard, Custodian, 1995. On Kempton Street in New Bedford, St. Mary's Home looks much the same as it always has, though its function has changed. At the time of this photograph, Raymond was still an important part of it.

John K. Robson

We had only ten Sisters here and they took care of everything. I was scared of the Sisters at first because I had never seen a nun before. All I saw were these big people standing there with white collars and all-black clothes. After seeing the first nun, I wanted to run out the back door, but after a while we got along pretty good. Sister Agnes St. Joseph took care of the boys and Sister Lois Gregory took care of the girls. Both were over six feet tall and close to 250 pounds. Sister Agnes St. Joseph was the one who threw me the left hook.

We would have assemblies in the auditorium and if you did anything wrong, Father Thompson would hit you in front of everybody to show the others that he was the boss and you had to follow the rules. He used to say he could punish you in his office, but by punishing us in front of all the kids, they would see what will happen if they disobey.

The worst punishment came after the boys had a pillow fight in one of the bedrooms and a nun got in the middle of the fight and got hurt. Our punishment was to sand down the chapel to its bare wood. At that time, the chapel was made of dark oak so it took a lot of work to sand it down. We would work two hours every evening, about five or six of us, and the whole thing took three or four months. After we finished the whole job, Father Thompson said, "It looks all right, but I want it back the way it was." So we had to stain it back.

St. Mary's was run like a military school, but they had to have the discipline. There were too many kids to let roam around doing what they pleased. Getting used to the system was hard but they had to do it. Forty-seven kids slept in the dorm and there was only one aisle down the middle of the bedroom. We crawled from bed to bed, to get to our own. The beds were made of steel and some had a footlocker, so it was a little rough there.

There were clothes rooms on each floor and each child had a drawer. There was a whole wall of drawers that slid out and they are still there today. Everything that wasn't in your drawer was hung up on hangers.

The boys wore knickers five days a week and we all wore uniforms to school. We also had some playclothes. All our clothes were passed down from one child to another. At 13, I was too big for my age- almost five feet, ten inches, so St. Mary's had to go out and buy clothes that would fit me. They paid for all my clothes, but my brother and sister fit in the hand-me-downs.

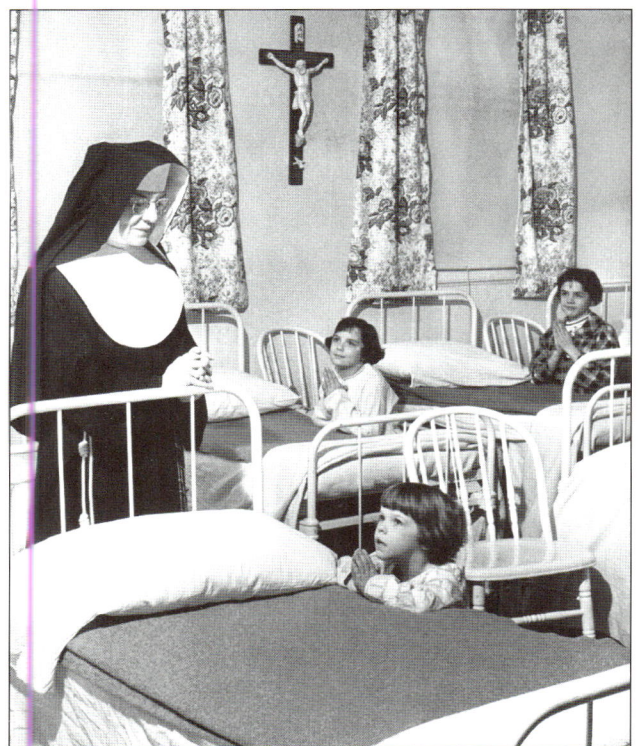

The Standard-Times

The Standard-Times

Oral Hygiene, *1944.*

Evening prayers, *1960 (left). Sister Margaret Francis, OSF, officiates prayers with Carole Bennett, 11 (under crucifix), Claire Pellerin, 4, and Kathleen Irwin, 12.*

Girls corridor, third floor, 1911.

Spinner Collection

Reading, 1949.

The Standard-Times

We got up at 6:00AM, went to Mass at 6:30 and did our chores before breakfast. School went from 8:30 to 10:30, then we went back to finish our chores. After lunch, we went to school again from 1 to 3:00 and had playground until 6:00. From 6:30 to 9:30, we went back to school for study hour— a quiet time. So we went to school three times a day.

There was no talking. We just took our books and did our work. I did not like school, I'm sorry to say. The major problem was going from a public school with individual grades to a Catholic school with one teacher for three grades. Grades one through three were together and grades four through six were together.

I started off in the fifth grade. Naturally, when you're sitting there listening to a fourth grade level story and, all of a sudden, the teacher is with the sixth graders talking about some king over in Europe, you forget about what you're doing and you listen to them. I hated spelling and I still do, so that was my toughest subject.

We had a dirt yard and there wasn't much we could do there. There were so many kids. I played baseball even though it wasn't my sport. We had a Boy Scout troop at the Home but the farthest we went was to South Dartmouth, where we camped at Holy Cross Fathers, a retreat for priests. We also played soccer and the custodian Al Mayo was our coach. Mostly, we built model airplanes and ships in the big playroom in the basement. There was also a playroom on the second floor. We were not allowed to have stuffed animals because they were a fire hazard. In the evening sometimes, we listened to the radio. The Sister made the choice on the program. Sometimes we'd hear "The Green Hornet" or "Roy Rogers."

When I first arrived, we had all cement floors, but they tiled the floors to put shuffleboard in for the boys and hopscotch for the girls. My favorite was the checkers that were twelve inches in diameter. We would push them along with a stick.

We went in lines to everything—to the dining room, to school and even to the movies. We went to a lot of theaters with the Sisters—the Olympia, the State, the New Bedford theaters. We had to walk down the street in single file, all 110 of us with two Sisters. We must have looked like a bunch of ants going down the road.

We did a lot of work at St. Mary's. We made our own beds, and washed our own clothes. The laundry was a small brick building across the street and there were huge wooden washing machines. I was in charge of my own laundry, my brother's, and the laundry of a couple of the younger kids. I did the sheets too, and we were in charge of our own ironing.

At mealtimes, I was in charge of the kitchen area. We served the children their food and did the dishes afterward in huge sinks. I washed dishes for four years. The children ate at big long tables with benches. A captain was in charge of each table. Sister would make soup in these big Army pots and it would last for three or four days. There was cheese on everything and, to this day, I cannot eat cheese. I cannot eat bologna and hot dogs either. Our best meal was on Sunday when we'd have chicken, ham or turkey.

The kitchen workers ate when the children were finished. I didn't mind because we got to eat the leftovers. The priests and Sisters didn't eat the same food as the kids and their leftovers were good. I also washed the basement floor and did many other chores.

When I first arrived, we didn't have showers so we had to take sponge baths. We had only three sinks along the outside wall of the corridor for 70 boys, so it was a little rough trying to get in there to wash. When we got showers, six on the girls' side and six on the boys' side, the world changed. It took a year to get the showers in. It was done by the Diocese with volunteer help.

Our dentist came down from Boston once a month with three volunteers who were dental students. We used to complain about the students to Father but he would say not to complain since it wasn't costing him a penny. Then one day he had a toothache and had to have his tooth out. Well, that was the last time we saw that dentist since Father was in agony for three days.

We also had a well-supplied medical facility at St. Mary's. Our tonsils were taken out here and any other minor surgery was done. In fact, one kid's appendix was taken out here 'cause he couldn't be rushed to the hospital in time.

Kitchen duty, 1949.

The Standard-Times

Boys' harmonica concert, 1947. The Catholic Charities' Appeal Fund, which raised money to support St. Mary's Home, launched their annual drive with this rhythmic ensemble.

Bill Howard, The Standard-Times

My father never saw us or sent us money 'cause St. Mary's gave us free room and board. He was supposed to contribute but he didn't. My mother eventually came back from California and we were so happy to see each other. We started going out with her on weekends and, after a court battle, we were discharged from St. Mary's. Since my father had put us there, the law said he would have to discharge us, but no one could find him. My mother took custody.

My brother, my sister and I went back to my mother's place on Acushnet Avenue to live. I had been at the home from age 13 to 17, and now I went right to work—first in a box company, then at New Bedford Luggage where I was a carpenter, then at Cornell Dubilier as a sheet metal cutter for four or five years.

On weekends, I would go roller skating at Lincoln Park—Friday, Saturday and Sunday nights—and I met my future wife on the skating rink, Lorraine Vieira. I thought she lived in Fall River and she thought I lived far away, but it turned out we lived eight blocks apart. I was 21 when we got married in June 1957.

We tried to get married at St. Mary's Home because I wanted the nuns to attend and, in those days, nuns couldn't go to any social events. I also wanted Father Thompson to marry us and say the Mass. Before going to St. Mary's, I didn't have any religion. I was baptized at St. Mary's, made my First Communion there on Christmas Eve and I made my Confirmation at St. Lawrence. I was also an altar boy at St. Mary's. So the church meant a lot to me.

But the Diocese would not give us permission to get married at St. Mary's because it wasn't a real parish, so we got married at St. Mary's on Tarkiln Hill Road. What really got us mad was that Father Hayes married us, but he couldn't say the Mass because he had already said two Masses that day and priests were not allowed to say three Masses in one day. So he got some priest from St. Joseph's down the street to say it—yet I couldn't have Father Thompson!

One day when I got home from Cornell Dubilier, my mother told me that Father Hogan had called. My wife and I didn't have a phone so he had to call my mother. He offered me the job of custodian at St. Mary's and I took it. When I went to give my two week's notice at Cornell Dubilier, they gave me a rough time so I left that day and started at St. Mary's on the following Monday, Labor Day. The year was 1958. I was 22 and I had the job for the next 29 and a half years.

In the past 30 years, St. Mary's has been through many changes. The year before I lived there, they took in only orphans. Then they were taking in kids from broken-up families like mine. There was nothing like child abuse and, if there was, the kids did not talk about it.

By the early '60s, St. Mary's was not getting enough financial support from the parishes and it began running out of money. Father Hogan went to the state for help. In 1965, St. Mary's was taken over by the Massachusetts Department of Social Services and everything changed. It became a residential treatment center. It had social workers and a psychiatrist.

The kids could no longer do work like washing floors because of state rules. I thought work was good for kids.

The kids were very different from when I was there. I had it rough as far as my family goes, but I never went through what the kids who came later went through. Some of these kids, I imagine, have four or five fathers in the family. I didn't have that problem.

The kids were more destructive and more disturbed than when I was living there. They would break toilets, doors and walls. When I was there, we would never do that. If we were mad at another kid, Father Thompson had a way of solving that. He would stick us down in the playroom with boxing gloves and we just fought it out. These kids today would kill each other.

After the state took over, St. Mary's was down to five nuns and they left the Home in 1983. The Home was now ready to be closed for good. We kept losing children because the state would send them to foster homes. When we were finally down to 30 children and 40 employees, we officially closed. The big statue of "Our Lady" that decorated St. Mary's Home is now at St. Mary's on Tarkiln Hill Road, overlooking the garden. I like to think of it there.

The building was empty for a year and a half and I stayed on as custodian. It was sad seeing tables and chairs and all the things in the Home cleared out and trucked off. We had no idea what would happen to the Home.

The state finally bought it and it was taken over by the Bristol County Sheriff's Department. I was laid off in June 1985 for about 24 hours, then I got a call from the sheriff who wanted me to stay on. It is now the home of Eastern Massachusetts Correctional Alcoholic Center and I have worked there for 9 and a half years. I supervise prisoners who have been jailed for drunk driving. The guys are on a 90 day program and they go to classes all day. Three guys work with me on building repairs.

It's a mighty big world out there and nobody's going to help you. I came from St. Mary's Home and ended up coming back to work here. I really didn't go too far into the world. I went to one year of high school before going to work. I also went to Voke at night for two years of carpentry and air conditioning. But I loved carpentry so that's what I put most of my time into.

We have three kids, Brian, Steven and Patricia. They were all brought to St. Mary's after their baptism, where they always had a special Mass for them. Sister Dativa put them up on the altar in the chapel so they would be blessed by the priest. They were good to our kids and I think it was great.

My boys came to St. Mary's constantly when I was working there and that's how Brian got interested in becoming a steam engineer. Steven is a long-haul trucker and my daughter works as a hairdresser in Wareham. We have five wonderful grandchildren.

I think life is great and to have kids is fantastic. It helped make my marriage beautiful and it's good to see them grown up. We did a lot of camping when they were growing up and they loved it. Today, Brian is a bass fisherman.

You have to work to keep your family going and some people can't cope with that. It's tough. Family life is very important to me. I taught my kids what Father Thompson used to say to me. He said, "You're here, we're doing everything we can for you. But when you get beyond the two front doors, what you make of yourself, you do it."

St. Mary's really helped me out. What they taught me, I went out and did it. St. Mary's means a lot to me because if it was not there, I would have been living on the street.

The Standard-Times

St. Mary's basketball squad, 1955. *Coach James Hesford stands with his eager warriors. The boys are identified as: kneeling, A. Pina, R. Silva, D. Rish, A. Pike, J. Upham; back row, K. Alves, E. Arredondo, N. Miller, R. Almeida.*

Early History of St. Mary's Home

St. Mary's Children's Home of New Bedford was established on September 30, 1894, to care for orphan children and the aged poor. It was run by the Diocese of Providence, of which New Bedford was then a part. By December 1894, there were 41 residents living in the Home. St. Mary's was run by the Sisters of St. Francis of Glenriddle, Pennsylvania.

Toward the close of 1889, strenuous efforts were made to raise money for the Home. A bazaar was held for a week and the children provided entertainment on three evenings. However, midway through the week, the bishop felt it was not profitable enough and something must be done.

The Standard-Times

He gave a beautiful ostensorium valued at $400 to be contested for by three parishes: St. Lawrence, St. John the Baptist and St. James. Competition was keen and the bidding was fierce. In the end, $4,000 was raised. St. Lawrence won.

A singing contest between an Irish girl and a Portuguese girl who lived in the Home was another popular feature. Crowds came to hear them and were unanimous in favor of the Irish girl as the winner. The week's totals realized $7,000 for the Home.

In 1909, the children had a memorable Thanksgiving, thanks to the contributions of New Bedford citizens. Besides sumptuous food packages, they also enjoyed the gift of a grand piano. The Star Store sent 25 pairs of boys' trousers.

The Portuguese Society staged a parade through the city to the Home to present their gifts. The parade was headed by a brass band, followed by a team of horses decorated with laurel and bunting, containing food and material to make clothing for the children. Upon arrival, they were taken through the building, which greatly pleased them.

Lincoln Park outing, 1951 *(right). Mother Superior Clarinda smiles at two youngsters about to ride the whippet, one of the rides enjoyed by more than 80 children at St. Mary's Home Annual Kiddie Outing, sponsored by the Allied Council of Clubs of Greater New Bedford.*

Bound for Lincoln Park, 1956. *Youngsters wave goodbye before leaving for their annual outing at Lincoln Park.*

The Standard-Times

On September 9, 1919, the children enjoyed a day of pleasure at Pope Beach, Sconticut Neck, thanks to the generosity of some good friends. Two electric cars arrived at the Home at 9:00AM to take 165 children, ranging in age from 3 to 15 years. At the end of the day "the Sisters reminded their tired but happy children that all these good things come from their Father in Heaven, who inspires kind benefactors to do good, and that, for the latter, they must ever pray."

In March 1920, the Home received visits from former male residents who had been years away from the Home. Two were soldiers who had fought in the war and one was wounded. They came in uniform. They shared memories with the boys of their years in the Home, talked about their behavior and the kindness shown to them by the Sisters.

They taught the boys the military step, the salute, the position at attention and position for inspection. They sang songs and told war stories, some sad, others funny, but all teaching lessons of obedience and discipline.

In 1930, many improvements were made at the Home: The Grinnell Sprinkling System was installed, making the Home completely safe from fire. Electrical wiring was improved, and the first floor hall, classrooms and reception room were rebuilt with quarter oak and covered with inlaid linoleum.

The classrooms were fitted out with desks and chairs for teachers and children, also beautiful pictures and maps. A fireproof stairway was laid in both halls from the first floor to the basement. New lavatories were put in and an ornamental fence was installed in front of the Home adding much to its beauty.

The Standard-Times

St. Mary's Home boys' choir, 1909.

Picnic at Sconticut Neck, 1913.

Spinner Collection

Natalie's passport, 1922

Unforgettable Days

JENNIFER DULUDE

For over 50 years, Natalie Lubavsky Kaplan's story remained hidden. At first, Natalie herself kept it from interested publishers at the Little, Brown Company. Later, it was gently tucked away in the cellar of a devoted daughter. Finally, librarians neatly filed it into manila folders at UMass Dartmouth's Jewish Archives, stored in a box labeled simply, "Natalie Kaplan."

When she died in 1977, few who read Natalie's short obituary would have guessed that a woman identified primarily as the "widow of Boris Kaplan" had a story worth telling. A longtime New Bedford resident, a mother, a retired licensed practical nurse, a member of several Jewish organizations—no one could say Natalie Kaplan hadn't made her contribution to local society. But little mention was made of her work as a nurse in Russia's Red Army, her emigration to America, or her struggle to raise two daughters in New Bedford.

Snapshot of Boris, Daniel and Natalie Pikelny (Kaplan), from their 1923 visa to the United States.

Those who knew Natalie say she would have wanted it that way. "She wasn't one for official titles and honors," recalls Rabbi Bernard Glassman, Natalie's professor at Southeastern Massachusetts University. Instead, Natalie Kaplan was content to spend her life working and giving without the benefits of awards and accolades, silently documenting her remarkable experiences and storing them safely in boxes and folders.

Did she know that someone would stumble upon her private diaries and letters, almost twenty years after her death, in a crowded room at the UMass Dartmouth library? Did she know that her masterful manuscript about life in revolutionary Russia, the manuscript that she herself had never really finished, would leave readers fascinated? Maybe not. But it seems that despite Natalie's reluctance to boast of her own accomplishments, she knew that she had lived through experiences few could imagine, and she made sure to preserve her manuscripts, diaries, and essays for others. And so it is that her story, a lesson in loss, sacrifice, perseverance, and strength, can be told today.

Saratov, 1917

In 1917, on a cold winter night in Saratov, Russia, Basil Lubavsky gathered his seven children around him. A broken man, his position lost and his life savings confiscated by a new regime of revolutionaries, he told his family of his dire situation:

Until now I have been able to give you a comfortable and happy home, but from now on I am an outcast. No matter how I try, it seems that I shall never be able to provide for you again. What shall we do? It's best that each one look out for himself. Go your own way and try to make your life as happy as possible.

Happy? That hardly seemed possible to 18-year-old Natalie Lubavsky. In the past year, she had watched as her beloved home by the Volga River was overrun with revolution, hunger, and disease. Now, her father, a man of respect in Saratov, was admitting defeat. And a cold Russian winter lay ahead of them.

Nothing could have prepared Natalie for the suffering the February Revolution would bring to her beautiful home in Saratov. In 1917, Saratov was the eleventh largest city in Russia, standing 200 to 300 meters above sea level and almost completely surrounded by tall hills. Its climate was more similar to a city of mainland Europe than northern Russia.

Natalie Lubavsky (far left) sits with three classmates and her sister Julia (far right), 1913.

Kaplan Family Collection

Saratov has been rumored to have gotten its name from a combination of two Turkic-Mongol words, "sary" and "tau," meaning "beautiful mountain."

Natalie surely would have agreed with this description of her city. As a young girl, in between school and chores, Natalie was busy discovering Saratov's natural beauty, enjoying its warm summer days, exploring its richly wooded hillsides, and roving along the shores of the great Volga River. Years later, in her manuscript, Natalie would remember Saratov's natural attractions:

Nature, day after day, still unfolds in a magnificent, mysterious way, its beauty and wonders. The nightingales are just beginning to sing, filling the still fragrant air with exquisite melodies. The giant oaks stand motionless against the starlit sky, and our beloved Volga stretches proudly before us, her cool waters murmuring drowsily at our feet. Little rowboats glide by occasionally and sounds of laughter and singing reach us across the waters.

Despite the idyllic beauty Natalie describes, however, by 1917 Saratov had earned a reputation not for its lovely hillsides and tranquil river, but for its strange population and rundown slums. Saratov's role first as a military center and later as a commercial center for the fishing, salt, and flour industries had created a population that was a confusing mix of well-to-do professionals, merchants and factory owners, and workers and peasants. Saratov University and World War I added new groups to Saratov's population: students, radical writers and artists, and political and religious refugees. By 1917, Saratov's residential area was divided into two sections—a rich, modern neighborhood for those with money, and disease-ridden, brick slums for the rest. Saratov's visitors labeled the city "dull, dirty."

Natalie had little firsthand knowledge of the dull and dirty side of Saratov. Her father, Basil Lubavsky, was a Russian Orthodox priest, and her mother, Catherine Lubavsky, was a teacher. As successful and respected professionals, Natalie's parents made a good home for their seven children, a home where religion and education were greatly valued. Born on September 1, 1899, young Natalie became accustomed to a certain amount of privilege by Saratov's standards—she lived in a large home staffed by servants, attended a reputable school, and wore well-tailored clothes. At 17, dark-haired, blue-eyed Natalie was a skilled writer and creative artist, but it was medicine that interested her most. After completing secondary school, she attended Saratov University, where she was certified as a Red Cross nurse and planned to become a physician. Then, revolution erupted, changing everything.

Saratov had long been home to a large population of *Bolsheviks*, Marxist revolutionaries who, at that time, were engaged in an ideological struggle for political and economic equality in Russia. In Saratov, these revolutionaries had a ready audience: poor workers and peasants.

Added to this already tense atmosphere were the social and economic strains of World War I: food shortages, energy and transport crises, and failing medical and sanitary systems. Finally, in 1917, the combination of all these factors resulted in the February Revolution and the overthrow of the absolute monarchy. Russia's autocratic government was replaced with a "Provisional Government," a mostly unstructured system of quickly elected political committees in each province.

While revolutionaries, peasants, and workers had hoped the overthrow of the autocracy would finally

Kaplan Family Collection

Natalie and her mother, Catherine, practicing music. "*Singing is one of the favorite pastimes of the Russians. They sing on every occasion—on warm summer nights near bright camp fires; on the fields under the scorching sun; in huts with the spinning wheels, on endless cold winter nights...*" [From Natalie's original manuscript, Unforgettable Days.]

give them opportunities for greater political and economic gain, they soon found that the February Revolution would bring only further instability and bloodshed. With the collapse of the old regime came fierce battles between the different revolutionary groups who hungered for control of the new regime. Caught in the crossfire, workers and peasants became the pawns of revolutionaries who needed soldiers for their armies, and established professionals lost their positions and savings. Food shortages and unsanitary conditions remained unresolved, resulting in growing famine and disease.

Such were the conditions Natalie and her family faced in the cold winter of 1918. Now that the monarchy had been overthrown and revolutionaries were fighting for communist rule, her father's position as a Russian Orthodox priest had been rendered obsolete. Once a man of great influence and respect in Saratov, Basil Lubavsky could no longer provide for his family. How would they heat their home? How would they eat? Natalie knew she must do something to help her family survive. School was no longer a luxury she could afford—she would have to find a way to earn money for her family. She would have to find work.

But finding work proved harder than Natalie had imagined. Even though she had training as a Red Cross nurse, Natalie could not find a position at local hospitals, as many of the vacancies had been filled by nurses who had left the battlefields after peace had been declared between Russia and Germany. But finally, in June of 1918, Natalie overheard two medical students talking about the opening of a new hospital to care for victims of an epidemic of Asiatic cholera spreading through Saratov. The next day, Natalie slipped secretly from her house and traveled across Saratov to apply for a position at the *Gubozdrav*, Saratov's Board of Health.

As she walked through the hot streets of Saratov, Natalie thought of the danger and risk that lay ahead of her if she were to take a position at the cholera hospital. Like everything else in Saratov, sanitary medical supplies were hard to come by, and she knew she would be exposed to highly contagious strains of cholera. But what else could she do? Destruction, dirt, and sickness were all the Revolution had brought to Saratov. With no end in sight, Natalie knew there would be a great demand for nurses willing to work in

Lubavsky family portrait, circa 1916. Natalie (standing, second left) with her five sisters, one brother, mother and nanny Masha (standing, third left), get together for a portrait at their Saratov home. These were quiet days just prior to the Russian Revolution.

Kaplan Family Collection

the dangerous cholera hospital. And besides, she had no other opportunity for work.

But even the doctors at the hospital were shocked by the willingness of a young and healthy woman to work in such disease-filled conditions. One young doctor in particular, Dr. Boris Pikelny, was particularly horrified by Natalie's decision:

"You are so young," he said. "Do you realize the danger of this disease? A nurse coming in such a close contact with a patient is liable to contract this dreadful disease so easily."

I tell him then about the long and weary weeks I spent looking for work. I tell him about my family and about its desperate need of help at the present time. "I have no choice, as you see, and am ready to do work of any kind."

The next day, against her parents' wishes, Natalie accepted a job in the cholera ward at Hospital #100.

Cholera Hospital #100

The conditions at the hospital were worse than Natalie had suspected. Only a few nurses were in charge of 150 beds, and the only medications available to fight the dreaded cholera epidemic were injections of camphor oil and tannic acid solutions. With the only bathtub in the basement of the hospital, the nurses were forced to carry their weak patients up and down three long flights of stairs to give scorching baths. Delirious, unruly patients begged for help, then accused the nurses of trying to kill them with the camphor oil injections.

Despite these conditions, Natalie threw herself into her position, faithfully using the few supplies she had to give injections, baths, and hot packs to her patients. Still, within her first week at the hospital, Natalie was faced with her first death:

Towards midnight, Masha, the woman near the door, begins to sink rapidly, though remaining conscious almost till the very end. I manage to give her a few hot baths. I use all my power to influence the senior student of the medical college, who helps doctors in their work, to make her an additional infusion of saline solution, which does wonders in some cases. But despite all this, soon after midnight, the lifeless body of the woman is taken away and placed on the floor in the empty room next to the ward.

This is the first death I have ever witnessed and it simply terrifies me. How utterly helpless and weak we are against the power of Nature! I feel death hovering in the gloomy room, stretching its greedy hands to the helpless humans lying before me, ready to snatch away the lives within them. And as the night crawls by, a few more beds become empty.

Natalie's medical training had taught her the procedures for fighting disease and death, but she had never been taught how to surrender to them. Again, the Revolution's legacy of destruction and sickness had presented young Natalie with a problem she could not solve on her own, and she couldn't help feeling that the situation at the cholera hospital was hopeless. But she had little time for reflection—other patients called her name, and Natalie had to go on working.

Through the hot months of June and July, Natalie spent long 12-hour days at the hospital, healing the ill and easing the pain of the dying. Slowly, Natalie learned to deal with the inevitable deaths of her patients, and the dark atmosphere of the hospital was brightened by the arrival of Maria Lartzeva, a tall, witty nurse with laughing blue eyes called "Marusia" by most of the staff. Even better, the hospital began offering excellent free meals to the

Kaplan Family Collection

Boris Pikelny with his sister and her husband, 1915. *At the Department of Health, Natalie observed, "I see a young man with dark wavy hair and large black eyes. He is not Russian, I think. The dark hair and black sad eyes belong either to a Caucasian or a Jew. He wears a uniform but his bearing is not military…From our conversation I learn that he is a doctor, had returned a few months ago from the Turkish Front after spending two-and-a-half years there…My intention to work in the cholera hospital frankly horrifies him."* [From Natalie's original manuscript, *Unforgettable Days.*]

Kaplan Family Collection

Natalie's parents and brother. "The Russian intelligentsia, in whose midst the first revolutionary ideas originated, soon found itself in the position of a stepchild of the movement for which it fought desperately during the old regime. It greeted the Russian Revolution with great joy and bright hopes, but the new regime proved to bring to many of them nothing but disaster. A large number of them lost their positions, many their freedom and many, even life. My father, also a member of this group, the only provider of our family, lost his position...His entire savings at the bank had been confiscated by the new government. And ahead of us lay a long severe Russian winter."
[From Natalie's original manuscript, *Unforgettable Days*.]

medical staff, no small feat during a food shortage. Not having seen food of this quality in months, Natalie and Marusia devoured their suppers and dinners. And best of all, Natalie was also able to provide desperately needed money for her family.

As time passed, the hospital no longer left Natalie depressed and dispirited. Breaking out of her role as just another dutiful Lubavsky daughter, Natalie was becoming much more: a vital part of a medical team and a financial supporter of her family. Befriending her fellow nurses and doctors, Natalie also regained some of the social life she had lost when she left Saratov University—well liked and admired, especially by many of the male doctors.

Natalie's rare moments away from the hospital and her family were spent socializing with her colleagues. Strangely, although she was surrounded by sickness and death, Natalie was beginning to feel more alive.

Natalie knew, however, that her position at the cholera hospital was temporary. As the summer came to an end, fewer and fewer patients filled the beds at the hospital, and Natalie's 12-hour days were replaced by shorter eight-hour shifts. Then, in August, a senior doctor visited the hospital to inform the staff that the cholera epidemic was nearing an end. Good news for Saratov, bad news for the cholera hospital staff. The senior doctor told Natalie that Hospital #100 would be closed shortly.

But the doctor also brought other news. While the epidemic was ending in Saratov, it was only beginning in the town of Yelan, and the local *Gubozdrav* needed six nurses for its hospital there.

Natalie had to think fast. Yelan was 200 *versts*, the equivalent of 132 miles, from Saratov by railroad, so she would be forced to leave her struggling family if she were to volunteer for such a position. Natalie quickly weighed her options:

If I remain in Saratov, I will be left without work; on the other hand, work in Yelan will enable me to help my family. While the shortage of food is felt very keenly here in Saratov, practically any product can be bought in the country, but the trip to the country is connected with great difficulty as every one needs a special passport to travel through Russia now. Here is my chance. I can travel freely to the country for a month or two and then return home loaded with all kinds of provisions for my half-starved family.

Without further hesitation, I step forward and offer my services.

Yelan, 1918

The thought of 19-year-old Natalie traveling 200 *versts* away did not please Basil and Catherine Lubavsky. Still, they knew that Natalie could not forego the opportunity to earn still more money and food for the family, and Natalie was able to convince them that Victor Ilin, a family friend who had also volunteered for work at the cholera hospital in Yelan, would keep her safe. A few days later, with just one bag of personal belongings and a supply of medical equipment, Natalie boarded the train to Yelan with Victor, her faithful friend Marusia, Dr. Boris Pikelny, and the rest of their medical unit: three doctors, three medical students, and four nurses.

When they arrived in Yelan, however, they were surprised to learn that the *Gubozdrav* in Yelan had heard nothing of their unit's arrival, and the threat of cholera had been greatly exaggerated. "Why," the official told them, "the few men that were sick with what our doctor thought was cholera are well now." Even worse, the unit soon discovered that Yelan was only a few *versts* away from the front lines of the battle between the Bolsheviks, the revolutionaries who had gained control of the Russian government, and the Don Cossacks, a counterrevolutionary group fighting for their share of the power.

The *Gubozdrav* official, a peasant soldier named Volkoff, told the unit that he could issue no new orders until he heard word from the *Gubozdrav* officials in Yelan. Meanwhile, Natalie and the rest of the unit would stay in the home of local peasants.

Unsure of their position in Yelan, the volunteers followed their orders and set out for their new quarters, a small house in a nearby village. Their hosts met them with open hostility, outraged at the prospect of having to share their home with "city people." Still, the volunteers were allowed a small hallway and two rooms in the modest house.

As the days passed and still no new orders came from the Saratov *Gubozdrav*, Natalie and her colleagues enjoyed a well deserved rest after months of hard work at the cholera hospital. Natalie and Marusia took long walks on the paths that run through the Yelan countryside, and when he was not working at the village hospital, Dr. Boris Pikelny joined them. Marusia, the daughter of peasants herself, managed to charm their hosts, a feat that earned the volunteers the privileges of home-cooked meals and better sleeping quarters.

For Natalie, the delay in Yelan fostered a new closeness with 29-year-old Dr. Pikelny, the doctor Natalie remembered from his stern warning about the dangers of the cholera hospital back in Saratov. On long walks in the country, Boris told Natalie about his childhood in a Polish province, his schooling at Warsaw University, and his experiences as a military doctor in the Russian Army. Then, when Victor and Marusia fell ill with severe cases of influenza, they spent long nights together helping them recover. When Marusia and Victor gained back their strength, Boris pulled Natalie into one of the nearby rooms:

When the rain seems to fall with more persistence than ever, and the lilac bushes lash and knock on our small windows with the pressure of the relentless wind, Dr. Pikelny tells me that he loves me and it seems now that I had loved Boris since the day I first met him near the tall latticed window of the Gubozdrav.

Taken by surprise by the love that had developed between them, Boris and Natalie nevertheless tried to make plans for their ambiguous future together, tentatively deciding to move back to Saratov as soon as possible. Boris would try to get a position at a local hospital, and Natalie, of course, would continue her medical education.

On the move in Eastern Europe, circa 1917. "This is what the Revolution has brought to us so far—destruction, dirt and sickness. It is the Revolution too that brings me here today, an 18-year old girl, ready to work in such a dangerous place as a cholera hospital." [From Natalie's original manuscript, *Unforgettable Days.*]

University of Massachusetts Dartmouth Library

Kaplan Family Collection

Boris Pikelny, from his Russian passport, circa 1922.

Revolutionary Russia, however, was not the ideal setting for a budding romance. After three weeks in Yelan and still no word from the Saratov *Gubozdrav*, two members of the medical staff escaped on a departing train. Hearing of their departure, Volkoff ordered the rest of the unit to stay in Yelan. "Since the authorities in Saratov are evidently not interested in the fate of your unit," he told them, "I will give you your orders." Two days later, Boris was ordered to take charge of a hospital train in Elmen, 60 *versts* south of Yelan, where the Red Army was in desperate need of medical staff to care for wounded soldiers. A day later, Natalie and Marusia were given orders to go to Elmen as well.

Elmen, 1918

Suddenly, although they had not officially "signed up," Boris and Natalie found themselves serving for the Red Army in the midst of Russia's Civil War. On a seven-car train converted into a makeshift hospital by the Red Army, Natalie became the unofficial head nurse of a ward overflowing with wounded and sick soldiers.

This was a strange position for a young girl who only a few years ago had rarely ventured outside of her beloved home by the Volga, but Natalie quickly adapted to the exciting atmosphere aboard the train. The spirit of adventure that she had developed at the cholera hospital in Saratov was aroused again in Elmen. Earning better wages as a nurse in the Red Army, Natalie was also able to send home more money to her family in Saratov.

But Natalie also witnessed an even harsher side of the Civil War than she had seen in Saratov—now, she was seeing first hand the death caused by the incessant fighting of revolution and counterrevolution. Weak and wounded soldiers flowed into the hospital, only to be sent back to the front lines as soon as their wounds healed. Her efforts here, Natalie thought, seemed even more pointless than her struggles at the cholera hospital. War, it seemed, was an even more formidable foe than disease. No amount of bandages or injections could stop the fighting between the revolutionaries.

Natalie also learned of the worsening situation spreading across Russia. In Saratov, without the benefits of modern newspapers and television broadcasters, Natalie had little information about the rest of her country. Now, nurses from other provinces brought news of the hunger and discontent that plagued the ancient city of Moscow. Soldiers and civilians weak from severe strains of influenza and other illnesses displayed the effects of widespread disease. Doctors told stories of half-crazed mothers seen mourning near deep ditches, where it was rumored their innocent civilian sons had been savagely executed and buried by counterrevolutionaries. Apparently, Saratov was not the only city suffering from the effects of the Civil War.

Months passed with little change, and the excitement of the train began to fade. Boris was frequently away at the nearby hospital in Rudnia, and Natalie was left alone on the train, surrounded by the incessant shooting of the battlefield.

Shooting, shooting. It means a busy day tomorrow. Even after my night's vigil, I will not be allowed to rest long. This infernal war—blood, destruction, terrible suffering, death—will it ever come to an end? How we hoped that the revolution would stop this merciless slaughter, but instead, it has brought us a new war, a war much more cruel, much more brutal—a war where brother fought against brother, and son against father.

Soon, however, good news came. The Red Army officials allowed Natalie a short leave to return to Saratov, where she could seek her parents' blessing on her engagement to Boris. After months away from her family, Natalie was finally going home. Gathering as much food, clothing, and money as she could, Natalie set off on the next train to Saratov.

As soon as she saw Catherine Lubavsky's thin face and tired, worried eyes, Natalie knew that conditions in Saratov had worsened since her departure for Yelan. Her brothers and sisters were weak and malnourished, and they quickly devoured the cakes Natalie had brought from Elmen. Basil Lubavsky, the once influential and vibrant priest, had been reduced to doing menial clerical work for a meager salary. And Masha, the beloved family servant that had been with the Lubavsky's for 15 years, had died from the physical and mental strain of the Civil War.

Still, Natalie's family was happy to hear the news of her engagement, and although Basil Lubavsky didn't like the idea of allowing his daughter to marry a man he had never met, he eventually gave his reluctant consent. With Catherine's help, Natalie made quick arrangements for the small ceremony, which was to be held in Elmen because Boris had not been granted a leave from his position. Managing to get a permit from the New Government for only a few yards of coarse cotton, Catherine and Natalie ransacked their drawers for old dresses and a few pieces of lace. Together, they pieced together Natalie's plain, cotton wedding dress. Only a few days after returning home, Natalie boarded the train back to Elmen.

With no better place for their wedding, Boris and Natalie were quickly married aboard a train bound for the Russian city of Kamishin. Their life, Boris would later recall, had become one continual round of riding.

Saratov, 1921

The newly married couple soon found that this transitory life would not do. As soon as they were able to get permanent leaves from the Red Army, Boris and Natalie moved back to Saratov, where Boris was able to get a small position at Saratov Hospital and Natalie was able to be closer to her struggling family. Unfortunately, Natalie's medical education had to be postponed again—the great Famine of 1921 had struck Saratov and the surrounding Volga region, and Natalie and Boris were hard at work helping the starving with few medical supplies. It was during these desperate times that Natalie also gave birth to their first child, Daniel.

Marriage to Boris and the birth of Daniel gave Natalie new responsibilities. She was no longer obligated solely to her mother, father, and siblings, she was also responsible for her own struggling family. She knew that she could no longer fulfill these obligations in Russia. How could she make a life for a son in a country ravaged by war and famine? The Pikelny's thought about emigrating to Palestine, but all of Boris' relatives had emigrated to America, so Boris and Natalie made reluctant plans to join them.

In July of 1922, Boris' brother, Samuel Kaplan, a successful New Bedford businessman, agreed to sponsor the Pikelny family. The following January, Boris, Natalie and Daniel were granted visas for their "visit" to America. With her husband and son, Natalie began the long journey from Saratov to America. She would never see her family or her homeland again.

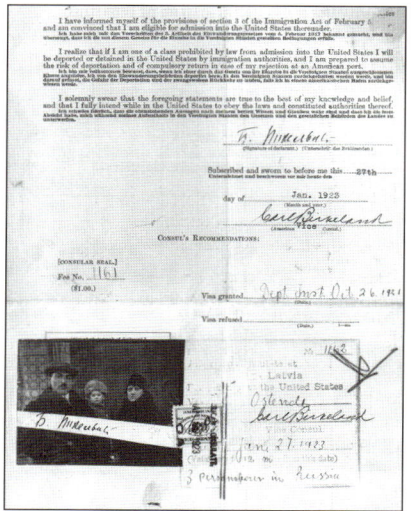

The Pikelny's visa to the United States, 1922.

New York City, 1923

The Pikelny's were the lucky ones—after 1918, the United States set small quotas for Russian immigrants, and few Russians were fortunate enough to have successful relatives who could serve as sponsors. Moreover, Natalie and Boris narrowly escaped the Soviet government's total ban on emigration in 1926. Had they waited just a few more years, they would have been forced to stay in Russia.

Exhausted, Boris and Natalie arrived at Ellis Island in February of 1923 after a long trip across the Atlantic Ocean. With immigrants from the West Indies, Germany, and England, the Pikelny family awaited admission to the United States. As she got her first glimpses of the American people in a small room there, Natalie felt optimistic about the new life she was about to begin. The Americans wore content smiles and nicely tailored suits. As much as she already missed her home in Russia, Natalie vowed to become an American:

My husband and I came from Russia—a country ravished by war and revolution. A country where most abject misery, poverty, disease, and starvation reigned supreme; a country where mistrust, suspicion, and fear were our constant companions, where death lurked around the corner at all times. It was all in the past. There was a new life ahead of us now. Someday we might be just like these Americans. We will never be hungry. We will have enough clothes. We will be happy.

But Boris and Natalie had not yet escaped the disease and death they had faced in Saratov. With the many immigrants that waited at Ellis Island came various diseases, and small Daniel became severely ill with the measles and Scarlet Fever. Boris and Natalie, with all their medical training, could do nothing to save their child. Only a few weeks after being admitted to the United States, two-year-old Daniel died, and a small funeral was held in New York City. It seemed as though misfortune was following them, Boris would later recall.

New Bedford, 1923

Still mourning their only child, Boris and Natalie Pikelny began their journey to New Bedford, where they were to live with Samuel Kaplan, Boris's brother, at 11 Briggs Street. Having lived in America for 22 years, Samuel Kaplan was an established businessman in New Bedford, with a net worth of over $35,000. He and his family opened their home to Boris and Natalie.

European immigrants on deck aboard passenger ship arriving in New York, circa 1915.

University of Massachusetts Dartmouth Library

New Bedford in 1923 was enjoying its last years of growth and development. A major destination for Portuguese, Irish, and French-Canadian immigrants in the early 1920s, New Bedford was known for its successful textile mills and the many employment opportunities that accompanied them. By the mid-1920s, however, with the growth of the textile industry in the South, many New Bedford textile mills abandoned the city and its workers; others dropped wages and increased workloads. Even before the Great Depression hit, New Bedford was facing hard times.

Surrounded by the strange noises and peculiar language of New Bedford, Boris and Natalie hardly noticed the beginning of New Bedford's economic struggles. During their first months in America, the young couple devoted all their time to "becoming Americans." Like his brother, Boris replaced their Polish-sounding last name to the more American-sounding "Kaplan." Determined to master the frustrating English language, Natalie enrolled in English courses at New Bedford Evening High School. And Boris devoted all his time not only to learning the new language, but also to studying for the Massachusetts medical exam. Boris and Natalie Fikelny became Boris and Natalie Kaplan—and they would not be dependent on Samuel Kaplan for long.

Despite her busy schedule, these were not easy times for Natalie. Away from her family, grieving for Daniel, and trying to learn her new country's customs, rules, and language, Natalie was also forced to confront unanswered religious questions. In Russia, where they were closest to Natalie's family, Boris and Natalie had never fully resolved the conflict between Natalie's Russian Orthodox upbringing and Boris' Jewish heritage. Now that the couple was living with Boris' family, Natalie was faced with difficult questions about her own beliefs and how she would raise a new family in America. If she were to have more children, would she raise them according to her own Russian Orthodox beliefs or Jewish philosophies? Or should they raise their children according to both religions? Natalie decided that one religion was enough for a family, and after serious thought, Natalie decided to convert to Judaism. It was a decision she never shared with Basil and Catherine Lubavsky.

Meanwhile, Boris's devotion to the English language and American medicine was rewarded. Only 18 months after arriving in America, Boris Kaplan passed the Massachusetts medical exam with the exemplary score of 83. He would later become the first licensed gastroenterologist in New Bedford. A *Standard-Times* article, "In this Country 18 Months, Now Full Fledged Physician," touted Boris's quick success and profiled the young couple's amazing experiences in Russia. They had yet to become naturalized citizens, but Boris and Natalie Kaplan were quickly gaining recognition and prestige in New Bedford.

Now that Boris had earned an American medical license, the Kaplan's had more financial and personal independence and no longer had to live with Samuel Kaplan and his family on Briggs Street. Boris opened his practice on Pleasant Street, then moved it to the couple's rented home on Clinton Street. Natalie, whose medical training at Saratov University and nursing experience in the Red Army was unrecognized in America, was unable to work in a hospital. Instead, she served as her husband's medical secretary and attending nurse. In 1965, she earned her LPN.

As Boris' practice was established in New Bedford, the Kaplan's enjoyed some well deserved peace and stability. They bought nicely tailored clothing at New Bedford's fine shops and department stores.

The Standard-Times

Natalie, 1927.

Kaplan Family Collection

Natalie with Leda and holding Esther. *Both Boris and Natalie credited America for giving them the opportunities they had been denied in Russia, and while they both loved and missed their homeland, they were determined to raise their children as Americans and speak perfect English.*

Natalie practiced her speaking skills by talking incessantly to her dog when no one was home. Despite her love of her country and its culture, she refused to speak Russian to Leda so that she would learn English only. And to perfect her writing skills, she wrote extensive diaries of Leda's development. If Leda uttered a new sound, took a new step, or visited a new place, Natalie documented it in her diary.

They went on weekend trips to Horseneck Beach, loving the sea air and cool ocean. Finally, the young couple was able to take pleasure in their marriage, something that had been difficult to do in the shadow of Russia's disease and hunger.

But something was still missing for Natalie. While she still mourned Daniel's death, Natalie longed for more children. Now that Boris had a growing medical practice, the couple began to try for more children. In 1928, Natalie gave birth to her first daughter, Leda.

Becoming a mother again was a great source of joy for Natalie, especially now that she and Boris were better able to provide for their family. Leda's birth only deepened Natalie's resolve to look and sound American. Often embarrassed by her strong Russian accent and imperfect grammar, Natalie embarked on a personal mission to speak and write perfect English.

She continued her English courses at New Bedford High School. Soon, Natalie's writing became more than just an exercise in improving her grammar. As the language barrier diminished, Natalie began to realize her talent as a writer. And with Boris always so busy with his patients and practice, Natalie needed some outlet for the natural creativity she had always been blessed with. Now that she had the time and opportunity, Natalie began to write a manuscript about her life in Russia, appropriately titling it "Unforgettable Days."

The revolution in Saratov, Natalie's work at the cholera hospital and as a Red Army nurse, the hunger and suffering of the 1921 Famine—all of Natalie's adventures quickly translated into a fascinating manuscript about life in revolutionary Russia. But writing about life beyond Russia, about her first awful weeks in America after the death of Daniel, proved too difficult for Natalie. The death of her son remained the one loss Natalie could not yet speak or write about. Even when a representative from Little, Brown Company expressed interest in Natalie's manuscript, she could not bring herself to finish her story. Writing about her new, flourishing family in her diaries was so much easier than writing about the family members she had left behind in Russia and the son she had lost in America.

By 1936, Natalie had a new baby to write about. In April she gave birth to a second daughter, Esther. With seven-year-old Leda, newborn Esther, and her work in Boris's office, Natalie's manuscript was overshadowed by her husband and children. "Unforgettable Days" was tucked away in a small desk drawer.

American Dream

While the Great Depression of the 1930s struck hard in New Bedford, Boris Kaplan's practice continued to thrive. In 1938, the Kaplan's moved into a large, 10-room house on Cottage Street, converting their downstairs dining room into an office and examination room. Natalie continued to serve as Boris' medical secretary, hiring a young servant girl to help care for her large house and growing daughters.

In her late 30s, Natalie was not only educated and talented, she was also experienced and wise—and she began to use her wisdom to educate those around her. A believer in "proper" and appropriate behavior, she took in Boris's nieces in the summer and spent long, hot afternoons teaching proper table manners. Feeling one of the servant girls needed a lesson about the "birds and the bees," Natalie decided one day to pull the girl aside to give a lesson about human sexuality—only to be shocked to discover that the girl was not only educated but experienced in such matters!

The late 30s brought some renewed economic prosperity to New Bedford as World War II broke out in Europe, and Natalie began to focus her efforts on important political matters. Still fiercely patriotic, Natalie devoted much of her time and resources to the Russian War Relief, playing an instrumental role in persuading First Lady Eleanor Roosevelt to speak in New Bedford. Never forgetting her own terrible first weeks in America, Natalie also did her best to help a new wave of German Jews who had escaped Hitler's regime and fled to America. For several summers, she housed two young Jewish girls while their immigrant parents established themselves in New York. And although she only heard from her parents occasionally now, in cryptic telegrams subject to inaccurate translations, she continued to send money to her family in Saratov.

Meanwhile, Natalie's girls were growing up fast. Sixteen year old Leda, a promising student, was a high school senior planning to attend Lesley College. At nine, bright, energetic Esther loved ballet and the stage. America had been good to the Kaplan family, and for perhaps the first time in her life, Natalie felt in control of her world. But life was about to confront Natalie with still more loss and yet another challenge.

Boris Kaplan had always been a silent and serious husband. His medical and military education in Poland and Russia had taught him the value of hard work, and sometimes it seemed as if Boris did little else. From the moment he arrived in America, Boris was determined to become a successful physician, and much of his time was devoted to establishing his practice and reputation. By the 1940s, Boris had achieved these goals; a respected gastroenterologist and brilliant diagnostician, he had published articles in several medical journals.

But all this hard work often took Boris away from his wife and family. Because his office was located in the Kaplan's Cottage Street home, there were few boundaries between their home and work lives, and the two were often blended beyond recognition. Even on family excursions to Horseneck Beach, Boris wore a suit and tie, always ready to go to work, or at least appear that he was only on a brief lunch time break. Although he rarely remembered Natalie's birthday, he would sometimes show up with jewelry and other unexpected gifts.

By the mid-1940s, Boris's life of hard work began to take its toll on his health. Perhaps it was the years of military service, the exposure to disease and hunger during Russia's revolution and famine, or the years of nonstop dedication to his profession; no one really knew why or how it happened. On Christmas Day in 1945, Boris Kaplan died suddenly of heart failure.

At 46, Natalie was left alone in the large house on Cottage Street with Leda and Esther—and little time to grieve for her husband. While Boris's practice had a growing list of patients, he had not become a doctor to become rich, and he never billed his patients; they only paid what they could afford, and during the Depression and World War II, few New Bedford citizens could afford to pay much. When Boris died, he had only just begun to make a decent doctor's salary, and Natalie was left with little money to care for herself or her daughters.

After four years of renting out Boris's office to another doctor, Natalie realized that she could no longer afford to care for her family or the large Cottage Street home on rent money alone. With Leda off at Fisher College (they could no longer afford Lesley College), Natalie and Esther moved

Kaplan Family Collection

Natalie and her children take time to smell the daisies, 1940. *Natalie instilled a love of nature in her children—every year, on April 19, the Kaplan's dressed in their Sunday best to watch the newly thawed stream at Russells Mills Farm run its course. It was one of the few ways Natalie and Boris would remember the natural beauty they had left behind in Saratov, where the crackling sound of melting ice along the Volga always marked the beginning of Spring.*

Much of Natalie's teaching was devoted to her daughters. The first day of each school year was an event to be celebrated with new dresses and family pictures on the front porch, and schoolwork was as much a priority for Leda and Esther as it had been for Natalie back in Saratov.

Kaplan Family Collection

Natalie and Boris, 1940s. Even on family outings Boris wore a suit and tie, always ready to go to work, or at least appear that he was only on a brief lunch time break.

Natalie in her garden, 1933 (opposite, top).

Natalie and Esther, 1946 (opposite, bottom).

into a small New Bedford tenement building. Their small apartment was a big change from the large house on Cottage Street, but Natalie told Esther not to worry. One door closes, another one opens, she told her daughter confidently.

Privately, however, Natalie did worry about their future. She knew she needed to find a job. She had always worked alongside her husband and was not licensed to work in a hospital. How would she continue to pay for Leda's education and support herself and Esther?

Natalie did not have to worry for long. When Natalie's former neighbors adopted a baby and needed someone to care for the newborn so they could attend a legal conference, they immediately thought of Natalie. Natalie agreed to stay for a week at her neighbor's house, as long as the couple left an extensive list of the baby's schedule, food preferences, best-loved toys, and favorite lullabies. Natalie and Esther packed up their things and moved to their neighbor's house for the week. When the couple returned, Natalie earned $100 for her week's work—quite a sum of money in 1950.

Soon, word of Natalie's expertise spread to other New Bedford families, and with the baby boom of the 1950s in full swing, Natalie found herself in high demand. Mothers recuperating from childbirth hired Natalie to help them care for their newborns and other children, and couples who needed a temporary nanny hired Natalie to stay with their children for anywhere from a week to a whole month. Natalie earned a reputation as a traveling Mary Poppins figure known not only for her medical knowledge, but also her easy rapport with children. Almost by chance, Natalie had started a successful and lucrative child care business.

Despite her success, however, these years were not easy on Natalie or young Esther. Moving from house to house, family to family, left little room for the stability and peace Esther had enjoyed on Cottage Street. These busy years also left little time for the activities that had always consumed much of Natalie's life: writing, exploring nature, and contributing to local organizations. But Natalie had little choice—like her work in the cholera hospital and the Red Army, Natalie did whatever it took to support her family. With the start of the Cold War, her family in Russia felt it was too dangerous to communicate with Natalie—even the occasional telegrams stopped arriving. Her daughters and clients were all the family she had left.

For almost twenty-five years, Natalie served as nurse/grandmother to many of New Bedford's growing children, often returning to the same families year after year. But in January of 1974, when Natalie traveled to Miriam Hospital in Providence, Rhode Island for a variety of tests and physical examinations, her doctors discovered progressive heart disease. She was given strict orders to stop working.

Without the work that had consumed her for so many years, Natalie felt empty and depressed. Esther and Leda were married and had their own lives and children to tend to with, and Natalie was left alone in a small apartment on Oesting Street in New Bedford. She had spent her entire life working for her family and contributing to worthy causes, and now her life seemed meaningless.

It was Esther who first suggested that Natalie enroll in some continuing education courses at Southeastern Massachusetts University, a suggestion Natalie felt was ridiculous. Why should a 74-

year-old woman go back to school? But Esther convinced Natalie that attending a few night courses would help give her life meaning again, and Natalie registered for a two-part course on "The World of the Old Testament" and the "Post Biblical World" with Dr. Bernard Glassman, who was also a rabbi at the Tifereth Israel Synagogue, where Natalie was a member.

At first, Natalie was intimidated by her young classmates, many of whom Natalie had cared for during her years as a nanny. But the years hadn't diminished Natalie's intelligence or creativity, and she soon found herself immersed in lengthy readings and term papers. At 74, Natalie was finally getting another chance at higher education, an opportunity that had been delayed so many times before.

Even as a student, Natalie continued her lifelong dedication to teaching others. Twenty years later, Dr. Bernard Glassman still remembers Natalie as one of his most inspirational and brilliant students. "Her body was young because her mind was open," he recalls. "She brought a wisdom of life to a bible class that made the other students come alive. She exemplified the Jewish tradition of education as a lifelong process."

When Dr. Glassman's course ended, Natalie enrolled in another course, "Elder Affairs in American Life and Politics," a course that renewed Natalie's sense of community activism. She began speaking and writing about the important role of senior citizens, telling of her own experiences as a student. In an article for the *New Bedford Standard-Times*, she wrote:

Our number is growing. Many of us still continue to lead an interesting and productive life. Many manage to fill the empty hours by travel, by doing volunteer work, by enjoying card games and other games. But there are also many lonely, sad people for whom time hangs heavily on their hands, who for one reason or another are unable to fill their free time.

To them I would like to say: "Here in New Bedford we are most fortunate to have S.M.U., a school of higher learning that offers us such marvelous opportunity to study many subjects and gives us a chance at the twilight of our life to fill our existence with new, exciting and truly most worthwhile interests.

For three years, Natalie continued her studies at Southeastern Massachusetts University and her dedication to New Bedford's community. When she died on January 26, 1977, Dr. Glassman, her teacher and rabbi, eulogized her as a giving and warm person, a woman who suffered painful transitions but never lost her love for life.

Several years later, when the Jewish Federation of New Bedford was looking for materials for its Jewish Archives at Southeastern Massachusetts University, Esther Kaplan Roderick opened the box of documents her mother had left behind. "I was astounded by what I found," Esther remembers, "and I just sat there and wept. She lived through everything and never complained, and when I really can't bear it anymore, I look at my mother's diaries and manuscripts and remember what my mother went through."

Natalie Kaplan's manuscripts, diaries, essays, and immigration documents are preserved in the Jewish Archives at the UMass Dartmouth Library.

Jennifer Dulude, freelance writer and Spinner intern, is a graduate student in the Writing program at UMass Dartmouth. She also masters home pages for use on the world wide web.

Kaplan Family Collection

Kaplan Family Collection

Whereas in many parts of the country, bloomers were cause for ridicule, New Bedford stands out as a place of sweet tolerance, a city open to the new liberating fashion for women. Unfortunately, bloomers lived a short life; they were simply too shocking for the time. But they made a statement that would be heard a century later.

The Progress of Bloomerism

PAUL ALBERT CYR

The clothes of the mid-Victorian woman were thick and bulky; the stays, corsets and hoops both mind-numbing and backbreaking. This elaborate dress, often weighing between 10 and 30 pounds, made it difficult for women to move about—and impossible for them to run. The tight lacing (associated in the popular mind with virtue) even made breathing a problem. Such restrictive clothing caused women to be helpless and incapable of useful exertion; it imprisoned and deformed them. But it was the fashion, and fashion reigned.

"In a highly patriarchal society such as the mid-nineteenth century," says Alison Lurie in *The Language of Clothes*, "the costumes of men and women tend to be clearly differentiated and anyone who adopts the dress of the opposite sex in public is likely to be considered shocking or even disgusting. Mrs. Amelia Bloomer's campaign for the divided skirt in the 1850s was greeted with ridicule and social ostracism."

Did bloomers come to New Bedford? How were they received? Was New Bedford a radical hotbed of bloomerism? Bloomer sightings, bloomer lectures, bloomer letters-to-the-editor and impassioned bloomer defense were all faithfully reported in the newspapers.

In the spring of 1851 the news of a new type of women's dress was one of the hottest topics in America. Popularized by Amelia Bloomer, her name became attached to the costume.

In comparing the two New Bedford newspapers at the time, you can see the personality and politics of each. The *Standard* embraced the new costume and ran twenty-four articles about it between May and September, some of them lengthy. The *Mercury* ran four articles during the same period, all brief.

Dress reform fit into a closely knit group of causes, including women's rights, the abolition of slavery and temperance. Amelia Bloomer wore her namesake costume to a women's temperance convention. Other early women advocates, like Lucretia Mott of Nantucket, had their early political training in the antislavery movement. These causes were all compatible with the philosophy of the *Standard*, its editor, Edmund Anthony, and its political patron, Rodney French.

The wearing of the Bloomer costume even became a patriotic gesture in some circles. The *Turkish* costume began to be called the *American costume* and seen as an act of independence from the domination of Parisian fashions.

These slices of life are from the *Republic Standard*, the weekly version of the *Daily Standard*.

May 22, 1851: *Bloomerism*

They are coming! The short skirts and Turkish trowsers. They are near—They have reached Taunton.

May 29, 1851: *The Bloomer Costume*

It is said that the dressmakers are going to put down the new fashion, if possible. We hope that if the dressmakers attempt to do any such thing, they will get put down themselves.

May 29, 1851: *Bloomerism in New Bedford*

We understand that one lady in this city has come out in the Turkish costume, and others are preparing to follow suit. More anon-that is to say, when we learn it.

Sheet music cover of the "new costume polka," or "Bloomer," 1851. Amelia Bloomer publicized a new feminine attire of full Turkish trousers gathered at the ankles, and her name was quickly attached to the outfit, although it was actually created by Elizabeth Smith Miller. The "Bloomer costume" was ridiculed by most observers, and it became a symbol of radicalism. Mrs. Bloomer wore the costume for a time, as did her neighbor Mrs. Elizabeth Cady Stanton, Susan B. Anthony, and other leaders of the women's rights movement, but they all abandoned the costume when it seemed to draw attention away from more important aspects of the movement.

Brown University

Boston, June 4, 1851. *A Friend to the Ladies.*

[An opinion written by Mary Vaughan, edited by Mrs. Nichols, in the Windsor (Vt.) Democrat, *scooped by the New Bedford papers.]*

My dear Mrs. Nichols,…Even in spite of ridicule, I am not ashamed to avow myself greatly in favor of a radical and decided change in the style and manner of wearing of female garments. Who that has felt the involuntary smile of happiness spread over the features, as the whale-bound bodice, and heavy skirts were laid aside, will deny that a crusade for the abolition of such torture, would be a blessed work?

Long and loud and verbose were the arguments urged against the wearing of corsets a few years since, yet I very much doubt if physical femininity suffered half as much from their use, as from the present style of dress.

The long tight bodice, (or if not *tight* it matters little) pushing downward the internal viscera, aided by the heavy skirts suspended from the hips and stuffed with cotton; are these not instruments of torture worthy of the "high and palmy days" of the Inquisition? Yet these are voluntarily assumed. We are but victims of our adherence to Fashion and desire to beautify ourselves according to her capricious decrees.

We have no right to expect pity, but we really do receive it, and from men with sense and judgment too. They urge upon the sex here, in most instances, the propriety of assuming habiliments *a la Turc*; but none have yet assumed sufficient courage to do it. The pantaloon has been too long a bugbear, figuratively, for women to assume the garment in reality, without the indulgence of some scruples.

We would rather as yet sweep the streets with our skirts and merinos, and even our delicate muslins, and stay away from the pleasant woods and flowery hillsides, and all the places where we may study God's character through nature, almost altogether, for fear of spoiling the same graceful drapery, than assume a garb which would give us ease and comfort and the unrestrained enjoyment of our natural powers. And why? Nothing but the fear of ridicule.

…The evils that spring from our habits of dress fall not entirely upon ourselves. Much as we may suffer, we may also see those sufferings renewed in our children, the enfeebled, pining victims of our violation of physical laws. Viewed in this light, the subject is one of fearful and vast responsibility. If we are to bring disease and physical inferiority, and perhaps death, upon our children, is not the subject one to be considered, weighed, and acted upon, with decision and without delay? Yours, Mary C. Vaughan.

June 5, 1851: *The Bloomer Costume*

To the Ladies. Our lady readers are aware of the Bloomer costume, consisting of a short dress and Turkish trowsers, coming into fashion to a considerable extent, and in different and distant parts of the country. It has been variously received in places where it has appeared, according to the tastes and fancies of the local community and probably also according to the social standing of the respective first wearers. Some have encountered it with ridicule; others have hailed it with real or affected admiration, and praised it to the skies.

As to gentlemen, it may be said they have no right to interfere in such a matter… but, in the words of the old Roman poet, a little varied, we may say, Whatever relates to the interest of womankind is interesting to us.

We are, then, in reality and in seriousness, in favor of the new fashion…First and foremost, it is a *modest* fashion…It certainly affords a sufficient protection to the person from the observation of rude and unfriendly eyes. The objection that it gives the female figure a

Ruth Edwards

Ruth Edwards

masculine semblance we regard as utterly futile. One has only to see a lady attired in a neat suit of the new style to be satisfied of the fallacy of this objection.

The new fashion has *neatness* to recommend it. The present criticism of ladies wearing long dresses, often of material and hue so fine and so fair as to exhibit the slightest soiling, trailing through the dust and mud of dirty streets, would be accounted superlatively ridiculous were it not so extremely common.

Again: the new dress is more *economical*…affords far greater freedom and play to the limbs and is therefore *more convenient*. It must be *most comfortable* and in our humble judgement, *more becoming and elegant*.

We had almost forgotten to add, what may have weight with a large portion of the ladies…gentlemen are almost unanimously in favor of the new fashion.

June 7, 1851: *The New Costume, Boston Journal*

About a year since, I followed to the grave a beautiful and affectionate daughter, whose sickness and death, I have some reason to believe, were induced by getting the bottom of her clothes wet in the winter, and sitting in that condition through the day. She went out of town to school, and walked a mile in going to and returning from the cars. And have not many thousands been brought to premature graves in this way?

The present style of dress does not sufficiently protect the body in cold weather. In getting in and out of carriages and rail cars, and in ascending stairs, the wearer is liable to exposure. On ascending stairs one hand must always be used, to draw up the clothes. In high winds, the ladies in the street find themselves sometimes in a most awkward position. I have frequently seen them stop and take both hands to hold their garments down while rude and unmannerly men and boys stopped short to gaze.

Ruth Edwards

I accord fully in the following remarks from the Commonwealth: "The general adoption of the new dress will do more for the national wealth than the mines of California, and more for the national health than all the discoveries in medicine, since Galen…"

June 10, 1851: *Bloomerism Flourishes*

Tuesday evening there were nearly 100 young ladies promenading our principle streets, attired wholly or partly in the new costume. In walking three squares we met about 25. The "Bloomers" *do make a fine appearance*.

June 10, 1851: *Bloomer Festival*

The Bloomer festival, given in compliment to the new costume, at No. 5 Washington Street, on the 4th, passed off in the most agreeable and satisfactory manner. The festival was attended only by ladies in costume, with the exception of two or three elderly ladies, who came as spectators, having daughters or friends present. It was very gratifying to see all those who had donned the new style were ladies of intelligence, fully competent to judge what comports with female delicacy and what does not.

At the dinner table several spirited and appropriate toasts were given, which, not being noted down at the time, we do not remember, much to our regret. We could not forget one from Rev. S. Lovell, however, which was as follows: "General Washington and Mrs. Bloomer—both saviors of their country;—the first by raising the colonists from the degradation of British rule, the second by raising our countrywomen out of the *mud* and *filth* of the streets."

Some excellent remarks were also made by Dr. Lee; who averred that we should be constrained to believe that all ladies who do not adopt the new style have either large feet, or are on the wrong side of *thirty*.

June 19, 1851: *The Bloomers Have Come!*

At length the eyes of our citizens have been favored with a view of the far-famed new style of dress. Two young ladies, daughters of one of our respected merchants, as good as they are fair, appeared in our streets on Friday afternoon, complete in the new costume, in beautiful changeable silk dresses, with white trowsers *a la Turc*, and neat Gypsy hats—they were accompanied by gentlemen. Of course their *debut* and promenade in this attire attracted considerable attention but the ladies understanding themselves, bore themselves with perfect *nonchalance*, and were treated by all observers with respect. All agreed that the new dress was very pretty and becoming. We heard not a syllable of dissent. Now that the ice is broken, we hope to see the new and convenient costume soon come into general use.

June 19, 1851: *A Bloomer Man*

The *Boston Bee* says that a man in the new camilla costume, with plaid trowsers gathered *a la Turc*, at the ankle, light skirt and waist, with his cocoanut covered by a real camilla straw hat, stalked down State Street, Thursday afternoon. He drew a wondering crowd.

June 26, 1851: *Bloomerism on the "Fourth"*

We understand that a large number of our fair ones are coming out in the Bloomer costume on the ensuing "fourth"…nothing could be more appropriate than the choice of such a day by the ladies in which to disenthrall themselves from the tyranny of foreign cumbersome and unseemly fashions! Three cheers for the Bloomer damsels, say we, and all manner of success. We cannot have a doubt that with their charms heightened by the becoming new dresses they will be more dangerous than ever.

June 26, 1851: *More Bloomers*

An honorable gentleman of this city accompanied his young daughter in a quiet walk through some of our most eligible streets on Saturday afternoon, the young lady being dressed in the new and far-famed costume complete. She seemed perfectly at home, and we heard very favorable remarks on her appearance,

Brown University

Brown University

Page of music from "The Bloomer Polka," written by Edward LeRoy and published in 1851.

Music sheet cover of "The Bloomer's Complaint," a very pathetic song (left).

Ruth Edwards

from gentlemen. The dress, as we remember it, was a cinnamon colored silk. We understand that the young lady attended church on Sunday in the same costume, and in company with several other ladies.

June 30, 1851: The "Bloomers" in Council. *Lecture of Mrs. Gove Nichols at Hope Chapel, on Thursday Night. (Reported for the New York Express).*

After a few preliminary remarks, Mrs. Nichols said that the reform was bound to succeed. Some ten years ago she had lectured in this city on the necessity of allowing women to hold property. She had heard it objected by gentlemen at that period that if the women were allowed to become property-holders, they would never marry-(laughter)-and now it was said that if they were allowed to wear a dress, in which they could walk about with ease, they would walk away from their duties to the lords of creation.

The right to hold personal real estate, however, had at last been conceded to women, and she did not think the men found it any more difficult to find wives than they did ten years ago, and she did not believe the dress reform which they would also have to accord to women, would cause her to be derelict to the duties she owed to man. Women but live to please men she averred, and if this reform in dress was only the caprice of the whim of the wearers, it could not succeed; but it is not; the men are as much in love with it as the women; the men wish the women to be free from the terrible bondage in which they have been so long held by stays and corsets; long dresses and muddy petticoats…

Mrs. Nichols acknowledged that she often felt the effects of a weak constitution and could not help thinking how much better it might have been for her had she been born of a healthy mother, and brought up free from the trammels of a torturing method of dress. In the long skirts, when she had walked ten miles, it had cost her as much exertion and she had been as much fatigued as if she had walked forty in the new costume. Men said the women were too cowardly to adopt a change in their dress, which would make them observed of all observers…

She had come to address those women who felt that there was a great work to be done, and were ready to put their shoulders to the wheel and do it. She came to speak to those who were willing to free themselves from their corsets and stays, and increase their area of Liberty. (Faint demonstrations of applause, at which Mrs. N. did not seem very well pleased, as she remarked, "Oh, that won't do; you don't call that applause!" Whereupon the good natured audience gave her a good round of approbation and a chorus of laughter.)

After Mrs. Nichols concluded her address, she came forward with several young ladies, each attired in full Bloomer rig…Quite a crowd were collected outside the Chapel, to see the Bloomers come out.

July 24, 1851: *A Bloomer Man*

On Wednesday evening about 8 o'clock, a man in a sort of semi-Bloomer costume, with Bloomer flat on his top-piece, and a light tunic which was in fashion a sort of compromise between a Bloomer skirt and a hunting-shirt, reaching down to his knees, and with wide light trowsers, made his appearance and promenaded a while upon Purchase Street.

The boys who had behaved with perfect decorum to the pantaloons of real, handsome, neat looking, *genuine*, Bloomers whom they had just met upon the street, assailed this "bogus" one with a howl of indignation, insomuch that after several vain attempts to appear indifferent and unconscious of notice, constrained to flee from the gathering storm, he plunged into an oyster shop to liquorize and imbibe some Dutch courage.

August 7, 1851: *Bloomerism in Nantucket*

The quiet town of Nantucket has been thrown into great excitement by the startling news of the appearance of a genuine, sprightly Bloomer, aged seventy-five, who was seen last week promenading through one of its principal streets.

August 27, 1851: *Mrs. Hale on the New Costume*

Mrs. Sarah J. Hale, of the *Lady's Book*, has the following compliment to the Bloomer dress wearers:

"In brief, it must be apparent to everyone that the prevailing female fashions are the most appropriate for the great diversity to be found in the female form and stature and that, consequently, they must continue to prevail so long as those diversities are thereby equalized or rendered, in a measure, uniform to the exclusion of the most formidable innovation that ingenuity and personal perfection may attempt to introduce. We would, however, give our hearty approbation to a reform in the length of ladies' walking-dresses, considering the present fashion out of all form of neatness and comfort."

If we are to understand this, it means to say that only those having "personal perfection" will adopt the new dress, and that the old style is much the best to practice deception with. She here virtually says, that when you see a form in the long skirts you do not know whether it is made up of cotton bags, bran bags, or flesh and blood, whether the rounded bust is counterfeit and the sudden expansion below the waist a bundle of hay or a real genuine human form. Really, if long skirts give such an opportunity for gross imposition, young men will take warning by Mrs. Hale's argument and see the "personal perfection" found encased in the Bloomer. This is decidedly the greatest compliment we have yet seen to the new costume.

– Providence Mirror

October 9, 1851: *Bloomer Wedding*

In South Abington on Sunday evening 28 ult., in the Congregational Church by Rev. Mr. Hayne, Mr. Bucklin S. Benson of Thompson, Conn. to Miss Ann P. Whitman of E. Bridgewater. The bride was dressed in the Bloomer style.

April 28, 1852

Mrs. Bloomer, at the recent Woman's Temperance Convention at Rochester, NY, appeared in the costume which bears her own name. Her dress and trowsers were of 'silver grey' silk, the prevailing color relieved by lighter figure; she wore a short turban. In the street, she wears a white beaver hat, in 'flat' style, and her appearance is very unique. Mrs. Stanton was also clad in the new costume. Her dress was black satin. Her hair, which is slightly silvered, was cut short, and 'shingled,' which together with the close fitting dress, gave her a rather masculine appearance.

Paul Cyr, Curator of Genealogy at the New Bedford Public Library, has been a contributing writer and editor with Spinner since 1981. "The best way to get a feel for life in New Bedford in the nineteenth century is to sit down with a run of local newspapers," he says. "The day-to-day occurrences are what make the long-term changes in people's lives. The personal is political."

Brown University

Amelia Jenks (1818-1894), American reformer and crusader for women's rights. She was born in Homer, New York, on May 27, 1818. In 1840, Ms. Jenks married Dexter C. Bloomer, a Quaker newspaper editor and reformer. Strongly influenced by the reform movements of her day, in 1849 she started a temperance journal, the Lily, *probably the first publication edited entirely by a woman. The magazine also espoused women's rights and women's suffrage, opposed unjust marriage laws, and advocated dress reform. Amelia Jenks Bloomer is remembered for the Bloomer costume, but she was primarily an editor and reformer. She died in Council Bluffs, Iowa, on Dec. 30. 1894.*

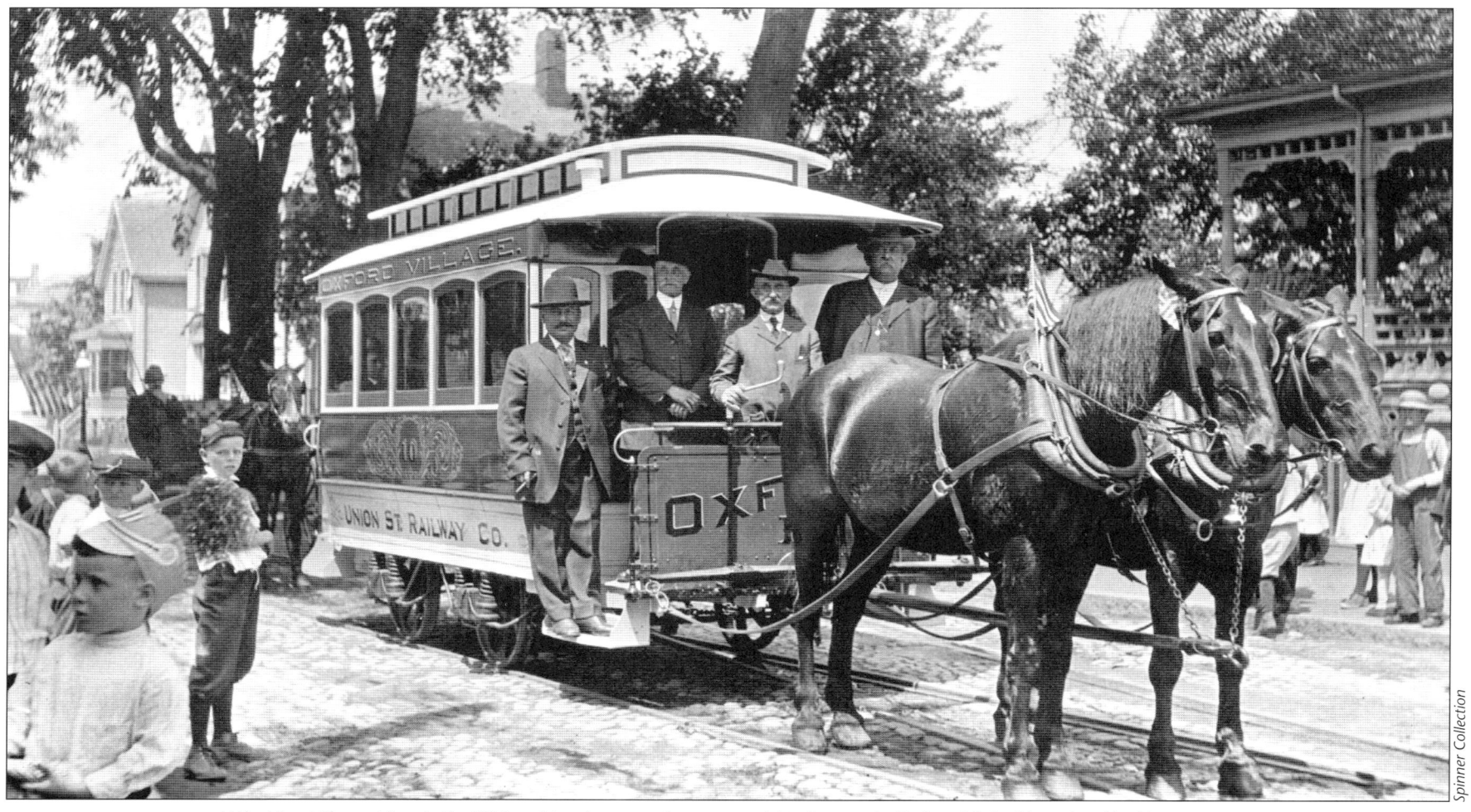

At the Mount Pleasant Barn in the 1920s, celebrants prepare for a ceremonial trolley parade. On board Oxford-bound car No. 10 are veteran drivers James Card and Frank Paine. Car No. 10 has been preserved and is currently on display at the Seashore Trolley Museum in Kennebunkport, Maine.

Trolley Days

JOHN ACKERMAN

    Seen from a low-flying plane today, New Bedford and its suburbs blend seamlessly into one continuous pattern of industries, harbors, schools, parks, malls and homes joined by a network of paved roads. The auto appears to define the landscape but, in fact, the pattern was laid down over a 75-year period by the auto's predecessors, the horsecar, beginning in the 1870s, and later the electric trolley.

    New Bedford's first horse car line was built in 1872 in order to link Pearl Street Railroad Station to the city steamship docks. Here, travelers boarded the sidewheel steamers for Martha's Vineyard and Nantucket.

    Until the New Bedford horsecar line was built, island-bound vacationers had to struggle with their baggage over the mile from the station to the wharves. Moreover, the Cape Cod Railroad had built a branch line to Woods Hole and the Vineyard steamer docks. The New Bedford and Taunton Railroad and the Island Steamship Lines, based in New Bedford, feared they would lose business to the new Woods Hole route.

The New Bedford and Fairhaven Street Railway, circa 1872. The No. One car (right), at the corner of Merrimac and Purchase Streets, was probably the first streetcar to run in New Bedford. The driver was cooped in and had to pass through the car to get off, or jump over the dasher.

Fairhaven-bound, circa 1872 (below). *An open car travels the route to Fairhaven along Purchase Street, heading south toward Union. These early streetcars were open at both ends with two long benches along each side and a platform for the driver. They could accommodate 14 to 16 passengers. There were no conductors except at rush hour, and passengers were expected to deposit their fares in a box at either end of the car. During the winter the floors of the streetcar were covered with straw so that people could push their feet under the straw to protect them from the cold.* [New Bedford: A Pictorial History]

From that first horse car line came a network of routes that extended from the center of New Bedford to the North, South and West Ends and to Fairhaven. The revolutionary effect of these little two-horse cars is largely forgotten.

Until the horse cars came, men and women in New Bedford and in every American city and town had no choice but to live within walking distance of their work. That necessity saw rows of little houses built across the streets from the New Bedford mills.

On the city waterfront, the mansions of the whaling magnates and their counting houses were only a block or two away from the less salubrious aspects of a nineteenth century whaling port: dance halls, saloons, brothels and such necessary but noisy businesses as ship chandleries, blacksmiths, carpenter shops, boatyards and ship supply houses.

A popular 1876 print of New Bedford illustrating the city as it might be seen from a balloon, shows a small city clustered around the present historic district, bounded on the north by the Wamsutta Mills, on the south by the present location of Commonwealth Electric and on the west by County Street. The intersection of Rockdale Avenue and Kempton Street was a rural enclave called Cannonville. Most of today's West, South and North Ends were open fields.

Spinner Collection

Trolleygrams

The expanding horse car line changed the city forever. Men bought or rented newly-built homes well away from the noisy mills and the turbulent waterfront, taking the horse car to work.

Powered by 12 horses from Prince Edward Island and with four cars ready to go, the New Bedford and Fairhaven Street Railway opened for business on Saturday, July 29, 1872. School children were allowed to ride free that first day. Regular fare was six cents.

A young man named Fred Coon was proud to be a hill-boy with this new form of rapid transit. He wrote of his experiences and the growth of the line from horse cars to electric in a handwritten manuscript now in the collection of the Old Dartmouth Historical Society.

He told of cold nights and skies full of stars as he waited at the New Bedford end of the Fairhaven Bridge with his hill horse. When the two-horse car rattled down the bridge from Fairhaven to begin the long climb to Summer Street, Fred was ready.

Spinner Collection

Fairhaven horsecar No. 10, circa 1890. *Union Street Railway's Oxford car on Main Street with motorman James E. Card holding the reins of his horse, Annie.*

Fairhaven car in front of the Corson Block, circa 1890. *Traveling through the intersection of Elm and Front Streets, the trolley advances toward the bridge to Fairhaven. Behind the car is the Elm Street hill, covering about 10 blocks west to Summer Street, where Fred Coon began his adventures as a hill-boy.*

In the early days, each car carried both a motorman and a conductor (at rear). The conductor collected the fares, assisted passengers and gave signals to the motorman.

Spinner Collection

Mount Pleasant Car No. Four at Rural Cemetery, circa 1887. Driver William Hiscox and his son take a break at the end of the line. The straw collar on one of the horses was used when the horse's neck became sore. The smokepipe on the roof of the car was used as an interior night lamp that also lit the colored bull's-eye denoting the car's route. [Trolleygrams, 1923]

Mount Pleasant Barn, 1887. Driver Thomas Farley, wearing the derby at center, is about to take his car downtown. He is flanked on the left by William Drew, car barn man, and Fred Gifford, at right with his dog. Everett Sowle, on horseback next to Gifford, was riding down to Kempton Street to relieve the animal. The Mount Pleasant Barn was located on Durfee Street near Summer Street—the end of the line that began at Rural Cemetery. [Trolleygrams, July 1922]

He ran alongside the moving cars, dropping the heavy hook he carried through a ringbolt on the floor of the horse car. As Fred ran beside the car, the driver cracked his whip and the three horses lunged ahead, straining to pull the car up the steep grade. At the top of the hill, the car paused. Fred lifted out his hook and walked his horse back down to the bridge to wait for the next city-bound car.

For his work, Fred received $1.00 a day—for a day that began about 8:30AM and ended around 11PM, with one-and-a-half hours off for dinner and supper. Drivers who worked much longer hours received $2.00 a day for a seven-day week. Fred Coon wrote:

Driving a horse car was an art. First, after the conductor gave the usual two bells, it was necessary to prevent the horses from bolting into their collars and giving them a sore neck or shoulder. If the car was on

Trolleygrams

level track, you would let off the brake and hold back your horses…if on an upgrade, the horses would start themselves on hearing the two bells and when the traces tightened, you slack off your brake and your horses have got the car moving.

Fred's narrative captures the horse car with sudden clarity:

The writer well remembers the old box cars in winter standing in the Fairhaven car barn with blankets on the horses on a cold winter night with straw on the floor and a kerosene lamp on each end of the car…before starting, the driver took off the blankets, folded them up and threw them over the dasher unless it stormed, when they were laid just inside the front door on the floor…

When the car started and the horses were trotting along, the windows in the car which were loose would jar all the way…coming across the bridge from Fairhaven to New Bedford, the driver would hang his reins over the brake and beat his hands together as teamsters do…

Disaster struck the new company soon after it opened. An epidemic of equine epizootic killed many of the horses and left many more too weak to work. In desperation, the company turned to oxen and bulls

Trolleygrams

Trolleygrams

to haul the cars, some with yokes, some with traditional horse harness minus the bridle. But the big beasts were slow and the city cobblestones hurt their feet and it was with relief the company went back to horses.

In 1884, areas not served by the horse car line began clamoring for service. In February of that year, the Acushnet Street Railway was organized to serve areas not reached by the older company. To increase its business, the new line opened River View Park in the North End and a pavilion and restaurant at Clark's Cove.

Ox power, November 1872. *Oxen replaced horses during the Great Epizootic Horse Influenza Epidemic of 1872. This car, at the Union and Purchase Street intersection, is headed for Steamboat Wharf with three oxen pulling.*

Spinner Collection

Lawton's Corner, Union and Purchase Streets, circa 1890. *During electrification of the system, when both horse and electricity moved the trolley cars, predictions of doom and disaster were pervasive. Mayor Morgan Rotch predicted that horses would, "never, never become accustomed to the sight of electric cars." Others predicted an epidemic of electrocutions from falling trolley lines. Despite these worries, there were no electrocutions, and only a few timid horses were frightened by the cars.*

On very sharp curves, a horse might balk in the middle of the turn and no amount of whipping or coaxing could move him. The car then backed up, the horses were given a short rest, and the conductor would give "two bells." If the horses pulled together with a rush, the car continued on. [Transportation Bulletin *and* New Bedford: A Pictorial History]

In less than two years, the competition was proving expensive to both companies. In 1887, they merged to form the Union Street Railway.

From then until Henry Ford's inexpensive Model T arrived on the scene, horse car lines and their successor, trolley lines, enjoyed steady growth locally and across the nation. Massachusetts was the only state that had more miles of trolley lines than of steam railways, thanks to the short distance between towns and cities and the availability of lakes and ocean beaches.

Fairhaven, Dartmouth, Westport, Freetown, Lakeville, Mattapoisett, Marion and Wareham were all served by trolleys based in New Bedford. Inevitably these towns became suburbs of the city and still are today although the paved road has long replaced the trolley track.

The railroads were not pleased with the arrival of their electric competitors. Although the auto was later blamed for killing local rail passenger service, the trolley did that first. Passenger service along the New Haven Railroad's Watuppa branch, from New Bedford through North Dartmouth and Westport to Fall River, was abandoned in the early 1900s, long before the auto was a threat.

The Standard-Times

Open trolley at west end of the New Bedford–Fairhaven bridge, circa 1910. *One of the joys of riding the open trolleys in New Bedford was having a special place to go: ocean beaches within the city limits, grand amusement parks and beautiful public parks and pavilions.*

With the new bridge in use at the turn of the century, open trolley trips to recreational areas such as Fort Phoenix in Fairhaven and Onset Beach in Wareham became popular summer junkets for active city dwellers and working people. "I have such fond memories of trolleys. I remember my mother taking us from Sconticut Neck to New Bedford every Sunday afternoon to visit relatives. The seats in the back were of a woven material and I remember how they looked and felt." – Barbara Sylvia

The trolley line along what is now Route 6, linking New Bedford, Dartmouth and Westport to Fall River and offering the joys of Lincoln Park, offered faster and more frequent service at lower fares; the railroad could not compete.

Many street railways built amusement parks to build up their weekend traffic; a few, a very few, survive today though no longer served by trolleys. Like most street railways in the early years of this century, the Union Street Railway enjoyed some years of steadily growing passenger service.

Local riders could take the trolley to Wareham, Onset and Monument Beach, and connecting lines to Lakeville, Freetown, Middleboro, Taunton and points beyond. Brockton was one of the cities reached by trolley from New Bedford. The ride took three hours but did not deter riders.

Open trolleys in the summer carried whole families on all-day trips through the countryside for $1 per family. Inns in the old country towns along the route were kept busy serving trolley travelers on weekends. The open cars also carried crowds to New Bedford beaches, to Fort Phoenix and to Cape Cod.

Onset beach was a typical and popular summer trip from New Bedford; it's still an outstanding beach offering such attractions as Kenny's, noted still for taffy as it was when it opened in 1895.

The impact of these country trolley lines on the small towns of New England was far greater than is realized today: In the mid '50s, *The Standard-Times* interviewed a Marion woman, then in her 90s. What was the most memorable event to take place in Marion in her long life? she was asked. "The coming of the New Bedford and Onset trolley," she replied. That memory was strong despite the fact the trolley line succumbed to auto competition in 1926.

Acushnet Park, 1920s. In its heyday, Acushnet Park was a popular South End attraction. On warm weekends, open trolleys disgorged hordes of fun seekers. The park opening in 1916 was a roaring success, attended by perhaps 40,000. Two hurricanes, a fire, changing tastes and changing times consigned the park to oblivion during the 1950s. The park was sold to the city and transformed into the present municipal East Beach.

New Bedford and Onset Street Railway car at Onset Beach, circa 1917 (bottom left).

The Standard-Times

Spinner Collection

149

New car delivery, November 1929 (top right). Streetcar No. 601 was one of twelve new cars added to the Purchase Street line. Built by the Osgood Bradley Company of Worcester, the cars were designed for one- or two-man operation. They seated 44 passengers and were comparatively light, weighing 34,000 pounds. They were designed specifically for quick acceleration.

A city for everyone, January 1934 (center right). During hard economic times, when many people couldn't afford an automobile, the trolley made urban centers accessible to remote rural areas. The city was a shopping Mecca for the region and during holiday season, hotels were filled and streets were bustling.

Onset car at Onset, circa 1910 (bottom right). Car No. 150, built by Jones Car Co. in 1901, was a 13-bench open car. Here, along Onset Avenue, the conductor gets out of the car to change the signal for the next trolley car.

Railway Post Office, May 3, 1947 (below). On the eve of the last run of the Union Street Railway, a group of trolley enthusiasts came to Pope's Island to salvage a piece of history. The old mail car was enshrined in the hearts of men who refused to recognize the electric railway was part of vanishing era. On its way to a museum in Branford, CT, the car was to be repainted and refurbished to its youthful splendor and run by the Branford Electric Railway Association. The next day, the Union Street Railway made its final run.

The frequent service and low fares of the trolley lines ended Marion's isolation and its dependence on a couple of trains a day. The trolley line put New Bedford within easy reach of all, not only for its stores and theaters and parks, but for its jobs.

The isolation of small rural towns in New England in the pre-trolley era, particularly in the long cold winters, is almost beyond understanding today. One of the most graphic descriptions of that time can be found in Edith Wharton's short novel "Ethan Frome." In that tragedy of love and hate and loneliness, she has given an unmatched description of rural life before the trolleys came.

But in the foreword of a late of "Ethan Frome," Mrs. Wharton writes that the isolation she had described in the novel had largely disappeared… thanks to the coming of the country trolley lines.

In its heyday, the rural New Bedford and Onset, an offshoot of the Union Street Railway, carried the mail from Fall River to New Bedford and Onset. Trolley freight cars did the job done today by trucks, delivering cargoes to businesses and industries along its route.

The Standard-Times

The Standard-Times

The Standard-Times

Paul Levasseur

A veteran Union Street Railway worker recalled the night he operated the last trolley from New Bedford to the Onset Lines Wareham car barn. His comment summed up the end of a country trolley line and the reason for its demise:

"I threw the switch and that was the end. Then I walked outside where my wife was waiting for me in our Model T." (That Wareham car barn as well as car barns in New Bedford still survive, long since put to other uses.)

The Standard-Times

Trolley graveyard, Popes Island, April 1939. *As was the custom, the old cars were often burned before being scrapped.*

Farewell, Union Street Railway, May 4, 1947. *Enoch Newsman, a motorman for more than 26 years, tips his hat in farewell as he leaves his empty car, No. 606, for the last time.* [Standard Times, 5/4/47.]

The Standard-Times

In 1935, the Union Street Railway announced a plan to replace all its trolleys with buses in five years. The cost of the buses and the advent of World War II delayed that plan until May 3, 1947, when the last New Bedford trolleys ran on the Purchase Street line.

A new lease on life was given to the ten newest Union Street Railway trolleys, the 600 series. After service ended in New Bedford in 1947, they were purchased and used for service on the Queensboro Bridge above New York City's East River. They carried riders to and from the elevator that linked the bridge to Welfare Island underneath the bridge. They were the last trolleys to run in New York City.

The Standard-Times

New York connection, July 1957. *One of the former New Bedford trolley cars was in service on New York's Queensboro Bridge. Here, the car still carries its New Bedford designation: "Route 1, Butler Street."*

Streetcar behemoth, February 1946. *In the trolley's waning days, it was seen more as a hindrance than an asset—too big for the old town's crowded streets; too slow and in the way of fleet moving cars; not as agile as the modern bus. It's demise was imminent, and few people called for a stay of execution. This view is from the fourth floor of the old Star Store.*

Trolley Memories: *"My friend and I would take the trolley to the local ski slope—around 1945 or '46, when I was about 13. When the snow was good for skiing, my friend Edgar would walk down to Liberty Street to meet me, skis over his shoulder, and we would walk the four blocks to Kempton Street and the trolley line.*

"The trolley seemed to whisk us to the New Bedford Country Club in no time at all. We would get off at Slocum Road and the trolley continued on to Lincoln Park where it turned and came back. After a full day of skiing, we would catch a late afternoon trolley for the ride back to Liberty Street." –Lee Butterworth

The Standard-Times

Trolley Sidebar

Any institution as long-lived as the Union Street Railway accumulated legends down the years. Two of them have come down to me, both from the early years of the trolley lines. I cannot vouch for their veracity…but I can vouch for the veracity of *The Standard-Times* reporter who passed them on to me:

The last trolley car from New Bedford to Padanaram used to run at midnight. The riders, most of whom had spent the evening in sundry city saloons, tended to be boisterous. One snowy winter night, they were even more so…so much so the conductor struggled forward to tell the motorman he could not control them and they were beginning to dismantle the trolley car from within.

"Stay up here with me," said the motorman. "When we get to the top of the hill at Elm Street, brace yourself." The conductor braced himself. The motorman opened his controller to the highest notch and sped down the hill. At its foot, he slammed on the emergency brakes.

Trolleygrams

No. 418 Luxury Car makes its way along Dartmouth Street to Padanaram, 1918.

Trolley pranksters: *"As kids, we'd go from the South End to the North End and get into trouble along the way. We'd pull the cord and the arm would drop. It would stop the trolley. Then we'd run like hell. The biggest thrill was to hitch a sled to the back. We did that all the time. We never paid to ride the trolley."* –Tony Braz, Jr.

"We used to drive the conductors nuts, but they were very polite. We took the green trolleys from the North End to the South End and we would stomp on the conductor's bell and hear it ring all the way from one end of the city to the other. They also used the trolleys to plow Acushnet Avenue and I remember standing there, watching." – James H. Jenkins

"My friends and I would get on at Kempton and ride up to Tarkiln Hill Road to school at Normandin. We would huddle in the back of the car and pull the wire down from the electric. The motorman would have to get out and run back to fix it. We would take that opportunity to run to the front end and take off with the street car." – Reverend Frank Morse

Fort Rodman car No. 605 at Hazelwood Park, circa 1930.

Rivet Street, end of the line, circa 1926 *(center). In November 1913, the Union Street Railway added what turned out to be their last extension of tracks. Three quarters of a mile of track running westerly on Rivet Street from Purchase to Bolton Street. The Rivet Street line was a response to the expansion of textile mills in the area and the residential and commercial neighborhoods cropping up around the workplaces. Unfortunately, this was one of the poorest paying lines and in 1935, one of the first city lines to be replaced by bus service.*

Summer Street car, circa 1920 *(bottom).*

Trolley Memories: *"I actually drove the trolley, which was quite an accomplishment for a little kid. My family lived at Westport factory and when the old Lincoln School on State and Reed Road was closed, I had to transfer to the Gidley School at Smith Mills. The trolley would come through the village and stop where the water slide now is. Here the conductor would take the controls—the accelerator and the brake mechanism—and put them on the other end of the trolley and drive the other way.*

"As a kid, I boarded the trolley in the village and made friends with the conductor, Joe Bushee. I'd help him move the controls and then he would let me drive. It was only about $^1/_8$ mile and only when no one else was on the trolley. This was a great thrill for a 12-year-old. I felt like a hero." –Donald Edwards

"Streetcars that ran from New Bedford to Fall River were a different type of car. They were like a suburban—big, heavy and strong-looking. Sometimes they'd lose time going through the city of Fall River and there's a place coming back, just before you get to Smith Mills, where there's quite a steep grade. So most of the motormen, especially at night, would wind their cars out and they'd get up to as much as 50 mph to make up time." –Neal Galligan

The drunks hurtled forward, piling up at the front end of the car in a mass of stunned, bruised and bleeding bodies. The conductor opened the door and, one by one, the dazed riders staggered or fell into the snow and stumbled off.

Padanaram commuters waiting for the city-bound trolley the next morning stared, appalled at the blood-streaked snow leading away from the tracks in all directions. Whether the truth was ever known, I cannot say, but I was told the midnight trolley from the city to Padanaram was a model of decorum ever after.

Ingenuity rather than a brake application marks the other story handed down to me.

Once upon a time, there was a motorman who used to operate the little, lightweight, four-wheel trolley car that ended its run in Oxford Village, North Fairhaven. The tracks simply ended abruptly in the street; the overhead wire continued a bit further on.

On several occasions, this particular motorman managed to run his car off the end of the track. The Union Street Railway then had to send a trolley work car to North Fairhaven equipped with a long rope to pull the little car back on the tracks. These special runs did not go unnoticed by the management.

The motorman was warned…one more time and he would be unemployed by the Union Street Railway. But, of course, he did do it again. Fear sharpened his wits. The electricity that powered his trolley came from the overhead wire, turned the motors and grounded out through the rails.

With his trolley off the rails, he needed a substitute ground. He went from house to house, begging for old newspapers. When he had enough he soaked them in water (water also conducts electricity) and laid them in two parallel rows from his stranded trolley back to the end of the rails. He pushed his

Private Collection

Private Collection

Private Collection

reverse key, opened the controller, and slowly inched the little car back to the rails. Apparently, he got away with it—and the legend suggests he never ran off the end of the track again.

John Ackerman's finely-crafted articles in The Standard-Times *have enjoyed a wide audience for close to a half century. John loves trains and trolleys and wonders whether trolleys may have played a part in getting him his job.*

As a journalism student in New York City, John had the opportunity to ride one of the former New Bedford cars across Queensboro Bridge. During his interview at the newspaper, he offered to write a feature story on New Bedford's homesick trolleys. The Standard-Times *published his story. "How much effect that story had on my being hired, I don't know," he says. "But I did the job from that day until I retired in 1994."*

Spinner Collection

Weld and Purchase Street, 1900.

Trolley snow plow, 1930s (top left).

The new 611 car to Fort Rodman, 1929 (top right).

The Union Street Railway station, Purchase and William Streets, circa 1906 (bottom right). *The company opened this new, two-story headquarters in 1906. While waiting for a streetcar, passengers could sit in a spacious waiting room or at the soda fountain; or they could even shop at the Talbot Company, a men's and boys' clothing store, also on the first floor. General offices of the Union, the Dartmouth and Westport, and the New Bedford and Onset Street Railways were on the second floor. In 1929, the Union Street Railway moved to a terminal on Middle Street and in 1930, this building was razed to make way for Cherry & Co.*

Lawton's Corner, circa 1900 (bottom left). *Named for Lawton's Drug Store, which occupied the northwest corner of Union and Purchase for many years, the corner was long considered to be at the heart of downtown. Here, two women prepare to board the Padanaram car. At left, the rear end of a mail car be seen. In 1899 the Union Street Railway was granted the contract to carry the U.S. mail between New Bedford and Padanaram. The streetcars made three mail trips daily except on Sunday.*

Private Collection

The Standard-Times

The Standard-Times

Spinner Collection

Heritage Harvest

KERRY DOWNEY ROMANIELLO

Acushnet peaches, ripe for picking, Ashley Farm.

Food history, like art history or economic history, tells the story of the way people lived in a certain time and place. It tells us about nutrition, family life, celebrations, customs and the technology used in cultivation. When you look back at what the Indians and settlers were serving up, you can read the larger social history of the two peoples. Since the 1600s, the Three Sisters—corn, beans and squash—have been basic American fare, thanks to the Indians, and corn has been the greatest gift of all.

In this slice of food history, we will go straight to the larder of the settlers and Native Americans. Over the years, their culinary worlds slowly mingled, and we can smell these delicious flavors in our kitchens today. The birthplace of "American food" really was right here, in this New England, in Plymouth and Boston and Old Dartmouth.

We will also visit three historic working farms—sparkling gems in a sea of suburbanization—that have helped preserve our culinary history: Gray's Grist Mill in Westport, Ashley's Peaches in Acushnet and Smith-Long Acre farm in Westport, now the Westport Rivers Vineyard & Winery.

Imagine the lush beauty and abundance of this corner of Massachusetts a mere 350 years ago. The sandy coast separates dense woods of beech and cedar trees from the Atlantic. Thick bushes of wild huckleberries, blueberries, strawberries, grapes and plums grow in clusters through the woods, bordering creek beds and meadows.

Imagine the rivers and the sea teeming with fish and shellfish, bluefish, shad, eels, smelts, herring, clams, scallops, oysters and lobster. The woods full of deer, the skies alive with fowl—pheasant, partridge, quail, duck and heron. Red fox, quick and crafty, pursue long-eared rabbits as tiny chipmunks collect walnuts, chestnuts, hazelnuts, hickory and acorns.

The Wampanoag Indians flourish in this culinary wealth, on land extending from Cape Cod to northern Rhode Island, where they hunt, fish, forage and farm, moving in harmony with the seasons and the moons.

***Awe-chaw-chick-ken-in-nu-og (hunter men).** Two hunters spring from their hiding place in the marsh, a familiar scene before the arrival of white men. The marsh grass and bullrush that provide cover are still plentiful today.*

Bartholomew Gosnold, the first white man to extensively record his landing in the New World, was astonished by the abundance of fish, wildlife and flora everywhere. When he crossed the bay from Cuttyhunk in a flat-bottomed boat he landed near the mouth of the river later known as Acushnet. There, on the western shore, he was met by a company of native men, women and children who "with all courteous kindness entertained him, giving him skins of wild beasts, tobacco, turtle, hemp, artificial strings colored [wampum], and such like things as they had about them. The stately groves, flowery meadow and running brook afforded delightful entertainment to the adventurers."

Robert A. Henry

At regularly held community feasts, Indian families sup together on samp (cooked corn meal), roast venison rubbed with dried cranberry and fire-seared fish. The Sachem, or Chief, stands by the fire when the meal is finished to share stories of the tribe and pay homage to the gods of the harvest.

Imagine the year, 1602, early in summer, and a ship sails south along the coast of a peninsula whose waters are so thick with codfish that the ship's captain, Bartholomew Gosnold, names it Cape Cod. The visitor from London is awed by the abundance he finds. In his report, he writes that his men, "...feasted and grew fat on the young sea fowl they found in their nests."

Captain Gosnold makes brief contact with the Indians during an excursion to "Hap's Hill" (Round Hill) and several days later these Indians row out to his camp. For three days they visit, trading goods and good will. The English sailors enjoy the foods brought by the Indians, especially a soft flat cake made of corn. A brief but meaningful exchange has taken place, one that could mean survival to those who come later.

Fifty years later, the settlers discover there are greater hardships in store than their arduous ocean journey. They must learn new techniques of hunting, farming and cooking. Fortunately, they have good teachers.

The Wampanoag Indians teach them about the "Three Sisters," corn, squash and beans and how to plant, harvest and handle them. They plant kernels of corn in holes, along with a small fish, and cover it over with kelp and a hill of stones to deter small animals. As the corn begins to grow, the stones are removed and beans are planted alongside. They will eventually climb the corn stalks as the two crops grow together. Careful rows of these plantings are sown so

John White

various squash plants of pumpkin, butternut and hubbard can stretch comfortably down the center and produce well. The soft earth is tended regularly with a rake of deer antlers tipped with quahog shells.

Other vegetables, fruits and nuts require foraging. The settlers are shown where to dig for onions, what herbs are safe to be served as teas and used as medicines, primarily bay and fennel, walnut, hazelnut and how to identify the chestnut trees. They pick berries and plums throughout the summer and sun-dry them, layered in loosely woven rush and reed baskets, to preserve them throughout the year. The dried fruit is pressed into jerkies, brewed with strong herbal teas, and ground into fine powders used to sweeten breads and thicken soups.

Acquiring meat and fish was another matter for the first settlers. No pigs, horses or cows stood complacently behind weathered fencing; no fishmonger's shop was yet established. Hunting and fishing were a great challenge for the settlers. The Wampanoags showed them how to set snares and traps designed to outsmart wary, clever wild game.

Early American supper. *This watercolor made by artist/explorer John White at the Virginia colony in 1585 is among the earliest artistic renderings of Algonquian life. It shows an Indian man and woman eating hominy, made with hulled and boiled kernels of Indian corn. The settlers adopted this meal and ate it with bits of fish and meat.*

Similarly, the settlers learned of pemmican, a food prepared from lean, dried strips of meat pounded into paste, mixed with fat and berries and pressed into small cakes. Pemmican had an excellent keeping quality and was made primarily for taking on journeys. The Chippewa tribe boiled dried cranberries, anibimin, and then seasoned them with maple sugar or combined them with other foods.

Roger Williams observed how the Narragansetts took dried berries, sautaash, beat them to a powder and mixed them with parched corn to make sautauthig, "a delicate dish... which is as sweet to them as plum or spice cake to the English." They also mashed fresh strawberries in a mortar and mixed them with corn meal to make bread. [A Key into the Language, 1643]

The settlers learned how to locate and handle turtles and find nests of wild birds for eggs. They learned how to make special spears that caught eels without damaging the flesh and how to locate the air holes of clams and dig for them.

The Indians used no salt; salting for preservation was unknown to them. Instead they rinsed venison or fowl, pounded it very flat and air-dried it, while gutted cod, bluefish and eels were smoked over coals until completely dry. The resulting stuff was reconstituted in stews or packed "as is" to sustain a traveler for long journeys.

Staples in the early American larder included syrup made from boiled sap tapped from maple trees, powders of ground nuts and seeds and the rendered fat of bear, cold-weather ducks and geese.

No food impacted traditional cooking as much as maize, or corn. Corn roasted whole and eaten on the cob, corn kernels steamed fresh or dried with beans to make msickquatash, or succotash, and a fine corn meal for porridge, corn in fried flat cakes, in coal-baked breads, and in sweet Indian Pudding, all preparations adapted from the squaw's kitchen. Cakes of corn stirred into a paste of roasted pumpkin, a variety of askootasquahs, or squash, were the parents of pumpkin pies and breads.

Giant community clambakes were also a culinary gift to the settlers. The process was simple but preparation required an entire day and everyone pitched in. The children gather quahogs, corn and onions. Young men spear lobsters and fish while women collect stones and driftwood. A giant hole is dug in the sand and a fire built in the bottom.

Damp driftwood is piled up, surrounded by rocks and covered with seaweed. When the rocks are hot, the food is spread out in an even layer, then covered with more seaweed and deer skins. The shellfish, vegetables and fish cook for hours in the smoky steam bath, mingling flavors and aromas. An entire tribe would feast well into the night on succulent oysters and clams, smoked onions and sweet, tender corn.

Clambakes grew to become important social events in our early communities. Allen's Neck Friends has been drawing large crowds since they began in 1888, and Remington's Pavillion at Hix Bridge in Westport was filled to the rafters for weekly clambakes until its destruction about 60 years ago.

The settlers did not come to this New World empty handed. They brought with them generations of recipes, European cooking techniques, sacks of seeds and eventually domesticated animals including pigs, cows and sheep. They planted fields of oats and barley and set their sheep and cattle to graze in the vast, golden-green meadows of native hay. As they adapted

Clambake at Horseneck Beach, 1920s. Clambakes on the beach are a long tradition in southeastern Massachusetts. Here, a wedding dinner is being celebrated.

In the 1890s, a well-known area clambake man listed the ingredients he needed for a successful bake, serving 100 people: 5 bushels clams, 10 loaves brown bread, 5 gallons coffee, 5 lbs. tripe, 1/2 bushel onions, 30 lbs. fish, 2 pecks sweet potatoes, 1 peck white potatoes, 10 dz. ears of corn, 75 lbs. lobster, 20 lbs. sausage, 6 watermelons. According to Gilbert Machado, a legendary Fairhaven bakemaster: "You can't just use any type of rocks. They have to be porous so they can absorb the heat without cracking. The seaweed has to be of the rockweed variety so that it will hold water. The weeds should be piled to a depth of one foot over the rocks before the clams are spread. If less seaweed is used, the clams will be burned."

Private Collection

to the new climate and soil, the two culinary worlds slowly mingled and linger in our kitchens today.

What was this mingling of flavors and aromas? Take peas and beans, for example. The Indians cooked dried peas or lima beans slowly, over hot rocks, buried in the ground, in a mixture of bear grease and maple syrup. In the colonists' version, salt pork and black pepper are added and the pot is set over low coals to cook overnight. Brown bread often accompanied these baked beans, along with a steamed pudding of rye flour, corn meal and molasses. Boston Puritans prepared this almost every Sabbath because of the ease of the dish, hence the name Beantown.

Sausages nestled with the seafood and corn under the cover of rockweed and canvas at Quaker clambakes, and cranberries replaced raisins in traditional breads, puddings and cakes. Cream stirred into soups and succotash and buttery crusts that enveloped pumpkin and wild berry "pyes" signaled the introduction of dairy. Cornmeal "Jonny Cakes" appeared at nearly every meal—with syrup or molasses at breakfast, surrounding a thick slice of ham for lunch and alongside pan fried eel as one component of "snakes and cakes" for supper.

These early southern New Englanders were solid drinkers, practiced in the techniques of fermentation. Hard apple cider, pear perry, dandelion wine and hearty barley ale were consumed (by some) up to the legal quantity of five quarts per day. Even corn was tested for its fermentability. Eventually, bourbon was developed from these first experiments.

A mere 30 years after Plymouth was established, the colonists were trading salt cod as far as the West Indies. Livestock and produce farms, built on the edge of far-reaching fields acquired from the Indians, popped up like buds. Merchant and village mills, town centers and general stores soon followed. Smokehouses and grain stores cropped up nearby.

In 1720, the Salt House, a saltworks on the water's edge of Salters Point was established. By 1840, over a dozen saltworks lined the shores of Old Dartmouth. The fishing industry boomed as virgin waters seemed to hold more than could be caught. Businesses and farms of varied size and description were the cornerstone of early New England life.

We can still see evidence of these days past when we visit a historical mill, drive through the lush farmlands of Westport and Acushnet, or when we share a supper of traditional New England fare. Most of these original businesses are not around any more, but a few gems still exist.

Three such entities have survived the uncertainties of time to help us preserve and witness our culinary history: Gray's Grist Mill in Westport, Ashley's Peach Farm in Acushnet and the Smith Long-Acre Farm, now the site of the Westport Rivers Vineyard & Winery.

Remains of an old grist mill, somewhere in Old Dartmouth region, circa 1900.

Spinner Collection

Gray's Grist Mill

Gray's Grist Mill on Adamsville Road in Westport is the keeper of our story with corn. Corn! It had greater impact on the southern New Englanders' diet than any other food. This Indian treasure saved us from pellagra, a disease brought on by niacin deficiency, and corn meal replaced unavailable flours in basic English cookery.

The "Jonny Cake" is one offspring from the marriage of new and old worlds. The cakes are made from the milled, dried kernels of Narragansett Indian White Flint Corn. This starchy, eight-row variety is native to this area and was developed by the Indians for grinding. Gray's Grist Mill still follows the original procedures for drying and milling "Jonny Cake" cornmeal.

The corn is planted around Memorial Day, grows and ripens until harvest in October, then is placed in a crib to dry for seven to nine months. The kernels are then removed from the cob and winnowed (air blown) to remove the "glume," the connective membrane that secures the kernels to the cob. It is now ready to grind.

Milling at Gray's Grist Mill. Tim McTague demonstrates the process of grinding corn. First he shucks the dried husks. The kernels are then removed from the husks and winnowed (below). At right, Tim grinds the kernels into meal.

John K. Robson

John K. Robson

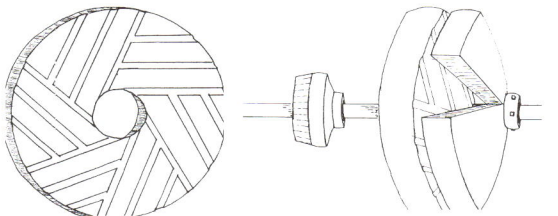

Nina Downey Levesque

The mill is a simple but imposing assembly of two enormous granite stones, a top stone and a bed stone. Both are cut with channels and the top stone is slightly concave. Kernels are fed into the hopper, a little at a time to prevent overloading, while the top stone rotates. As the stone turns, the corn is rolled through the channels and follows the concave structure outward. This progression from course grain to flour or meal is called "gradual reduction." The meal is then hand sifted and bagged.

Where did the name "Jonny Cake" come from? Gray's miller Tim McTague offers two possibilities. These flat cakes were often packed for long journeys, giving them the name "Journey Cake," that eventually slanged-down to "Jonny Cake," or perhaps they were named Jonny because of how commonly they were consumed. Tim refers to them as the "Yankee Tortilla."

The building itself was constructed in 1675 by Philip Taber and served as a village mill, rather than a merchant mill. James L. Gray purchased the mill and most of the surrounding businesses in 1878 and the mill still holds his name. The building went up for sale in the early 1980s and was purchased by Mr. Ralph Guild, who wished to preserve his favorite historical landmark.

Tim McTague is still amazed by the number of visitors the mill attracts and the impact it has on them. He generally "mills by demand," according to order but he is there and happy to show visitors around from Thursday through Sunday in summer and on weekends during the off-season. Go through Gray's Store, out the side door, and there's the mill, in a small building with the sloped roof.

Loaded family station wagons, RV's of retirees, and the convertibles of summer honeymooners fill the parking lot as these curious-seekers cross the doorway into Gray's Grist Mill. Perhaps the "oohs and aahs" are exclaimed not only for what the mill isn't—steel, sparks and loud noise—but for what it is: a functioning business that gives us a look 300 years into our past at who we were and who we still are.

Mill stone assembly at Gray's Grist Mill. Cross section view (far left) shows the concave top stone that turns over the bed stone (left).

Ready for sale. Mathew Olkavikas bags the sifted meal.

John K. Robson

Heritage Coast Recipes

Gray's General Store, Adamsville, RI, 1995. Facing Adamsville Road is the old general store, a town landmark, where jonnycake meal can be bought.

Thin Jonnycakes

2 cups Jonnycake meal
¾ cup cold water
½ teaspoon salt
1½ cup milk

Combine meal, salt and water. Stir in milk. Fry 3" cakes on a well-oiled, medium-hot skillet until edges are brown, then flip. Makes 20-25 Jonnycakes.

Thick Jonnycakes

2 cups Jonnycake meal
2 cups boiling water
1 teaspoon salt
¼ cup milk

Mix meal, salt, and boiling water. Let stand 5 minutes. Stir in milk. Fry 2½" cakes on a medium-hot, well-oiled skillet until browned, then flip. Makes 12 Jonnycakes.

Thick or thin Jonnycakes can be served for breakfast or as a side dish for supper. The meal itself is very versatile and can be used for polenta and cornbread. A small amount adds texture to homemade pizza crust.

Gray's Grist Mill. In the rear of the general store is the grist mill, where Tim McTague stands by the door.

Indian pudding (provided by Gray's Grist Mill)

2¼ cups milk
½ cup molasses
1½ teaspoon ginger
¼ teaspoon salt
4 tablespoons butter
½ cup Jonnycake meal
2 lightly beaten eggs

Scald 1¼ cup milk. Stir in butter, meal, eggs, molasses, salt and ginger. Pour into 1½ quart buttered casserole. Let stand 5 minutes. Pour 1 cup milk over the top. Bake at 300° for 1½ hours.

Cranberry Sauce

1 pound whole cranberries
⅓ cup sugar
¾ cup fresh apple juice

Combine the ingredients in a sauce pot and simmer over a medium-low flame for about 8 minutes, until the cranberries have burst. Serve warm or chilled.

Boston Baked Beans

½ pound Great Northern white beans
1 tablespoon mustard
4 slices bacon
1 onion, finely minced
3 cloves garlic, peeled
¼ cup molasses
¼ cup maple syrup
water

Cover the beans with water in a large pot and bring to a boil over high heat. Lower the heat to medium and allow beans to simmer for 20 minutes. Drain the beans in a colander, then transfer them to a large casserole. Toss the remaining ingredients with the beans, then cover the beans with twice their volume of water. Bake at 300° for 6-8 hours, or until tender. Check the water level of the beans as they cook and do not allow them to dry out. Add more water if necessary. Season with salt and pepper to taste.

The Smith-Long Acre Farm / Westport Rivers Vineyard & Winery

Rare is the farm that has remained in a family through the generations! For that matter, working farms of any type are becoming a rarity. But look again. Here and there, you will find a farm that is not only surviving, it is thriving, thanks to the imagination and grit of the present owners.

Such qualities have transformed the old Smith-Long Acre Farm on Hixbridge Road into the Westport Rivers Vineyard & Winery. Bob and Carol Russell, who purchased the farm from the Smith family in 1982, had the courage to dream and to begin growing a new crop—white grapes to make lush Chardonnay and Reisling wines.

Westport Rivers Vineyard & Winery contains the largest planting of *vitus vinifera* rootstock in New England. Their white European grapes are the hearty, short-season varietal that, with proper care, produce stellar wines. The Russell's celebrated their first harvest in 1989.

Once a vine is in the ground, it is good for 25 to 30 years, but there is much work to be done in season, such as spring trimming, mid-growth cutting and watching for insects and root rot. In the fall, when the grapes reach 20-30 degrees brix (the measure for determining how much sugar is in the grape), they are harvested, crushed, allowed to ferment and eventually turned into sparkling wines for dinner tables throughout New England.

Bob Russell is a New Jersey native and a metallurgist by trade. Carol Russell's father and grandfather operated the Germania Wine Cellars in Hammondsport, New York.

Russell Family at work and toasting the harvest. Robert Russell (with white sweatshirt), son Rob, wife Carol and faithful companion Morgan, tend to their winery.

John K. Robson

Though the property has a history of different owners since the original Dartmouth Purchase in 1652, it has always remained farmland. The Smith family acquired the farm in 1888 for $2500 and named it "Long Acre Farm" because of the extraordinary distance from the most northern point on the property to its most southern point.

The crops and livestock were varied and extremely well managed. Dairy cattle, chickens and horses lived in the protective cover of the stately barn, and potatoes, corn and grain stood in neat rows in manicured fields.

Perhaps the most notable crop the Smiths tended was the Macomber Turnip. This white-fleshed rutabaga was invented at a neighboring Westport farm in the 1870s by Adin and Elihu Macomber. This marvelous local invention was suited to our climate, stored beautifully and was easily afforded by people of

Grandpa Smith tilling the old Smith Farm, circa 1930s.

Russell Family Collection

modest means, but most of all, it tasted delicious. Soup of simmered diced turnip, dried meat, beans and corn would provide a hearty meal on a cold winter evening.

The Smith farm earned a reputation far beyond the town. The March 26, 1973 issue of *Poor Bill's Almanac* published a story from a 1938 publication containing an article on the Smith Farm. The author writes, "…there is nothing quite so satisfying as the sight of a farm well managed. That feeling is more pronounced in the case of a farm…because of the knowledge that the land is being devoted to the production of necessities."

This devotion to honest work in a family business continues on that same property with the Russell family. Their belief in the "stewardship of the land" and their "commitment to the preservation of our home" has led them to their successes. They hope more people will make similar efforts to preserve and promote what they call "The Heritage Farm Coast," an area rich with possibilities for farm, fish and wine.

Russell Family Collection

John K. Robson

Robert and Carol Russell and their homestead.

William, the grain reaper (top left). The inscription reads: "Uncle William, Grandpa Smith's brother, using a grain reaper or binder. The dark horse was called Fan Mare and the white one called either Clink or Dexter. Uncle William spoke with a heavy Scottish accent and lived with Grandma, Grandpa, and niece, Janie."

John Smith going to market, 1930s. His produce bagged, Mr. Smith is off to New Bedford for deliveries.

Russell Family Collection

Ashley's Peach Orchard

Bringing in the harvest, 1965 (right).

Ashley produce wagon *(opposite page, left). The old wagon was refurbished by Ernie Ventura and helps promote the peach farm to motorists along Main Street in Acushnet.*

Crops of Ashley Farm *(below & opposite page).*

Nina Downey Levesque

Journey through North Fairhaven along Main Street and it will take you through the center of Acushnet and into some of the area's most magnificent farmland. On the Ashley Farm in Acushnet, orchards of peaches, plums, nectarines and apples flourish under the attentive care of Diane and Ernie Ventura. The property has been in Diane's family for over 200 years. Diane proudly points out that she is the fifth generation in her family to turn out Ashley peaches.

"When you run a peach farm, some people think that all you do is pick the peaches when they're ripe and sell them!" says Diane. In fact, peach season in Acushnet begins in earnest during March, when the orchard becomes a full-time job. "A peach tree usually has a life span of 15 years. We did constant replanting for the first five years, bringing the orchard nearest the house back to life. We buy new trees as little twigs and it's five years before they begin to produce. We have to pull out the old trees with a rented backhoe, and Ernie hand-pulls the extra roots. We hand-water the young trees in 50-gallon drums and constantly prune.

"In May, we rent bees at blossom time to ensure proper pollination, and we maintain a rigid spray schedule, using the least hazardous materials. By now, the trees are starting to form peaches. In June, we're thinning 80 percent of the fruit off the trees."

After all this work?

"We have to give the best ones the space and strength to grow," Diane replies. "We do each branch by hand, which is arduous and time-consuming. The ones that fall to the ground become mulch. When the branches get overladen with fruit, you must prop them with sticks. Peach trees are very willowy and break easily. During the last week of July, the fruit is usually ready. Different trees have different varieties, and they come ripe at different times. Each variety has a different flavor.

"Peaches are the riskiest fruit to grow in New England," says Ernie, who wipes his brow and lays his tractor to rest. "Peach trees are easily injured in winter, but we're on Long Plain here and the high elevation and prevailing winds work in our favor. The only way for us to maintain quality fruit is to keep this a small operation. We both do everything—lug, water, prune, pick."

Peach season in southeastern Massachusetts begins the first week of August and ends the third week of September, a glorious time for peach eaters and a frenetic time for peach growers. The Ventura's admit they only barely make a living, but both agree you couldn't buy their quality of life for a million dollars.

Diane says, "I love the air, the orchards; I love watching the trees blossom, the fruit ripen. I feel

Ron Rolo, The Standard-Times

blessed knowing my father and grandfather and great-grandfather and great-great-grandfather lived here and worked this land. It's a piece of heaven."

With the help of her cousin-in-law, Bill Kells, the family genealogist, and letters and journals left by William Allen Ashley, Diane's great-great-grandfather, the history of the farm has been assembled.

Joseph Ashley was the first relative to arrive in Plymouth, in 1675. According to Mr. Kells, he is suspected to have been a privateer, mainly because he purchased his property on the Rochester/Freetown line with 50 Spanish dollars, not a common currency in usual commerce. His descendant, William Ashley, purchased a portion of the existing land in Acushnet around 1790.

The farm remained small until it was left to William Allen Ashley and his bride Hannah Crapo Ashley. After William returned from a five-year whaling voyage in June 1867, he put his full attention on the farm. According to their journals and letters, Hannah had kept a firm handle on the farm in her husband's absence, even taking produce to the new open market in New Bedford.

Diane and Ernie Ventura read these journals almost daily because they tell about Saturday callers, church on Sunday and a busy seven-day work week, a life much like their own. Mr. Ashley also recorded the sale or additions of crops and livestock. Eggs, beans, corn, potatoes and onions were harvested and sold at the market, apples were brought to the mill for pressing, and allusion to the well-being of the cattle were all included in the 1884 journals.

1895 saw the addition of rhubarb, grapes and asparagus while 1896 brought the planting of cabbage. Cucumbers arrived in 1903, tomatoes were first mentioned two years later. One entry, made in 1879, outlines his interest in peaches, naming several varieties, like Groth's Early Red and Reeves Favorite, none of which are available today. There is no mention again until 1905 when he writes that there was "one bushel picked."

Today the Ventura's grow 30 varieties of peaches and they won't sell a single one until it is perfectly ripe. Diane feels a certain satisfaction in keeping the continuity of family history intact. She walks the same path her ancestors walked and she works the same lands with the same determination and belief in hard work.

Diane's favorite quote from her great-great-grandfather's journals: "All those who pass through the door of success find it labeled push." —William Allen Ashley, 1893.

Words to live by? They are for the Ventura's.

Kerry Downey Romaniello grew up in South Dartmouth and cooked up a storm as a child. She graduated from the New England Culinary Institute in Vermont and Madeleine Kamman's School for American Chefs in St. Helena, California. Kerry, formerly a sous chef for the Beringer Vineyard in Napa Valley, is a food and wine consultant for the Westport Rivers Vineyard & Winery.

Ventura Family Collection

Nina Downey Levesque

"Best Wishes," from Annie, Fall River, June 1914.

The Fall River Nanny

From the Diary of Annie Elizabeth Ward

In 1914, a young Englishwoman came to America to visit and vacation. After five months, she decided if she were going to stay on, she'd better pay her own way. Annie Ward became a nanny in the home of Mr. & Mrs. Russell Leonard on Robeson Street in Fall River. At this time, Mr. Leonard was head of the Wampanoag Mill but is better known as the longtime head of the Pepperell Manufacturing Company.

Annie's journal tells of her two years in Fall River and her happy times with the Leonards, juxtaposed with ominous letters from her homeland, which rumble with the sounds of World War I. She falls in love and worries about betraying her dearest friend who is fighting a war.

This bittersweet memoir is full of joy and foreboding, full of the romance of young people and the harsh reality of war. There are also some delightful scenes of old Fall River; of dancing and silent films; of picnics and parks. On a shopping trip, Annie and her friend, Christine, try on every hat in the store: "wide-brimmed hats, full crowned hats, some with ribbons and plumes, one even with a flower arrangement."

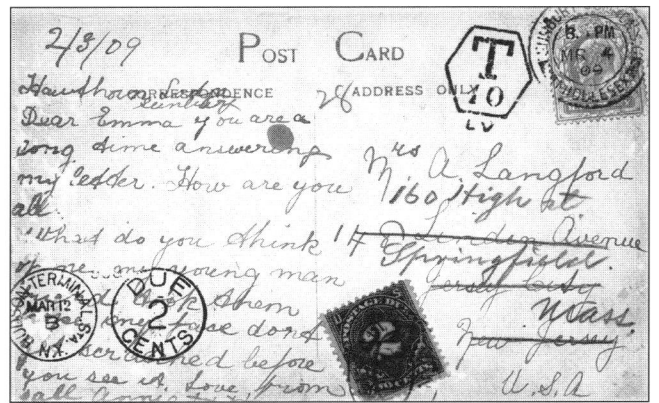

Mail from Annie to her friends in the U.S., 1909. Courtesy of Susan Hill.

Friday, 2nd January, 1914

Life has been busy for me since I joined the staff at the Leonard's household. The time has been so enjoyable and I have met so many people. The Leonards are such friendly people. Mr. Leonard is the head of the Wampanoag Mills here in Fall River, which is the biggest manufacturing town of cotton cloth in America with 111 cotton mills. It is the largest city in southern Massachusetts with a population of 119,295 (so Mr. Leonard informs me).

Russell Leonard is a tall, dapper man who cares a great deal about his work. He is very young for such an important post, being only 23, but he accepts the responsibility with relish, and works very conscientiously. He is often away for days on business and when home seems to enjoy talking to me about Fall River and his work in the mill, usually at dinner in the evening.

Last night during dinner he told me about a mill strike which took place in Lawrence, Massachusetts almost two years ago on January 12, 1912. Then the men, women and children went on strike to protest over a reduction in their wages.

I did not declare this to Mr. Leonard, but my sympathy went to the strikers. It is a hard life working in the mills, and the rewards are few, so a reduction in wages must have been a cruel blow.

I also have great admiration for the way in which the women of America are fighting for the right to vote. I feel the time has come for us to have more of a say in our own lives.

Saturday, 3rd January, 1914

The weather today is bitterly cold, there have been several snow flurries during the day. I think I may have caught a chill. Mrs. Leonard is extremely graceful and beautiful, every inch a lady. She has an artistic flair, and this reflects in her clothes, which are beautifully cut, and the inside decoration of the house, for which she is much admired.

Friday, 9th January, 1914

I have been confined to bed these past few days. The chill I spoke of turned into an unpleasant heavy cold. I have been taking Blackberry Vinegar three times a day for my cold and Bid (the cook) has been sending up an awful concoction of linseed oil, liquorice roots, sugar, lemon juice and rum for the cough when troublesome.

Mrs. Leonard has been most attentive throughout my short illness, bringing me soup and sitting with

Wampanoag Mill, 1996. Along the Quequechan River, the mills where Mr. Leonard worked still stand. Today, the sound of looms and machines are replaced by the rustling of busy outlet shoppers, diners and office workers.

Joseph D. Thomas

me. In return, she likes me to tell her about the family back home. And so I tell her of my mother, Elizabeth, my father, John, and my brothers, Jack, Tom, Sam and Fred, and my sisters, Edie and of course Emma, and all my nieces and nephews, at the last count, seventeen in all, twelve girls and four boys!

Sunday, 11th January, 1914

I feel so much stronger today and therefore have been sitting out in a chair. I have not spoken before of the house here in Fall River, so shall remedy this immediately.

Mr. Leonard tells me that the name 'Fall River' comes from the Indian word 'quequechan' which means falling river. Fall River seems to be divided into different areas. The house here is in the Highlands area. Many businessmen and mill owners live here. The houses are large with backyards, and there is much space in between each house.

Most people who work in the mills live in the south end of the city in an area known as Corky Row where the tenement houses, to say the least, are cramped. Many Irish immigrants live in Corky Row. The south end seems to have all different nationalities, although the French Canadians keep mostly to the Flint area.

Our house here is on Robeson Street, number 1096. As the number indicates, it is a long street, about four miles long. It begins at Bedford and ends near St. Patrick's Cemetery.

Sunday, 14th June, 1914

Today was a beautiful day, the sun was so warm. I took Helena to North Park, which is a public recreation park, not far from our home on Robeson Street. We had a lovely time and I made the acquaintance of a man called Charles O'Brien. He asked me to accompany him for a walk in the evening. I accepted. The evening was a very pleasant one.

Monday, 22nd June, 1914

Today Helena is two years old. It being such a glorious day, and Mr. Leonard not having to go to the Mill, it was decided that we should go for an automobile ride. Helena sat on my lap while Mrs. Leonard had three month old Field, Helena's baby brother.

We drove for some miles until we found a suitable place to stop. We had a picnic there and began the journey home at 6 pm. Helena became very tired on the homeward journey and fell asleep on my lap, her thick hair cascading down over my knees. Why do children look so adorable when they are asleep?

Annie's neighborhood, Robeson Street, 1996. The residence at 1096 Robeson Street is the first house (second building) from right, behind the small tree. This was Annie's first home with the Leonard's. Intersecting Robeson Street, at right, is Stanley Street, where the family later moved. At left is the Highland School; in the distance is the Braga Bridge.

Joseph D. Thomas

Courtesy of Walter Mitchell

Academy Building, circa 1880. *At the corner of South Main and Pleasant Streets, in the Borden Block, Fall River's Academy of Music officially opened its doors in 1876. In addition to concerts, the Academy also featured live theater, ballroom dancing, and eventually, moving pictures. Her diary shows that the Academy was Annie's favorite hot spot for dancing, movies and entertainment.*

Thursday, 25th June, 1914

Had a letter today from Phyllis Horton, my friend at home in England. Everybody seems well, but the situation generally does not seem good. There is a fair amount of unemployment and much "squabbling" Phyllis says, by several countries in Europe.

Friday, 26th June, 1914

I've realized I have not yet mentioned Bid. She is not only the cook of the house, but a wonderful Irish lady and my very good friend. She is a little older than me, although I dare not ask her age for fear of getting my ears boxed!

She has been with the Leonards for many years, and in fact brought up Mr. Leonard since he was orphaned at eleven years of age. Her real name is Bridget Kennedy, and, like me, is short and fat. She always wears her straight brown hair tied back in a bun at the back of her head, which in turn brings out the color of her lovely hazel eyes.

We spend many evenings together, talking and sewing, as she rocks continuously in her beloved rocking chair. Her chair is her pride and joy. Bid was very good to me during my first few months here. During the long winter evenings she taught me how to tell fortunes, which is her other passion.

Monday, 29th June, 1914

Mr. Leonard tells me that a Duke in Europe has been assassinated. He was Austrian and I believe his name was Ferdinand. It doesn't sound at all Austrian to me.

Thursday, 2nd July, 1914

Tonight I went to Devoll's Dancing Academy for the first time with one of the girls who helps Bid in the kitchen, Marie. Marie met her fiance there, William. They appear to make a nice couple. William is tall and thin, sporting the usual moustache, and looked very dapper tonight in his double-breasted lounge suit and Panama hat. Marie complemented William in a quiet way, wearing her hobble skirt and pretty lace blouse.

Devoll's gives private dance lessons at very reasonable rates. Tonight we were taught the Foxtrot. I danced with several different partners, and had a real good time.

Thursday, 30th July, 1914

I'm afraid I have been bad yet again and have not written an entry in my diary for two weeks. The truth is I have been so busy, and my life so wonderful, I have not had time to think about writing. But now I feel I must write down the reason for this shortcoming. I think I am in love!

I have met a wonderful man by the name of Charles O'Brien. We met quite by chance one bright sunny morning six weeks ago. I had taken Helena to North Park as it was such a beautiful day. She took her ball to play with. Unfortunately, a sudden breeze took the ball off into the trees.

Helena and I began a search at once, and had almost given up hope of finding it when a dark haired clean shaven young man appeared at Helena's side and enquired whether the ball he held in his hand was the item she was looking for so diligently. Helena was delighted. She gave a small curtsy and muttered, "Thank you, sir."

I naturally thanked him also. He touched his fine hat and told me it was a pleasure, then enquired of my daughter's name! Of course I then enlightened him as to Helena's name and my own services as her nanny. It seemed natural for us to sit down among the trees and continue our conversation. I must admit to being

Ruth Edwards

overwhelmed by the young man. As he talked he seemed to possess a certain magnetism which set him apart from other men I had met.

Oh, I am being called for downstairs, I must go now, I shall write more tomorrow.

Wednesday, 5th August, 1914

Mr. Leonard reported to me at breakfast this morning with some gravity, that Great Britain is at war with Germany! It seems that since the assassination of the Austrian Duke Ferdinand, events have been escalating. On August 1st, Germany declared war against Russia, then declared war on France on the 3rd, with Great Britain doing the same against Germany yesterday. I am so shocked! I have written home to the family for further news.

Saturday, 8th August, 1914

I regret I have been greatly in demand these past three days and have found no time for putting pen to paper. The Leonards had a big dinner party on Friday evening, consequently, Thursday and Friday were busy with preparation for the evening. Mrs. Leonard seemed to need my opinion on arranging the flowers, and I assisted Bid, Marie, Christine and the others in the kitchen, as a great deal of food needed to be prepared and cooked. I do not think the occupants of 1096 Robeson Street could survive too many dinner parties in one year!

Sunday, 9th August, 1914

Today is a rest day. The house seems so quiet today. The Leonards and Helena have gone out in the automobile with a picnic, to an unknown destination. They say they will drive until they find a suitable place to stop and have their lunch. I'm pleased they found the time to be together, so much of their life is spent apart…

Ruth Edwards

North Park postcard, circa 1900. *Located in the highlands close to the Leonard's home, North Park was one of the city's most important recreational sites. The park is designed by the famous landscape architect Frederick L. Olmstead, whose most famous work is Central Park in New York. In North Park, Annie met "a wonderful man by the name of Charles O'Brien."*

Courtesy of Walter Mitchell

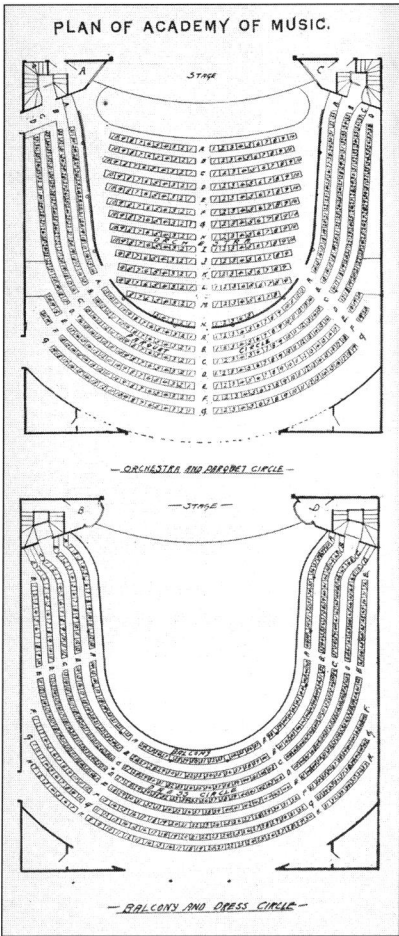

Academy of Music seating plan. With a seating capacity of 2,000, the Academy was the city's largest theater and host to shows of national renown, starring such famous performers as Fritz Kreisler, Joseph Jefferson, Ruth Chatterton and Sara Bernhardt. In 1910, Edwin Booth performed and received 50 percent of gate and $1500/night. Seats selling for 25 to 75 cents increased to $2.50. [Victorian Vistas: Fall River, 1901-1911]

Charlie Chaplin and Jackie Coogan In a scene from "The Kid," 1921, (opposite page).

I now have time to tell more about Charles O'Brien. He is tall, approximately six feet, (he towers above my height of 5 ft. 1 inch) with thick, straight black hair, is clean shaven and a snappy dresser.

The first time I met him he was wearing a single breasted lounge suit. His trousers had an immaculate crease down the front and turnups. He wore a bow tie and carried a walking cane which gives the appearance of a very distinguished and well-to-do young gentleman.

It is very easy to converse with him, he is so friendly, but gentle and kind. I am at a loss to see what the attraction is for me, with my dumpy figure and hair which refuses to do as it is told! After our meeting in the park, he took me to the Academy on the following Saturday, where we saw a Charlie Chaplin movie, which was very funny. He presented me with a bouquet of violets and afterwards walked me home to Robeson Street. No man has ever made me feel so happy, wanted and special. How wonderful it is to be in love!

Monday, 10th August, 1914

I have been reading up on Charlie Chaplin in a movie review. He is such a very popular man, everybody loves him. I was surprised to learn he born in England. It says this year he was signed a contract which gives him over $1000 a week, thus making him the highest paid star ever. If all goes to plan, he will make 34 films this year in 34 weeks. How incredible!

Thursday, 13th August, 1914

Have heard today that we (Great Britain) have now declared war against Austria-Hungary. This is surely madness!

Monday, 17th August, 1914

I have at last heard from home. I had a letter from my brother Fred yesterday. He tells me all are well at home in French Street. Mother is fit and healthy and sends her love. How I wish she could read and write herself.

My brothers Sam and Jack have joined the army to fight the Germans and so has my dearest friend, Bert.

Fred says all unmarried men below the age of 30 have been urged to volunteer for service but everybody at home believes this will be a short war with all the men back home for Christmas jingling money in their pockets. I certainly hope that is true.

Thursday, 20th August, 1914

Today I had a letter from Bert, informing me that he has 'joined up.' His mother was not keen for him to do so, but he says he was firm with her and told her it was his duty to his country. Why could he not have been firm with her over our future I wonder?

He has joined the Royal Engineers with his older brother, Bill, as a private and they do not fight but use their skills to help the other soldiers. As Bert has apprenticed as a carpenter, this is the work he will be doing.

It rests my mind to know that he will not be taking part in the fighting, but my conscience is not clear when I think of Bert at home, waiting to be ordered overseas, and myself here in Fall River…and Charles O'Brien.

What would Bert's feelings be if he knew? I feel wretched…

Why must life be so complicated?

Wednesday, 26th August, 1914

There are bad reports in the newspapers. They say Great Britain has sent 100,000 men overseas since war broke out, but the Germans are better armed than the British, and also well led. There has been a large battle at a town called Marnes in France, three days ago. The British were forced to retreat.

How I wish I knew whether my nearest and dearest were safe. I feel farther away from those I love than ever before.

The President of the United States, Woodrow Wilson, is reported to have proclaimed neutrality in the war, He will not take sides.

Thursday, 27th August, 1914

Marie, Christine and I all went dancing at the Academy. Had a real good time. Christine introduced me to a young man known as Tiverton Joe, a strange character. He struts about like a peacock full of his own self-importance, yet I wonder whether this is his true self, or if it is all an act.

Tiverton is a town to the south of Fall River, in the state of Rhode Island. It is only a short distance away.

Saturday, 29th August, 1914

All the girls came in to my room this evening. We had a lot of fun playing the victrola.

Sunday, 30th August, 1914

Went to Church in the morning. Nobody here in Fall River seems to be concerned about the war in Europe. To them, it is so many thousand of miles away. Charlie came to see me and stayed all evening.

Spinner Collection

South Main Street and the Academy neighborhood, circa 1914. *During the city's industrial heyday, theater and the arts thrived in Fall River. After each performance, horse cars would be at the front door ready to take patrons home to any part of the city.*

The Academy began showing moving pictures when the Count d'Hauterville exhibited his "views" before a standing room audience in 1902. Appealing to the tastes of children, the Professor's patented shows featured views of "Little Red Riding Hood" and "Alladin of the Wonderful Lamp." By 1914, the popular work of Chaplin and other stars were marquis events. By 1928, the Academy was converted into a movie theater, and in 1980, it was converted into apartments. [Victorian Vistas: Fall River, 1901-1911]

Monday, 7th September, 1914

Christine and I went dancing at the Academy. It is a huge building, there is so much to do there. There are two theatres, one for plays, and vaudeville, the other shows movies. There is also the dance floor. We had a marvellous time, but, as usual, the ladies outnumbered the men. There is never enough to go round!

Tuesday, 8th September, 1914

Terrible news has been reported in the newspapers. Battles are taking place in France at a town called Marne. The deaths and casualties are said to be horrific, and they are calling it the greatest battle in the world. I feel deeply worried, alone and so helpless. I have made friends here, yes, but there is no one who understands.

Courtesy of Walter Mitchell

Saturday, 12th September, 1914

Charles came to see me tonight, which cheered me up greatly. We talked at length about the war, this seemed to help me. I told him all about Bert, and our long courtship, also Bert's mother, and all the problems that entails, and lastly of the conflict between my strong feelings for Charles and the sentiment and regard in which I hold Bert.

Charles reassured me, telling me that he is happy for our friendship to continue, and is glad to know more of my background and my ties back home in England.

Saturday, 19th September, 1914

Christine, Bridget and I took the trolley to Lincoln Park. This is an amusement park and is great fun. It lies between Fall River and North Dartmouth, 12 miles to the east. We both had a wonderful time. Took the trolley home, also, back to Fall River.

Sunday, 20th September, 1914

Have realized I have now been with the Leonards for over a year. How the time has flown. I have grown so fond of Helena, I hope she has of me also. I am really so happy here that I sometimes feel guilty for doing so. Am I crazy?

Friday, 25th September, 1914

I have had a letter from Bert! It has travelled such a long way, from France to England, inside a letter to his mother, who forwarded it on to me here. The letter is undated and is a short letter, mainly just to let me know he is well. It must have been written during the time the Battle of Marne was taking place.

He sends his love and tells me his brother Bill and himself are kept busy making duckboards for the

Spinner Collection

Ruth Edwards

Bid, the cook.

Kids at Lincoln Park, circa 1910 (left). LIncoln Park was built by the street railway companies of Fall River and New Bedford to increase ridership on their trolley lines. It featured roller coasters, ferris wheels, arcades and ballrooms. From the time it opened at the turn of the century, until its closing in the 1980s, Lincoln Park was the area's most exciting amusement arena for kids and the young at heart.

trenches which the men appear to live in. He doesn't speak of the battle, I expect he is not permitted to write about such things.

Also enclosed is a photograph of Bert and his regiment, taken before they left England. Mrs. Brock put it in, she said, because Bert had sent her two copies. Does this mean the old lady is having a change of heart where I am concerned?

Friday, 2nd October, 1914

The weather has been much better today. I took Helena with me shopping. I have been able to save a few dollars for a new winter coat, the one I brought from England is looking worn and shabby. I managed to buy a reasonably priced navy blue one. It feels really warm and Helena said she liked it. It is a single breasted coat, which ends 3" from my ankles. The sleeves have cuffs and it has a half belt at the back of the coat. I was also able to get my laced boots repaired.

Friday, 9th October, 1914

My heart is breaking as I write this entry. I had a letter yesterday from my brother Fred informing me that Sam, my youngest brother, dearest Sam, has been killed. How, why did this have to happen? My poor little Sam. The details, as ever, are scant. Mother was informed by telegram that Sam had been killed in action during battle at the Marne last month. I am so distressed, I cannot write any more.

Monday, 12th October, 1914

I went to church yesterday to pray for Sam, Jack, Bert and all the others in this awful war. I pray that Christmas will come quickly, aren't all the experts saying it will be over by then?

Wednesday, 4th November, 1914

I have not felt the inclination to write for the last two weeks. I have felt low and homesick, the news from home is all bad. The Germans have started to use poison gas on our troops in their effort to win this diabolical war.

Thursday, 12th November, 1914

The nights are drawing in now, and becoming decidedly chilly. Tonight I have been reading more about Charlie Chaplin, who must be the most popular man in the States today, more so than President Woodrow Wilson, often playing a comic drunk. They say his success is attributed to the way he is able to portray both humor and sadness simultaneously.

Tuesday, 24th November, 1914

I am increasingly feeling that I should go home and help in the war effort. I had a letter from my friend, Phyllis Horton last week. She has found a

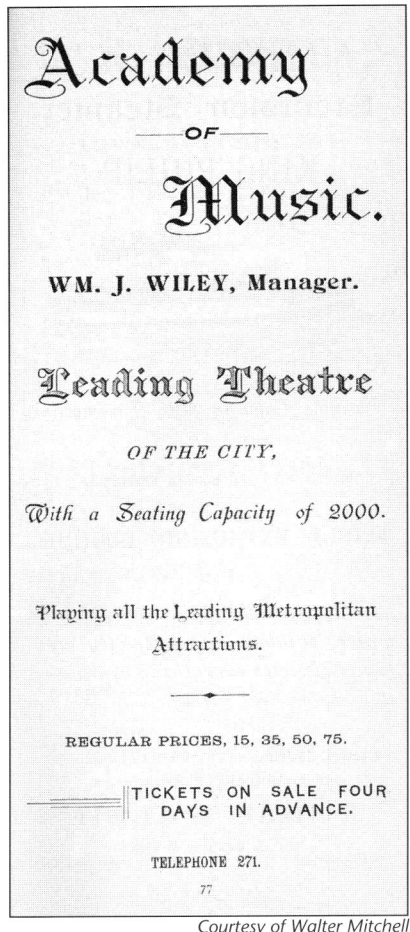

Courtesy of Walter Mitchell

Annie Ward, at home in Middlesex, England, 1909 (right).

worthwhile job in a munitions factory. She tells me that with so many men enlisting for the services, women are taking the place of men in factories and in the fields in Britain. I feel so useless here, I can do nothing to help. If I was able to return home, I could perhaps obtain a job on the land, or even a factory, although I have no experience, but, then, who has.

Unfortunately, my thoughts are just that, thoughts. I have not enough money saved yet to afford the journey home.

Friday, 27th November, 1914

I feel so much better having come to a firm decision. The war has occupied my thoughts for several months, I've not been able to think of anything else.

I had a long talk with Bid too. She is so wise I feel at ease with her. She has convinced me to adhere to my decision about eventually returning to England, if it is what I really want, but at the same time to enjoy the time I have left here in Fall River, however long that may be. I think I will take that advice.

Thursday, 10th December, 1914

Preparations for Christmas have begun in the Leonard household. The Leonards, as in previous years, will be entertaining, which means much hard work for those in the kitchen. I have been trying to lend a hand with the cleaning, as Mrs. Leonard naturally wants the whole house spic-and-span for her visitors.

Wednesday, 16th December, 1914

Mr. Leonard did not rush off to his office as usual this morning, but stayed awhile and spoke about the war. He understood, he said, my frustration over the war in Europe. But he assured me that many manufacturers and bankers all over the States were aiding Great Britain and her allies in every way possible, although this was not common knowledge as President Wilson and his colleagues at the White House wanted to maintain neutrality for the present.

Courtesy of Susan Hill

Sunday, 27th December, 1914

What a week! It sure has been busy. The excitement for me started on Tuesday 22nd, my 28th birthday, then onto the Academy for a wonderful evening of dancing. To experience Charles attempting the fox trot was hilarious. We had a wonderful night, I arrived home at 1AM, but I didn't care! It was pretty hard getting up at 6AM the next morning.

Christmas too, of course, was wonderful, if a little more sedate! The Leonards, as last year, spent the morning with Helena, and the gifts Santa Claus had brought. Her little brother, Field, is of course too young to understand, he's only nine months old.

Myself and the other staff were asked in, one by one, during the afternoon, to receive their gifts from Mr. & Mrs. Leonard. I was given a beautiful cameo broach which I was very pleased with. Helena stayed with me in the evening while the guests were downstairs, until I put her to bed. We played with her new china doll that Santa had bought her, and tried on the velvet dress from her mother. I'm hoping to take her to the park tomorrow to try her new whip and top, it's painted in a glorious red.

Friday, 8th January, 1915

I stayed at home and sewed all evening. The newspapers are full of an amazing event which, it is reported, happened at the battlefields in France. It appears that both the British and German soldiers ceased fighting on Christmas Day. For a few hours there was an informal truce. There are even reports that each side shook hands and played football together! Unfortunately, the fighting was renewed at midnight.

Thursday, 4th February, 1915

Marie and I went shopping together this afternoon. I'm afraid I was frivolous and bought myself a muff. It is a barrel-shaped muff, they have come back into fashion, and has a brown ribbon attached to it, so I can hang it round my neck.

Friday, 5th February, 1915

It has been a busy day today as we are moving house tomorrow. Moving, it seems, is the best way to bring out a temper. Bid has been very touchy about the way her pots and pans, and especially the best cutlery have been packed. At one stage, she unpacked a whole box and proceeded to repack it in her own way.

Such utter chaos! We spent our last night at Robeson Street playing cards. Everything else had been packed away!

Saturday, 6th February, 1915

Oh, what a day for moving. The snow fell thick and fast in the morning, making an awkward task more difficult. Everybody seems delighted with the house, including myself. Stanley Street is a side street off Robeson Street, about halfway down Robeson Street. Mrs. Leonard cannot wait to get started on adding her own personal touches to the new house. She is naturally artistic and will, in time, redecorate the whole house, I have no doubt.

Saturday, 13th March, 1915

Mr. & Mrs. Leonard, Helena, Field and I went for a nice ride in the auto to Tiverton. The weather was cold but sunny. I dressed in my warm coat and made sure I took along my new muff, and wrapped Helena up warmly.

Ruth Edwards.

Ruth Edwards

In the evening I went with Christine to see Charlie Chaplin in his first film for Mack Sennett and his Keystone Film Co. It was called "Making a Living." We had a real good laugh. We were still laughing at the end when as usual, he hitches up his baggy pants, twitches his moustache and walks off down the road.

Tuesday, 16th March, 1915

Charles took me dancing tonight, we had a lovely time. He dances so beautifully, he is so light on his feet, he appears to glide along. It makes dancing such a pleasure. Home 11 p.m.

Thursday, 25th March, 1915

Had a busy day. I went to Roads Corner with Christine, then went for a long walk. We left the hustle and bustle of town and walked through the countryside until eventually we found a suitable place to stop. The birds were singing, pleased that spring is on its way at last.

Everything seemed pleased to be alive, including myself. Christine and I just laid for some time on the grass, saying nothing, soaking up the warm sun, each with our own thoughts. Amid the peace, my thoughts turned to war. I have heard nothing from the family, and am feeling very anxious. How helpless and useless to them I am.

Saturday, 27th March, 1915

Went down town with Christine. I bought a hat after some fun trying them all on. There was such a variety. We tried on wide-brimmed hats, tall crowned hats, some with ribbons and plumes, one even with a flower arrangement. There were some with brims, some without, some made of beaver, others made of velvet or straw. I finally settled on a straw hat which is worn tilted to one side, trimmed with a red satin ribbon and tulle.

Sunday, 2nd May, 1915

A lonesome day. I had a very bad inflamed eye. I made an apple poultice, using two cooking apples, which I had chopped and boiled in water until soft, then put two spoonfuls into a square of muslin, and put it on my eye, but it did not seem to help a great deal. Stayed at home all day.

Mr. Leonard showed me a New York newspaper he obtained recently. It shows an announcement by the Cunard shipping line of their forthcoming Atlantic voyages. Next to it, however, is a warning from the Imperial German Embassy reminding travellers that a state of war exists between Germany and Great Britain, and her allies, that this war zone extends to the water, and that passengers travel at their own risk. Is this going to make my hopes of getting home more remote? Mr. Leonard says most people are disregarding the warning. Perhaps they are right to do so.

Monday, 10th May, 1915

It is now being reported that many lives have been lost on the sunken *Lusitania*. There were 1,357 passengers on board plus the crew of 700. Among the passengers were many well-known people such as Alfred Vanderbilt, a very rich American. It seems the torpedo struck at 2 o'clock as many people were having their lunch. Some of the survivors have been reported as saying there was a frantic rush for the lifeboats which were much too few, and some of these crashed into the ship and were rendered useless. It must have been a terrible time for all those on the ship, so very frightening.

Wednesday, 12th May, 1915

The press have been criticizing President Wilson for his lack of action over the sinking of the *Lusitania*. They say he should demand an apology from the Germans and an assurance that such a catastrophe does not occur again. All he has said so far is, and I quote, "There is such a thing as a man being too proud to fight. There is such a thing as a nation being so right that it does not need to convince others by force that it is right."

I hardly feel that this statement helps the victims and their bereaved families. He should do something, preferably get involved in this war, and help America's allies. I certainly wish I could do something, anything.

Friday, 14th May, 1915

There was more news of the *Lusitania* in the paper. It is now likely that 1,200 lives were lost, 128 of them Americans, with 750 survivors. Bodies are being swept up on the Irish beaches daily. The Cunard company has offered rewards for bodies found of 1 (pound) each, but 2 (pounds) for every American and 1,000 (pounds) for Alfred Vanderbilt. That seems rather sordid to me.

Saturday, 15th May, 1915

I took Helena to the Park in the afternoon. I saw Charlie and made a date to meet in the evening. It was a pleasant evening, which we spent strolling round the park, talking. Unfortunately the weather changed suddenly. A fierce storm blew up, the heavens opened and we had to run frantically under the nearest oak tree, to retreat from the hailstones. We laughed at ourselves, we were so wet through. Then a wonderful thing happened. Charles asked me to marry him, and stay here in the U.S. with him.

It is so hard to put the way I felt at that moment onto paper. I was surprised, shocked, extremely pleased and worried, all rolled into one. I love him, I know that, but do I love him enough to leave my family permanently? I managed to stutter "I will have to think on it" which seems totally inadequate and also unkind, but Charlie said no more. We remained under the tree, watching the hailstones fall, saying nothing.

Saturday, 22nd May, 1915

Charles asked me if I had thought anymore about his proposal last Saturday. I tried to explain that while I love him, I feel a responsibility towards my family at home. My brothers and sisters are married, and soon my mother will need someone to look after her. I have a feeling my brother Fred is going to need some support too in the future, and of course there is Bert. He is away fighting in an awful war, and I have

Ocean Liner Lusitania, *in New York Harbor, 1914. Struck by a torpedo from a German U-Boat, the sinking of the* Lusitania *caused world-wide outrage and prompted the United Stated to enter the war. Of the 1,959 passengers and crew, 1,198 perished.*

The Standard-Times

betrayed him. My mind is in a turmoil—what should I do! Should one follow one's heart or one's conscience?

Monday, 24th May, 1915

I had the shock of my life today. The telephone rang at the house this morning and it was for me. I picked up the telephone with trepidation. It was Ethel telling me we were going home. I was so surprised. I managed a tiny squeak and asked "How?", whereupon Ethel, my friend who works in Springfield, told me that Emma had wired the money, on Albert's instructions. I sat in my room for a full fifteen minutes afterwards pondering the news. Perhaps it was true that God did work in mysterious ways, this was his way of answering my question, telling me what I should do.

This evening I managed to meet Charles in North Park. I told him of my intentions, it was very painful for both of us, the hardest thing I have ever had to do. I wept while I was with him, and again when I reached the seclusion of my own room. Why is life so hard and so full of hurt.

Wednesday, 26th May, 1915

I have spent most of the day packing. Bid came to my room rather late tonight. She said she had a farewell gift to give me. I followed her downstairs where she presented me with her beloved rocking chair, one of the most precious things she owns. Tearfully, I told her I could not accept, it was too great a gift to give, but in her no-nonsense manner she insisted I take it, and remember her each time I used it. Eventually, emotions overcame both of us, and we clung to each other in a final display of our deep friendship. I shall never forget her and will treasure the rocking chair always.

Thursday, 27th May, 1915

I left Fall River for the last time at noon today. I had said goodbye to Mr. Leonard early this morning before he left for the office. Mrs. Leonard hugged me and told me to take care. I kissed and hugged my dear Helena so tightly I'm surprised she did not cry out. I will miss her so much, I will miss them all. As I loaded my luggage on to the jitney, I glanced round for one more view of the beautiful house that had been such a happy home. Mrs. Leonard and Helena were waving frantically, and through a window I saw a tear-stained face looking at me. Bid.

Saturday, 29th May, 1915

The day started early for us. Arthur helped us and our luggage to the dock. After what seemed like an eternity, we finally were through customs and our

Annie's North Park neighborhood, circa 1912.

Courtesy of Walter Mitchell

luggage was loaded onto the ship. I was very worried about the rocking chair. I'm still anxious, I can only hope it has been loaded and secured properly.

As I write we have been sailing now for almost two hours. Again, as with my first journey across the sea, there was no one to wave me goodbye, but as we pulled away from the dock, I silently said a goodbye to each and every one of the wonderful people I had met, and some of whom I had grown to love. Wherever my life takes me I shall never forget them, and shall remain with them, if only in my thoughts.

Memoranda, 29th May, 1915

Goodbye America…Will I ever see you again?

Notes from Susan Hill, Annie's granddaughter.

Ms. Hill discovered Annie's diary among her possessions after her death.

I sat back in my rocking chair with mixed emotions after reading the diary. I felt drained and exhausted mentally, wanted to have a good cry, yet at the same time, felt euphoric and privileged. Here I was, sitting in that old rocking chair, Bid's beloved possession, now my pride and joy, as it was once hers, all those years ago.

The short time Annie had spent in the U.S had been a truly magical time for her. Never again would such an opportunity come her way. After returning home in 1915, she found work in a munitions factory in Staines, Middlesex, making shells to help the war effort.

In 1920, at the age of 34, she married Bert Brock. After several miscarriages and a stillborn, she gave birth to her only child, Frederick, in 1923, when she was 37.

Mr. & Mrs. Leonard moved to Boston in 1922, taking Helena and Field, their new daughter Joan, and Christine and Bid (who remained as their cook until they retired).

They remained there for two years before moving back to Fall River where Russell Leonard took up the position of the head of the Pepperell Manufacturing Co. which he held for 25 years. He died in 1949 following a heart attack. Helen Leonard died in an automobile accident in 1968.

Little Helena grew up and married Bart Brownall in 1933 and had seven children. She is now in her 80s and lives in Florida.

Ruth Edwards

Annie Ward, back home in England, 1918.

Courtesy of Susan Hill

Bibliography

Allen, Everett S. *The Black Ships.* Boston: Little, Brown and Company, 1965.

Araujo, Darlene. "Macomber Turnip Report." 1991.

Barton, Elizabeth. *The Compleat Blueberry Book.* Courier Printing Co. 1974.

Boston Bee. Boston, 6/19/51.

Boston Journal. Boston, 6/7/51.

Bloomer, D. C. *Life and Writings of Amelia Bloomer.* 1895.

Boss, Judith A. *Fall River: A Pictorial History.* Virginia Beach: Donning Company Publishers, 1981.

Boss, Judith A., and Joseph D. Thomas. *New Bedford: A Pictorial History.* Virginia Beach: Donning Company Publishers, 1983.

Crosby, Constance. "The Indians and English use them much…" *Cranberry Harvest.* New Bedford: Spinner Publications, Inc., 1990.

Cummings, O. R. *Union Street Railway: Transportation Bulletin No. 85.* Warehouse Point, CT: National Railway Historic Society, 1978.

Dexter, Lincoln A. *The Gosnold Discoveries in the North Part of Virginia, 1602.* According to the Relations of Gabriel Archer and John Brereton. Sturbridge: N.p., 1982.

Ellis, Leonard Bolles. *History of New Bedford and its Vicinity, 1602-1892.* Syracuse: D. Mason & Co., 1892.

Ferrary & Fiszer. *Sweet Onions and Sour Cherries.* New York: Simon & Schuster, 1992.

Herald News. Fall River. [Between Heaven and Hell] 11/28/81, 3/13/82, 3/29/82, 5/12/82, 5/13/82, 5/18/82.

Josselyn, John. *New-Englands Rarities Discovered.* Mass. Historical Soc., 1972 (1672).

Kaplan, Natalie. "Unforgettable Days." Unpublished manuscript. Center for Jewish Studies, Library, University of Massachusetts Dartmouth, 1930.

McCabe, Marsha, and Joseph D. Thomas. *Not Just Anywhere: The Story of WHALE and the Rescue of New Bedford's Waterfront District.* New Bedford: Spinner Publications, Inc., 1995.

McCabe, Marsha, and Joseph D. Thomas. *Spinner: People and Culture in Southeastern Massachusetts, Volume IV.* New Bedford: Spinner Publications, Inc., 1988.

Morning Mercury. New Bedford. [Children of Sol-e-Mar] 6/9/24, 10/26/24, 1/8/31, 1/31/32, 8/19/39.

Notre Dame de Lourdes Memorial Booklet. Fall River. 1983.

Peirce, Edward C. Family Scrapbook, 1900-1955.

Providence Journal. [Between Heaven and Hell] 8/15/88, 5/12/82, 5/14/82.

Republican Standard. Weekly newspaper. New Bedford. [The Progress of Bloomerism] May 1851–April 52.

Rozin, Elizabeth. *Blue Corn and Chocolate.* Alfred A. Knopf, Inc. NY. 1992.

Squanto and the First Thanksgiving. Video. Rowayton: Rabbit Ears Productions, 1993.

Ryan, Kathleen Komiskey. *Secrets of Old Dartmouth.* Reynolds Printing, Inc. New Bedford, MA. 1963.

St. Luke's Hospital Medical Library. Scrapbooks 1932-1958.

Silvia, Jr., Philip T. *Victorian Vistas: Fall River, 1901-1911.* Fall River: N.p. 1992.

Spinner Publications, Inc. Photography archives, original manuscript collection, oral history collection. New Bedford.

Standard-Times, The. New Bedford. [At St. Mary's Doorstep] 4/23/47, 6/12/55, 9/30/56, 1/21/60. [Between Heaven and Hell] 5/12/82, 513/82, 5/15/82. [Children of Sol-e-Mar] 1/13/47, 1/14/47, 4/18/48, 4/10/49, 8/15/51, 1/25/53, 1/27/58. [Judgment Day] 8/18/52, 8/19/52, 12/1/52, 5/22/53, 6/23/53, 5/23/54, 2/1/55.

Standard, The. New Bedford. [The Old Order Changeth] 3/4/11, 3/12/11. [Children of Sol-e-Mar] 5/4/24, 11/24/29, 1/31/32, 12/19/41.

Thomas, Joseph D., and Marsha McCabe. *A Picture History of Fairhaven.* New Bedford: Spinner Publications, Inc., 1986.

"Trolleygrams." Bulletins. New Bedford: Union Street Railway Company, June 1922, July 1922, May 1923.

Squanto: The Indian Who Saved the Pilgrims. Creative Education. Mankato, 1974.

Index

A

Abrams, Mr. 64
Academy Building 174, 178
Academy of Music 174, 176, 178
Accuracy, rumrunning boat 82
Ackerman, John 90
Acushnet, MA 157–58, 161, 168–69
    Long Plain 168
    Main Street 168
Acushnet Park, New Bedford 149
Acushnet, tow boat 82
Adamsville, RI 164
    Adamsville Road
Ainsley, Joe 90
Akron, OH 61
Allard, Helen 51
Allen, Captain Eli 74
Allen's Neck Friends 160
Allen's Neck School 84-87
Allied Council of Clubs of Greater New Bedford 116
Almac's 28
Almeida, R. 115
Altman, Mr. 64
Alves, K. 115
Andrea-Doria, ocean liner, collision with 91
Angell, William 61–62
Animal Rescue League 90
Ann, Sister Carole 12
Anthony, Edmund 136
Anthony, Susan B. 136
Argo Merchant, oil tanker 88, 90
Arkwright Finishing 27
Arredondo, E. 115
Ashley Family: Hannah Crapo 169, Joseph 169,
    William Allen 169,
Ashley, Mayor Charles S. 52
Ashley's Peach Orchard 157, 161, 168-69
Asiatic cholera 122
Associated Press 15, 31, 98
Assonet, MA 33
Atlantic Ocean 73, 128, 158
Attleboro, MA 83
Attleboro Sam 83
Austria 174–76
Azores Islands 93-94

B

Babbitt, Edwin 54
Barrington College 48
Batchelder, William 54
Battle of Marne, France 177–79
Bebis, Reverend Constantine 100
Bedford, England 173
Bennett, Carole 111
Benson, Bucklin S. 141
Beringer Vineyard 169
Bernhardt, Sara 176
Berube, Marc 30–31
Bid, the cook 172–75, 178–81, 184–85
Black Duck, rumrunning boat 72, 80–82
Blais, Father 22, 37
Blanchett, Charles A. 64
Blessed Sacrament Church, Fall River, 18
Bloomer, Amelia 135–36, 138, 141
Bloomer, Dexter C. 141
Bloomer Polka 139
Bloomer's Complaint 139
bloomers 135–141
Bolsheviks 121, 125
Booth, Edwin 176
Boston Bee 139
Boston Journal 138
Boston, MA 19, 36, 44, 60, 62, 65, 69, 73, 79, 96,
    113, 137, 139, 157, 161, 185
Boston Post 67
Bourne Counting House 90
Boutin Family: Marilyn 23; Robert V. 23–27
Boutin Reality 26
Braga Bridge, Fall River 90, 173
Brando, Marlon 91
Branford Electric Railway Association 150
Braz, Tony 153
Bristol County Sheriff's Department 115
Britto, Bill 103
Brock Family: Bert 176, 178–79, 183, 185; Bill 176, 178
Brockton, MA 149
Brooke, Senator Edward 107
Brothers Casavant 19
Brownall, Bart 185
Butterworth, Lee 152
Buttonwood Pond 99

C

California 110, 114, 138
Cambodians 38
Canada 19, 82
Cannonville 144
Canterbury Cathedral 36
Cape Bial 80
Cape Cod 44, 90, 149, 158–59
Cape Cod Railroad 143
Cape Verdeans 104
Capone, Al 79-80, 83
Captain Quahog 90
Card, James E. 145
Cardinal, The, motion picture 91
Carmelite nuns 53
Carrol, Milton 54
Carvalho, Nancy Peirce 55–71
Castagnoli, J.M. 18–19, 35
Castonquay, Pierre 29
Catholic Charities' Appeal Fund 114
Catholic Memorial Home 33
Central Cafe 63
Chamberlain, Cynthia Kaye 100
Chamberlain Manufacturing 67
Chantegulf, U.S. Navy boat 81
Chaplin, Charlie 176, 178–79, 182
Charette, Mr. 24
Charles W. Morgan, whaleship 90
Charlton's Dock 81
Chatterton, Ruth 176
Chicago, IL 35, 67, 78
Chippewa tribe 159
China 23, 25
cholera hospital. *See* Hospital #100
circus tent 91
Clarinda, Mother Superior 116
Clark, Myra H. 46
Clark's Cove, South Dartmouth 41, 44–45, 147
Coggeshall, Everett 78
Cole, Mr. 36–37
Commonwealth Electric 144
communism 23, 25, 122
Congregational Church, South Abington, MA 141
Conroy, Police Chief Raymond 20
Coogan, Jackie 176
Cook, Donald 54
Coon, Beverly 48–49
Coon, Fred 145–47
Cornell Dubilier 114
Correia, Robert 21
Corrigan Mental Health Center 27
Corriveau Funeral Home 34
Corson Block 145
Cosgrove, Robert 15, 31
Council Bluffs, Iowa 141
Cox, Wally 91
Cremonini, Ludovic 11–12, 18, 26, 35
Crispim, Lucille Gomes 41–43, 46–48, 53
Cronin, Bishop 36
Crowell, Howard 54
Cullen, Pete 96
Cunard Shipping 182–83
Cuttyhunk Island, MA 158

D

Daily Standard 136
Dartmouth, MA 60, 81, 85, 91, 96, 98, 157, 161, 169
    Clark's Cove 41–53, 147
    Lincoln Park 114, 116, 149, 152, 178–79
    North Dartmouth 48, 59, 148, 178
    Padanaram Village 79, 153–54
    schools
        Allen's Neck School 85, 87
        Gidley School 154
        Lincoln School 154
        Russells Mills High School 85, 87
        Smith Mills School 154
    Salters Point 161
    Smith Neck Road 57
    South Dartmouth 44, 57, 59, 82, 112
    streets
        Allen's Neck Road 84
        Reed Road 154
        Slocum Road 152
        State Road 59, 154
Dativa, Sister 115
David Duff & Sons Coal Co. 71
Dedham, MA 35, 64
Democrat, The 137–141
Democratic Party 60

Depot Social Club 60, 62
Deschene-Costa, Rachel M. 33–34
Destremps, Louis 18, 26
Devoll's Dancing Academy 174, 176, 178, 181
d'Hauterville, Count 178
Diocese of Providence 116
Direct Sales and Finance Company 59
diseases
    Asiatic cholera 122
    infantile paralysis 45
    influenza 125-26
    malnutrition 42, 45
    osteomyelitis 45–53
    pallagra 162
    polio 49, 74
    rickets 45
    scarlet fever 128
    scoliosis 42, 45
    typhoid pneumonia 85
Donne, John 38
Drew, William 146
Duff Building 71
Duff, John and Mark 71
Dufresne, Arthur 62
Durant, John 90
Durant Sail Loft 90
Dussault, Sister Helene 12

E

East Bridgewater, MA 141
Eastern Mass. Correctional Alcoholic Center 115
Eaton, Mr. & Mrs. 58
Edgar's Department Store 28
Edwards, Donald 154
Eighteenth Amendment 73
Ellis Island 128
Elmen, Russia 126–27
England 174–85
English, Augusta 52
Epizootic Horse Influenza Epidemic 146–47
Espirito Santo Church, Fall River, 20, 24
Estrella, Joanne 30
Ethan Frome, short novel 150
Europe 131, 174, 180
Evening Standard 85, 86

F

Fairhaven, MA 94, 144–146, 148, 160, 168
    Fort Phoenix 148
    Main Street 145, 168
    Oxford Village 154–55
    Pope Beach 117

Sconticut Neck 117, 148
Fall River, MA 9–39, 58–59, 69, 78, 90–91, 114, 148, 150, 154, 170-85
    Academy Building 174, 178
    Academy of Music 174, 176, 178
    Barresi Heights 28
    Borden Block 174
    Braga Bridge 90, 145, 173
    cemeteries
        Notre Dame 39
        Saint Patrick's 173
    Chamber of Commerce 26
    churches
        Blessed Sacrament 18
        Espirito Santo 20, 24
        First Congregational Church 28
        Immaculate Conception 38
        Mount Saint Joseph 36
        Notre Dame de Lourdes 9–39
        Saint Anne's 38
        Saint Jean Baptiste 38
        Saint Jean's 30
        Saint Mathieu's 26
        Saint Roch's 18, 26
    City Hall 25
    Community Development Agency 21, 28
    Corky Row 173
    Flint Village 9–39
    Globe section 39
    Government Center 9
    Highlands 30, 173
    Historical Society 25
    Jobs for Fall River 21
    name origination 173
    Office of Historic Preservation 9, 39
    Office of Tourism 39
    parks
        Heritage State Park 39
        North Park 173–175, 184
    Police Department 20
    Quequechan River 172
    Saint Vincent de Paul 28
    schools
        Bishop Connolly High 30, 36
        Durfee High 35
        Highland School 173
        Notre Dame School 12
    SCORE 26
    streets
        Alden Street 20
        Bedard Street 12, 20, 22–39
        Chicago Street 31
        Choate Street 22
        County Street 29, 33, 34
        Downing Street 34
        Eastern Avenue 16, 27, 31, 37–38

        Eight Rod Way 37
        Mason Street 38
        Meridian Street 24–25
        North Main Street 34
        Notre Dame Street 11–15, 32–37
        Oak Grove Avenue 28
        Pleasant Street 16–39, 174
        Roads Corner 182
        Robeson Street 171, 173– 176, 181
        Saint Joseph Street 11, 20, 38
        South Main Street 174, 178
        Stanley Street 173, 181
    Superior Court 62, 63, 64, 71
    Tax Assessor's Office 21
    YMCA 39
Famine of 1921, Russia 130
Farley, Thomas 146
Farm Security Administration 96
Fayal, The Azores 93
February Revolution. *See* Russian Revolution
Felder, Mr. 27
Ferdinand, Duke 174–75
Fernandes, Mrs. Gilbert F. 42
Figueira, Alfred 60–64
fires
    Notre Dame de Lourdes 8-39
    Great Fall River Fire 59
    Pairpoint Manufacturing 105
First Congregational Church, Fall River, MA 28
Fish, Johnny 83
Fisher College 131
Flanders' Field 50
Flight Into Egypt, window 19, 36
Fonseca, Mary 21
Forand, Russell 51
Ford, Henry 148
Fort Phoenix 149
Foxboro, MA 64
France, World War I 175
Francis, Joseph F. 60
Francis, Sister Margaret 111
Franco-American Hall 26
Freetown, MA 148–49, 169
French, Rodney 136
French-Canadians, Fall River 9–39
Fresh Air Kids 104

G

Gallagher, Leathia 51
Galligan, Neal 154
Gendreau, Bernard 11
Gendreau, Conrad 12
Gendreau Construction 11
Gendreau, Ernest 29

Gene Hubert's Aluminium Products 32
Germania Wine Cellars 165
Germany 131, 175–77, 183
Gibbs, Kathryn 49
Gifford, Fred 146
Giles, Mary 74, 83
Gillespie, Janet. *See* Grindley, Janet
Gingras, Norm 90
Glassman, Dr. (Rabbi) Bernard 120, 133
Glenriddle, PA 116
Goat Lady, Noelie Houle, 91
Gomes, Lucille *See* Crispim, Lucille Gomes
Goodyear Manufacturing 96
Gorham, Harold 68
Gosnold, Bartholomew 158-59
Grace, Charles Manuel "Sweet Daddy" 102
Gray, James L. 163
Gray's General Store 163-64
Gray's Grist Mill 157, 161–63
Great Depression 56, 59–60, 96, 129–31
Great Fall River Fire 59
Gregory, Sister Lois 111
Grenier, Rev. Normand 12, 24–25
Grindley, Janet 74, 8
Grinnell Sprinkling System 117
Gubozdrav (Board of Health)
    Saratov 122–23
    Yelan 124–25
Guild, Ralph 163
Gulf Hill Dairy Farm 45

H

Hale, Sarah J. 141
Hammondsport, NY 165
Hap's Hill 159
Harkins, Bishop 19
Harriman, Arthur N. 60, 66
Hartford, CT 30
Hartnett, Denise Sentner 29
Harvard Foundry of Ville-Dieu, France 19
Hathaway, Arthur 54
Hayes, Father 114
Hayne, Rev. 141
Healy, Leonard 62
Helen, rumrunner boat 72
Herald News 15, 22, 31, 39
Heritage Farm Coast 164, 167
Heritage State Park, Fall River, MA 39
Herter, Governor Christian A. 55, 64–65
Hesford, Coach James 115
Hill, Susan 171, 185
Hiscox, William 146
Hitler, Adolf 131
Hix Bridge, Westport 160

Hogan, Father 114–15
Holy Cross Fathers 112
Home of the Sweetheart Rose 59
Home Owners Loan Corp. (HOLC) 60
Homer, NY 141
Hoover, President Herbert 83
Hope Chapel 140
horsecars 143–49
Horton, Phyllis 174, 179, 122
Hospital #100 123–24
Houle, Noelie (The Goat Lady) 91
House of DePrato 35
House of Prayer Church, New Bedford 102
Howdy Doody 47
Humane Society 96
Hungary 176
Huston, Walter 91
Hyannis, MA 91
Hyannisport, MA 107

I

Ilin, Victor 124–25
Illinois 83
I'm Alone, rumrunning boat 81
Immaculate Conception Church, Fall River 38
immigration 128-29, 131
Imperial German Embassy 182
Indian pudding 164
Indiana 35
Indians 107, 157–62
    Chippewa 159
    Narragansett 162
    Wampanoag 107, 157–60
Ingersoll, Amory & Company 58
Inquisition 137
Irvin, Kathleen 111

J

Jeffers, Lorenzo 107
Jefferson, Joseph 176
Jenkins, James H. 153
Jenks, Amelia. *See* Bloomer, Amelia
Jesus Mary Academy 20, 24
Jewish Archives 133
Jewish Federation of New Bedford 133
Jones, Amelia H. 44–45
Jones Car Company 150
jonnycakes 161–65
    recipes 165
Judaism 129, 131-33
Judith, Sister 108
Jurgens, Francis 62

K

Kamishin, Russia 127
Kaplan, Boris. *See* Pikelny, Dr. Boris
Kaplan, Daniel. *See* Pikelny, Daniel
Kaplan, Esther 130–33
Kaplan, Leda 130–31
Kaplan, Natalie Lubavsky 119–33
Kaplan, Samuel 127–29
Karam, Robert 21
Kells, Bill 169
Kendall and Taylor 44
Kennebunkport, MN 142
Kennedy, Bridget. *See* Bid
Kennedy, John F. 90, 107
Kennedy, Ted 106
Kenny, John 83
Kenny Method 50
Kenny's 149
Kerwin garage 98
Keystone Film Company 182
Kimball, Pvt. Dean 13
King, Eleanor Smith 47
King, Governor Edward J. 20
Kiwanas Club 43
Krantzler, William 103
Krantzler's Antiques 103
Kreisler, Fritz 176

L

Lachance, Aime 11, 22
Ladies Home Journal 57
Lady's Book 141
Lafayette Bank 23
Lafayonaise, Alliette 51
Lajeunesse, Mr. 63
Lakeville, MA 53, 148–49
Landau, Abraham 102
Language of Clothes, The 135
Lareau, Elsie 41–42, 47, 50, 53
Lariviere, Mr. 64
Lartzeva, Maria (Marusia) 123–26
Last Judgement, The, painting by Cremonini 19, 26
Lawler, Francis L. 63, 66-67
Lawrence, MA 172
Lawton's Corner 147
Leach, Miss 51
League of Women Voters 60
Lee, Dr. 138
Lee, Richard 62
Leonard Family: Field 173, 181, 185; Helen 171–85; Helena 173–85; Joan 185; Russell 171–85
Leonard, Mark 54

LeRoy, Edward 139
Lesley College 131
Liar's Club 74
Liberia 88
Liberty motors 77, 79
Lider, Harry 62
Life Magazine 70, 91
Lily, The, magazine 141
Lincoln Park, North Dartmouth 114, 116, 149, 152, 178–79
Lindsey's Antiques 32
Little, Barbara 48–50
Little, Brown Company 119, 130
London, Jack 63
Long Island, NY 80
Lovell, Rev. S. 138
Lubavsky, Basil 120–24, 127, 129
Lubavsky, Catherine 121, 124, 127–29
Lubavsky, Natalie. *See* Kaplan, Natalie Lubavsky
Lubavsky, Julia 120
Lurie, Alison 135
Lusitania, ocean liner 182–83
Lyman, Grace 48–49, 51
Lyons, Maurice M. 61–63, 66–68, 71

M

MacAusland, Dr. William R. 44
Machado, Gilbert 160
Macomber, Adin 166
Macomber, Elihu 166
MacPhail, John 54
Madeleine Kamman's School 169
Maloney, Dennis 30
Manchester, Carlton Sr. 74, 75–83
Maple Grove Cemetery, Westport, MA 86
Marion, MA 148–50
Marnes, France 177–78
Martha's Vineyard, MA 72, 143
    Gay Head 107
Marxist revolutionaries. *See* Bolsheviks *and* Russian Revolutionaries
Mary Langdon, rumrunning boat 82
Masonic Temple 107
Masquesatch 83
Massachusetts
    Department of Social Services 114
    medical exam 129
    Senate 67, 70
    State Police 60, 82
Masse, Roland 12, 18, 35–38
Mattapoisett, MA 148
Maumejean Brothers 19
Mayo, Al 112
McIntyre, John W. 62–63

McTague, Tim 162–164
Medeiros, Caroline 41–42, 46–48, 52–53
Mein, Robert 54
Mello, Mary Soares 49
Mello, Mr. 64
Men's Mission 90
Merrill's Wharf 90
Michaelangelo 35
Middleboro, MA 149
Middlesex, England 180
    French Street 176
Miller, Elizabeth Smith 136
Miller, N. 115
Miriam Hospital 132
Mitchell, Walter 176
Mix, Tom 47, 51
Moby Dick, motion picture 91, 106
Model T Ford 148, 151
Monument Beach, Wareham, MA 149
Moore, Pvt. Thomas J. 13
Morning Mercury 42, 45–46, 136
Morse, Reverend Frank 153
Moscow, Russia 126
Mott, Lucretia 136
Mount Pleasant Barn 142, 146
Mount Saint Joseph Church, Fall River, MA 36
Mystic, CT 90

N

Nantucket, MA 90–91, 136, 141, 143
Nantucket Shoals 88
Napa Valley 169
Narragansett, RI 159
Narragansett Indians 162
Nash, Clarence C. 47
National Guard 21
Native Americans 157–62
New Bedford Country Club 110, 152
New Bedford Hotel 71
New Bedford Luggage 114
New Bedford, MA 11, 27, 44–45, 54–71, 78, 89–117, 119, 127–41, 143–55, 167, 169
    Animal Rescue League 90
    Bay Village 104
    bridges
        New Bedford-Fairhaven Bridge 94, 148
    Buttonwood Pond 99
    churches
        Greek Orthodox 100
        Saint James 116
        Saint John the Baptist 116
        Saint Joseph's 114
        Saint Lawrence 116
        Saint Mary's 114-15

City Council 56, 62-63
City Hall 60-61, 67
ferries
    Island Steamship Lines 143
Fire Department 65
Firefighters Charities Inc 43
Fort Rodman 154
harbor 59, 81, 82, 98
historic district 106, 144
library 141
mills 144
Municipal East Beach 149
North End 65, 100
parks
    Acushnet Park 149
    Buttonwood Park 98
    Hazelwood Park 154
Pearl Street Railroad Station 143
Police Department 60, 65
    vice squad 60, 63, 71
Presidential Heights 110
street railways
    Acushnet 147
    New Bedford & Fairhaven 144–147
    New Bedford & Onset 149–151
    New Bedford & Taunton 143
    Union Street 145, 149–154
School Department 46
schools
    New Bedford High School 130
    New Bedford Vocational School 101, 115
    Normandin Junior High School 153
    Textile School 70
    Thomas A. Rodman Grammar School 94
South End 149
streets
    Acushnet Avenue 62, 65, 71, 114, 153
    Bolton Street 154
    Briggs Street 128, 129
    Butler Street 152
    Clinton Street 129
    Cottage Street 56, 130–132
    County Street 144
    Durfee Street 146
    Elm Street 145, 153
    Front Street 145
    High Street 63
    Kempton Street 102, 107, 109–110, 144, 146, 152–153
    Liberty Street 152
    Linden Street 62
    Merrimac Street 144
    Mount Pleasant Street 146
    Oesting Street 132
    Purchase Street 62, 94, 140, 144, 147, 152, 154
    Rivet Street 154
    Rockdale Avenue 144
    Sixth Street 102
    Summer Street 145, 154
    Tarkiln Hill Road 114–15, 153
    Union Street 144, 147
    Washington Street 138
    Water Street 105
Transportation Committee 60
West End 107
New Bedford-Fairhaven Bridge 94, 148
New Bedford Port Authority 60
New Bedford Times 84
New England Culinary Institute 169
New Haven Railroad, Watuppa Branch 148
New Jersey 165
New Video Group 83
New York 182, 94, 96, 131
New York Camera Club 94
New York City, NY 26, 36, 53, 73, 83, 104, 128, 152, 155
    Central Park 175
    East River 152
    New York Harbor 183
    Queensboro Bridge 152, 155
New York Express 140
New York press corps 107
Newport, RI 27
Newsman, Enoch 151
Nichols, Gove 137–41
Norfolk, MA 68
    County House of Correction 64, 69
North Dartmouth, MA *See* Dartmouth, MA
North Dartmouth Mall 59
Norton, Thomas 21
Notre Dame Cemetery, Fall River 39
Notre Dame de Lourdes Church, Fall River 9–39
Notre Dame de Lourdes Church, Paris 26
Notre Dame School, Fall River 12
Notre Dame University 35

O

O'Brien, Charles 173–78, 181–84
O'Brien, Judge Daniel 62
Old Age Assistance laws 60
Old Dartmouth Historical Society 145
Old Stone Fleet 59
Oliver, Doris 46
Olkavikas, Mathew 163
Olmstead, Frederick L. 175
Onset, MA 149, 150
Osgood Bradley Company 150
osteomyelitis 45–53, 47, 50
    maggot treatment 50
Our Lady of Lourdes Feast 11

P

Pacific Coal Company 71
Paine, Frank 142
Pairpoint factory 105
Palestine 127
Palmer, Ab 74, 76–83
Paradis Funeral Home 33–34
Paradis, Mr. 34
Paris, France 19, 26
peaches 157, 168-69
Peck, Gregory 106
Peirce, Alma 61, 65–66, 68–69
Peirce Cottage Gardens 59
Peirce, Edward Cook 54–71
Peirce, Edward Sr. 59
Peirce, Estelle Cook 56, 66
Peirce, Helen 54, 56–57, 60, 67
Peirce, Nancy. *See* Carvalho, Nancy Peirce
Peirce the Florist 68, 71
Peirce, William 59
Peirce, Winsper & Company 58-59
Peladeau, Sgt. Robert 14
Pellerin, Claire 111
Pelletier, Claire 12
Pennsylvania State Police 94
Pepperill Manufacturing Co. 171, 185
Perras, Louis 62
Pertras, Mr. 64
Phillips, Marion 51
Picard, Alphonse 38–39
Pierian Spring 87
Pike, A. 115
Pikelny, Daniel 119, 127
Pikelny, Dr. Boris 119, 123–33
Pikelny, Natalie. *See* Kaplan, Natalie Lubavsky
Pilgrim Casket 34
Pina, A. 115
Plymouth, MA 157, 161, 169
Poet of Cape Verde 104
Poirier, Edmour 32–33
Poirier's Bakery 24, 32–33
Poland 131
Pont, Elsie Lareau. *See* Lareau, Elsie
Poor Bill's Almanac 167
Popes Island, New Bedford 61–62, 150–51
Portugal 44. *See also* Azores
Portuguese 43, 52
Portuguese Society, The 116
Preminger, Otto 91
Prevost, Father 18
Prohibition 61, 73–83
Proulx, Albert Jr. 27
Proulx, Christopher 27
Providence Bible Institute 48

Providence Mirror 141
Providence, RI 19, 48, 132
Puritans 161

Q

Quakers 141, 161
Quebec, Canada 91
Quincy, MA 91

R

Railway Post Office 150
Raphael 18
Rapoza, Daniel 21
Red Army 126–32
Red Cross 20–21, 28, 121–23
Remington's Pavillion, Westport 160
Republican Standard 136–37
Revolutionary War 73
Rhode Island 16, 72, 158, 177
Rish, D. 115
Rivard Family: Audrey, Bobby 110; Brian, Steven 115; Patricia 110, 115; Raymond 109–117
River View Park 147
Rochester, MA 169
Rochester, NY 141
Roderick, Esther. *See* Kaplan, Esther
Roe, Leathia 51
Roe, Richard 66
Rohlf Studios, New York 36–37
Ronan, Stephen 10
Roosevelt, Eleanor 131
Roosevelt, Franklin Delano 60
Ross, Miss 49
Rotch, Mayor Morgan 147
Round Hill 159
Royal Engineers 176
Rudnia, Russia 126
rumrunning 73–83
Rural Cemetery 65, 146
Russell Family: Robert 165–169; Carol 165–169; Rob 165
Russells Mills Farm 131
Russia 120
    emigration ban 128
    Famine of 1921 127, 130
    Provisional Government 121, 127
    World War I 175
Russian Army 119, 125
Russian Civil War 126
Russian Orthodoxy 121–122, 129
Russian Revolution 120–125, 131
Russian Revolutionaries 122–127

S

Saint Anne's Church, Fall River, 38
Saint Bernadette 26
Saint Helena, CA 169
Saint Hyacinthe, PQ, Canada 19
Saint James Church, New Bedford, 116
Saint Jean Baptiste Church, Fall River, 38
Saint Jean's Church, Fall River, 30
Saint John the Baptist Church, New Bedford, 116
Saint Joseph 34
Saint Joseph, Sister Agnes 111
Saint Lawrence Church, New Bedford 114, 116
Saint Luke's Hospital 44, 45, 51, 99
Saint Mary's Children's Home 108–117
Saint Mary's Church, New Bedford, 113–115
Saint Mary's Home 94
Saint Mathieu's Church, Fall River, 26
Saint Michael's Liturgical Arts 35
Saint Patrick's Cemetery, Fall River 173
Saint Roch's Church, Fall River, 18, 26
Saint Vincent de Paul, Fall River, 28
Sakonnet 80
Sale, Mrs. 51
Salters Point, Old Dartmouth 161
Salvation Army 28, 29, 32
San Miguel, The Azores 93
Saratov, Russia 120–124, 126–127, 131
Saratov Hospital 127
Saratov University 121, 124, 129
Sargent, Governor Francis 107
Saturday Evening Post 54, 57–58
Schwartz Rehabilitation Center 106
Sconticut Neck, Fairhaven 117
Scunnet River 81
Sears, Edward 54
Seashore Trolley Museum 142
Seeger, Pete 106
Sennett, Mack 182
Sentner, Dennis, Lucille and Mark 29
Shea, Fire Chief Louis 16
Sherman, Carrie 85–87
Silva, R. 115
Silvia, Milton 89–96
Simmons, Edward B. 69
Simon, Katherine 27–28
Simon, Mr. 64
Sisters of St. Francis 116
Small Business Administration 21, 33
Smith College 58, 60
Smith Farm 166
Smith, John 166, 167
Smith, Nona 100
Smith, William 167
Smith-Long Acre Farm 157, 161, 165. *See also*
    Westport Rivers Vineyard & Winery
Sol e Mar Convalescent Hospital 40–53
Sol e Mar Hospital, Portugal 44
Sol e Mar Volunteers 42, 43
Somerset, MA 27, 33, 38
South Abington, MA 141
South Dartmouth, MA *See* Dartmouth, MA
Southeastern Massachusetts University 96, 106, 120, 132–33. *See also* UMass Dartmouth
Sowle, Everett 146
Spanish-American War 75
speakeasies 78
Springfield, MA 184
Staines, Middlesex, England 185
Standard 136
Standard–Times, The 14, 50, 61–64, 68–69, 71, 89–96, 104, 111, 117, 129, 149, 151, 153, 155.
Stanton, Elizabeth Cady 136, 141
Star Store 116, 152
State House, Massachusetts 55, 65
Steamboat Wharf 147
Stockholm, collision with *Andrea Doria* 91
Stone Bridge 81
Sullivan, Mr. 62, 64
Swain School 96
Swansea, MA 38
Sylvia, Barbara 148
Sylvia, Charles 21
Sylvia, Tim 99
Syndicate, the 73, 76, 78–79

T

Taber, Philip 163
Tabor Academy 106
Taibbi, Mike 72
Taunton, MA 16, 136, 149
Tavares, Gilly 64
Temperance Movement 73, 136
Terry's Beauty Shop 32
Texeira's Barber Shop 32
textile mills 129
Thanksgiving 116
Thibault, Paul 32–33
Thomas, Antone 62–71
Thompson, CT 141
Thompson, Father 111, 113–15
Tierney, Rosemary 56
Tifereth Israel Synagogue 133
tin Lizzies 10
Titian 18
Tiverton, RI 177, 181
    Nanaquacket Pond 81
Trinity College 30
Tripp, Archer 74, 79–83
trolleys 143–155, 178
Truman, Harry 91
Turcotte, Paul 12
Twenty-first Amendment 83

U

U-Boats 183
UMass Amherst 39, 60, 83
UMass Dartmouth 96, 106, 119
    Jewish Archives 119–20, 133
Union Convalescent Nursing Home 65
Union Street Railway 71, 145, 149–53
United States
    Coast Guard 72, 76–83
    Navy 74
Universal Roofing Company 11
Upham, J. 115

V

Vancini, Paul 94
Vanderbilt, Alfred 182–83
Vaughan, Mary 137–41
Ventura, Diane and Ernie 168–69
Vermont 169
Victorian Society of America 39
Vieira, Lorraine 114
Vietnam War 101
Village Store 75
Vineyard Haven 82
Vineyard Lightship 77
Viveiros, Lt. Robert 13
Volga River, Russia 120–21, 126–27, 131
Volkoff, Russia 125-26

W

Walpole, MA 64
Wampanoag Indians 107, 158–60
Wampanoag Mill 171–72
Wamsutta Mills 144
Ward Family: Annie 171–85; Edie, Elizabeth, Tom 173; Emma 173, 184; Fred 173, 176, 179, 183; Jack, Sam 173, 176, 179
Ware, Laura 46
Wareham Car Barn 151
Wareham, MA 148–150
Warren, RI 16
Warsaw University 125
Washington, DC 61, 67
Washington, General George 83, 138
Webster, Dr. 51
Welfare Island, NY 152
West Indies 161
Westport and Dartmouth Lobster Co. 79
Westport, MA 29, 33–34, 38, 61, 73–83, 86, 148, 157, 160–64
    beaches
        Cherry & Webb 80
        Horseneck 160, 75, 130-31
    bicentennial 74, 83
    bridges
        Hix Bridge 160
        Point Bridge 75–76, 80, 83
    harbor 76, 80
    Liar's Club 74
    Remington's Pavilion 160
    rivers
        Westport River 75
            East Branch 75-76, 80
    streets
        Adamsville Road 162
        Hixbridge Road 165
        Reed Road 78
    Village Store 75
    Westport Point 73–83
Westport Point Bridge 76
Westport Rivers Vineyard & Winery 157, 161, 165–69
Wharton, Edith 150
Whatzis, rumrunning boat 77
Wheeler, Charles 67, 71
Wheeler, Estelle. *See* Carvalho, Nancy Peirce
White, John 159
Whitman, Ann P. 141
Wildes, Elizabeth 84
Williams, Roger 159
Wilson Funeral Home 65
Wilson, Woodrow 177, 179–80, 183
Windsor, VT 137
WNBH 61
Wobecky, Albert 101
Woman's Temperance Convention 141
women's rights 136, 141
Woods Hole, MA 82, 143
Woods of Dartmouth festival, UMass Dartmouth 96
Worcester, MA 150
Works Progress Administration, (WPA) 55, 59-60, 70, 80
World War I 50, 121–22, 171, 177–83
World War II 130–31, 152

Y

Yelan, Russia 124–26
Yellenti, Nicholas 54
YMCA, Fall River, MA 39

About the Editors

Marsha McCabe, senior editor and writer at Spinner Publications, is a national award-winning columnist for *The Standard-Times*. She is the author of *Not Just Anywhere: The Story of WHALE and the Rescue of New Bedford's Waterfront Historic District*. Her novella, "The Woman Behind the Counter," is featured in *Spinner IV*.

Joseph D. Thomas, publisher, editor and contributing writer at Spinner Publications, is a professional photographer and is responsible for art editing and design at Spinner. He has published eleven books and numerous small publications about the history and culture of southeastern Massachusetts.

John Robson, a freelance photographer, has worked in design and photography for Spinner since 1985. His commercial clients include design agencies, newspapers, schools and businesses in the New Bedford/Fall River area

Ruth Caswell, Managing Editor of *Spinner V*, brings strong business and research skills to Spinner. She is particularly interested in town and family history and is a volunteer at the Westport Historical Society.

Spinner Publications, Inc.

Spinner Publications is an independent, nonprofit small press. In addition to publishing, Spinner is involved in developing cultural programs in the community and education programs in the schools. We have organized art and photography exhibits, and a cultural/labor history archives and display known as the New Bedford Textile Museum.

Spinner books have examined how consequences of the Depression, the cotton textile industry, and urbanization have affected the region. Our books have looked at the role of women and children in the mills and on the bogs through Lewis Hine's haunting, early 20th century photographs. We've studied the development of the cranberry and fishing industries, and the rescue of a waterfront historic district; portrayed the Portuguese, Cape Verdean, French-Canadian, Irish, Anglo, Native American and other cultural groups in the region.

In 1985 and 1995, Spinner was awarded a Certificate of Commendation from the American Association of State and Local History for "excellence in the preservation, interpretation and distribution of local and regional history." In 1994, Spinner received the Fontera Award from the Labor Education Center at UMass Dartmouth, recognizing our "commitment to educating all people, especially through the lessons of the past, about the meaning of social justice, the integrity of the human spirit and the importance of struggle in the creation of a truly democratic society."

Spinner has received two Official Citations from the Commonwealth: for our contribution to the "African Experience in Massachusetts" exhibit and for our work to "record and preserve the heritage and culture of the working women and men…of the textile industry in New Bedford and southeastern Massachusetts." The Massachusetts Cultural Council recognizes Spinner as "a leader in enriching the cultural life of the Commonwealth."

Forthcoming titles include: *Portuguese Spinner*—which considers the history of Portuguese culture and migration to southeastern Massachusetts; *Atlantic Pearl*—the first book in a series recounting the history of the fishing industry in southeastern New England; *Spinner VI*—another volume in our series of short stories, biography, oral history and photography; and *The Heritage Coast Cookbook Series*

For our latest catalogue, or for information about Spinner books in print, calendars, forthcoming books, reprints, the Spinner photographic archives, and Spinner programs and activities, please contact us at:

P.O. Box 1801, New Bedford, MA 02741 • 508-994-4564
http://www.ultranet.com/~spinner • email spinner@ultranet.com